COMMENTS ON
HOOK ME UP, PLAYA!

"Lawrence Funderburke has reminded all humanity the importance of faith in God, discipline, work ethic, routine, financial responsibility, and accountability. As an athlete he has transcended the stereotype of today's athlete and entertainer. He has given us the roadmap of how to achieve and maintain academic excellence and become a celebrated college and professional athlete without compromising your virtues in an age where moral relativism has become commonplace. This book will become a timeless treasure for a younger generation growing up in single parent households and overcoming unprecedented obstacles in achieving moral and financial peace."

—Armstrong Williams
Nationally syndicated columnist and radio and TV talk show host
striving to show all sides of the political, social, and economic debate
www.armstrongwilliams.com

"Lawrence Funderburke's new book, *Hook Me Up, Playa!* is the perfect complement to one of my favorite mantras—FAILING TO PREPARE IS PREPARING TO FAIL…. Funderburke's incisive analysis of so many issues that are critically important to all of us is an enjoyable, riveting but also eye-opening tale that will help us understand what our lives truly entail….While pouring through this epic work, I constantly kept asking myself, 'Where was this book when I was growing up??????' Lawrence Funderburke has lived the biggest of lives and this timely masterpiece allows everybody to now experience what it's like to really be, 'in the BIG game'…. *Hook Me Up, Playa!* is a compelling project by a powerful force and spirit….This is serious—are you????"

—Bill Walton
Basketball Hall of Fame 1993

"I wish *Hook Me Up, Playa!* was around when I was in the NFL. Great reading and valuable information that guides you through the nuances of being a pro athlete. Those who do not know how to deal with investment scams, overzealous fans, and the transition from playing professionally to competing in the 'real world,' will benefit from this book. This book is a home run and one of a kind for fans and athletes alike."

—Tom Skladany
Three-time All American Punter at Ohio State University ('74–'76)
All Pro Punter-Detroit Lions ('78 and '81)

"The complexities of preserving capital are very difficult not only for the common person, but also for the athlete. *Hook Me Up, Playa!* is a must-read for those who seek preservation of capital and peace of mind."

—Ronnie Lott
ɔ Football Hall of Fame 2000

"Many pro athletes when their careers conclude try to continue living as they did while playing. Lawrence does an outstanding job discussing financial issues once an athlete leaves the game. It is relevant to non athletes also."

—**Brent Price**
Ten-year NBA veteran

"*Hook Me Up, Playa!* should be required reading for all young athletes. Lawrence does an excellent job of exploring the importance of an education to student-athletes. He touches upon specialization and the problems this phenomenon causes on a young person's body. With specialization parents are much more involved in their child's athletic careers. This book is extremely valuable to parents, especially along this issue. For every LeBron James there are a million kids who get burned out and sacrifice their education for the unrealistic dream of becoming a professional athlete."

—**Mark Murphy**
Eight-year NFL player ('77–'85) for the Washington Redskins
Trial attorney for the Justice Department ('89–'92)
Athletic Director at Colgate University ('92–'03)
Athletic Director at Northwestern University

"Thank you for writing this book for many types of people. This book is for people who need forgiveness, and for those people who have cheated or stolen from unsuspecting acquaintances. There are perspectives for anyone who needs advice on how to manage their financial future and encouragement for young men and women to continue their education to secure that future. I would recommend this book to anyone who is considering becoming a professional athlete, or who will have a considerable change in their economic status that will need honest, integrity-based management and advice."

—**Rick Harville**
Chaplain
Los Angeles Lakers

"*Hook Me Up, Playa!* is an educational, insightful and real look at the dynamics that occupy the lives of pro athletes, aspiring young athletes, and their families and friends. Lawrence, using the totality of his own experiences and the wisdom and experiences of others, has written a book that holds up faith, lifelong education, financial literacy, and character development as controllable and essential elements in living a productive and fulfilling life. Knowing that his motivation is to help and inform others, I admire, applaud, and respect his efforts."

—**Clark Kellogg**
Former college basketball (Ohio State University) and NBA star (Indiana Pacers)
College basketball analyst for CBS Sports

"*Hook Me Up, Playa!* is an intriguing book that offers a unique perspective of the trials and tribulations of the professional athlete. This book is a great read for all, no matter what your interest level in sports is."

—**John Paxson**
Former Chicago Bulls star
Three-time NBA Champion
General Manager, Chicago Bulls

"Players need to know. When players start being accountable, once people see that players are informed, now they are going to say, 'We got to come up with something else.' On a more personal note, no matter what sport you're in, it's something we all experience."

—**Greg Vaughn**
Former Major League Baseball All Star

"What I hope this book would do for athletes who are going to play professionally some day is to teach them to be responsible, that they need to grow up real fast. They need to grow up in a way to where they take responsibility for their lifestyle, their assets, their relationships, and their family."

—**Charley Hannah**
Former NFL player
Starting offensive lineman for the 1984 Super Bowl Champion
Los Angeles Raiders

"*Hook Me Up, Playa*! is going to be an eye-opener for guys that play professionally, because they are going to see what other players go through just like they do. The second thing this book is going to do is show outsiders how difficult it is to be a professional athlete, let alone to stay one."

—**Rickey Dudley**
Veteran tight end
Tampa Bay Buccaneers
Member of the 2002 Super Bowl team

"This book should be a handbook for all professional athletes. There's nothing out there like it, and it's basically going to be a one of a kind. I think parents have to realize that a Michael Jordan or a Wayne Gretzky comes along very rarely. Every day someone believes their son is going to be the next NBA or NHL star, and it's not that easy. Athletes have to surround themselves with good people off the court or ice. All the author's inquiries are basically situations that an athlete goes through numerous times in their career. It happens to everybody, no matter what sport they play. This could be a good book for someone that thinks they can become a professional athlete. *Hook Me Up, Playa*! gives them the heads-up on what's out there."

—**Kris Draper**
Professional hockey player
Stanley Cup Champion
Detroit Red Wings

"This book touches all elements of being a professional athlete—social, economical, and emotional. We're all aware of the expected. Read *Hook Me Up, Playa*! to find out about the unexpected. This book came too late for me, but on time for you. Thank you, Lawrence."

—**Dave Stewart**
Former major league pitcher
Oakland Athletics and Toronto Blue Jays
World Series Champion

"In this book Lawrence Funderburke shares the reality of the lives and expectations of professional athletes. He reinforces the importance of maintaining a good balance and surrounding yourself with a strong support system in order to truly succeed in sports and life. It's a breath of fresh air that is a must-read for athletes and sports fans alike."

—**Pat Brisson**
Managing Director, IMG Hockey
Represents over 60 NHL players

"Awesome. I loved it and highly recommend it!"

—**Sergei Federov**
Center for the Anaheim Mighty Ducks
Won three Stanley Cup titles (1997, 1998, & 2002)
Six All-Star appearances (1992, 1994, 1996, 2001, 2002, & 2003)
Won the Hart Memorial Trophy (MVP) in 1994
Twice won the Frank J. Selke Trophy (best defensive forward) in 1994 & 1996

"*Hook Me Up, Playa!* is a simple crash-course in life for anyone who is involved in the inner-workings of a professional sports team. Lawrence easily covers a broad range of concerns that will face any young professional...athlete or otherwise. From finances to social issues, his personal and first-person examples open the reader's eyes to a world that many assume is easy, but in reality can undercut you if you are not prepared. Lawrence has given back to the sports community by writing this must-read book."

—**Jim Kozimor**
NBA Announcer
Sacramento Kings

"I think *Hook Me Up, Playa!* is a great book for athletes and entertainers of all ages, because it can be used as a guide for what to expect and how to deal with situations most of them face in there lives. I loved it because it opened my eyes and made me realize that I wasn't the only one going through the trials and tribulations of being a pro athlete."

—**Ben Gordon**
NBA Sixth Man of the Year '05
NCAA Men's College Basketball Champion
University of Connecticut '04

"Having been an agent for thirteen years and personally representing Lawrence Funderburke for eight years, I feel qualified to say that *Hook Me Up, Playa!* is a must-read book for any young professional athlete as well as their families and friends. Lawrence has seen professional sports highs and lows first-hand, and has overcome many obstacles to become the ultimate spokesman for the way professional athletes should conduct themselves on and off the court."

—**Andrew Vye**
Kauffman Sports Management Group

"The issues of expectedness, worldliness, and forgiveness not only face the player, but the spectator as well. Few have made it to the notoriety of Lawrence Funderburke and even less ever grasp that with privilege comes tremendous responsibility...fiscally, morally, and spiritually. Maybe after looking into the fishbowl world of an athlete, even the public will appreciate it's not 'all honey and no bees.'"

—Ken Whitten
Senior Pastor
Idlewild Baptist Church, Tampa, Florida

"*Hook Me Up, Playa!* is the closest thing to reality drama in book form. It doesn't get any more real than this. This book is a must-read for every high school or college athlete that aspires to reach the pinnacle of athletic success—the 'real world' of professional sports. Young athletes and their parents need to be aware of this lifestyle and what it entails before that time arrives. Fans are in for quite a shock too."

—"Bailiff" Byrd
From the hit television show, "Judge Judy"

"*Hook Me Up, Playa!* sheds light on the world of the professional athlete as well as any of those in the public limelight. This unique perspective can be a valuable tool for anyone who is interested in what pressures there are in being a public figure or a professional athlete. It's a must-read."

—Mike Uckele
Certified Nutritionist
Consultant for many professional athletes
www.physiotech.uckele.com

"*Hook Me Up, Playa!* is a book that's not necessarily about why a high-caliber professional athlete is the way that he is, because that's only the way the public perceives him to be. It's about why he has to present himself the way that he does. When you get to know some professional athletes, they are some of the kindest people you'd ever want to meet. This kindness is what makes them so vulnerable. This book proves why an athlete needs to act differently in the public's eye."

—Dr. Scott Paton
Chiropractor
Certified Athletic Trainer
www.patonchiropractic.com

"Lawrence leads you on a fast-paced, riveting journey through the lives and circumstances of the hook-me-up attitude. It's as fast-paced as the lives that athletes lead on and off the field. *Hook Me Up, Playa!* captures the thoughts and the mindset of the past, present, and the up-and-coming professional athletes in the sense that this is what they go through in terms of their feelings, actions, or behaviors. It's definitely a must-read."

—Rick Oliver
Registered Certified Reflexology Therapist
Works with several professional athletes
www.rsoreflexology.com

"*Hook Me Up, Playa!* doesn't glorify professional athletes in the slightest way, although compassionate giving is commendable under some circumstances, because much of what is presented of them in the media is superhuman. But what they actually experience off the field or court is quite remarkable too. How they cope with these debilitating situations is just as unbelievable as their feats in their respective sports are, and I am being serious."

—**Dan Springmeyer**
Mentor to several professional athletes in the Sacramento area

"For the first time a book documenting the painful experiences of professional athletes and the perceptions that follow. I had dreams and aspirations of making it to the pros, but fell short of my goal. However, I had a backup plan just in case I didn't make it—a college degree. Lawrence emphasizes this as a prerequisite to every high school and college athlete who desires to reach the professional ranks. Every young person, parent, and sports fan needs to read *Hook Me Up, Playa!*"

—**Rodney Gowens**
Former men's college basketball player
University of Wyoming '85

Hook Me Up, Playa!

An insider's look into the financial fortunes, misfortunes, and fortunate lessons learned from today's mega-paid professional athletes.

Lawrence Funderburke

Wetherby Press

For further information, contact the author at:
Wetherby Press
The Studio 419 Group
P.O. Box 24320
Tampa, Florida 33623
(813) 774-6877

Hook Me Up, Playa!
by Lawrence Funderburke

Library of Congress Control Number 2005924359
ISBN 0-9767471-0-3 (paperback)

Dedication

"Do not say to your neighbor, 'Come back later; I'll give it tomorrow'— when you now have it with you."

—Proverbs 3:28 (NIV)

To sports fans, current and future athletes, and young and old alike from various walks of life, the information contained in *Hook Me Up, Playa!* is dedicated to you.

Preface

IN OUR INCREASINGLY MATERIALISTIC CULTURE, where many people are driven by a desire for power, possessions, and beauty, the professional athlete's lifestyle is often portrayed as the most desirable in society. By all outward appearances, athletes are healthy, wealthy, famous, and powerful. Given these things, how can they possibly be anything but happy and carefree? This perception, which is fed largely by the media, is accurate in some respects, yet distorted in many others. The "other side" of the lifestyle of the professional athlete is unknown to most people.

Few studies have been conducted on the real issues and concerns surrounding the lives of professional athletes. This is partially due to the absence of accessible and reliable data as well as the public perception of professional athletes—a perception that is often protected because of its real monetary value.

As a sport psychologist with more than fifteen years of experience working with NBA players and other elite athletes, I have seen the not-so-glamorous side of professional sports. In my career I have counseled professional athletes on issues involving:

- Lack of academic preparation, professional preparation, and training for work in the outside world once their athletic career is over
- Relationship crises resulting from the athlete's unusual lifestyle and travel demands
- Financial problems resulting from the inability to handle their finances and/or poor advice from people they trust
- Health problems caused by physical injuries, and
- Depression and anxiety caused by the uncertainties that are typical of the professional athletic career.

In general, it takes professional athletes four to eight years to adjust to life after their career ends. This assumes that they have a good support system and that they have taken steps to prepare themselves (by completing their education and obtaining some work experience) for the transition to the more traditional workplace. In the absence of a support system and this type of preparation, many athletes never adjust to their new life out of the limelight.

In *Hook Me Up, Playa!* Lawrence Funderburke examines some of the primary issues and concerns of the professional athlete's lifestyle in an effort to reveal the other side of the glamour and hype. Through his personal experiences, Lawrence has developed the skills to cope with the obstacles faced by athletes. Here, he brings his insights to public attention.

Of particular importance, Lawrence provides valuable information for parents, coaches, and young people (athletes and non-athletes alike) about the critical need for education, personal responsibility, and planning ahead for a secure financial future.

For the first half of the twentieth century, sports, for most people, was just a pleasant way to spend a sunny spring afternoon, sometimes engaging in a little friendly rivalry. Those days may not be over entirely, but they are waning. Professional sports is now a multi-billion dollar business and entertainment industry. No longer can we assume that the needs of professional athletes and those training and preparing for a career in professional sports will be met by teachers, coaches, managers, leagues, and other people in positions of power.

As a society, we must develop an awareness of the issues and problems facing professional athletes—and the young people who wish to follow in their footsteps—to ensure that they do not fall through the cracks and lose themselves in a media-created fantasy world from which they may be unable to return.

I believe Lawrence's leadership and his book will be a major step toward developing this awareness.

Dr. Cristina B. Versari
President
Director, Sport Psychology Program
San Diego University for Integrative Studies

Cristina Bortoni Versari holds a master's degree and a doctorate in psychology, with a specialization in sport psychology, from the United States International University.

For more than fifteen years, Dr. Versari has counseled high-profile sports figures (individuals, couples, and teams) in areas such as career development, educational planning, life planning, performance enhancement, stress management, and relationship management.

Under Dr. Versari's leadership, the NBA/NBPA Education and Career Development Program provided counseling services to twenty-nine NBA teams and more than 450 players. She developed numerous seminars and training programs for NBA players, and was the official psychologist for the Brazilian men's basketball team in the 1992 Olympics and the 1994 World Championship of Basketball.

Dr. Versari is President and Director of the Sport Psychology Program at the San Diego University for Integrative Studies, and has conducted numerous national and international workshops and training programs for athletes, coaches, businesspeople, and academicians.

She is also editor of the online magazine *Performance and Sport Psychology*. Her innovative work as a sport psychologist has been featured in *Psychology Today*, *Sports Illustrated*, the *Los Angeles Times*, the *San Diego Union Tribune*, and the *San Diego Business Journal*. In addition, she has appeared on MSNBC, Fox News, and Court TV.

Contents

Acknowledgments

ANY AUTHOR WORTH HIS OR her salt will tell you that there are always dozens of people without whose faith, help, friendship, and guidance the book would not have been possible.

In being true to myself, I will first thank the Creator for blessing me all these years. Christianity has given me the peace that I have longed for and come to enjoy as a servant of Jesus Christ.

Heartfelt gratitude and appreciation go also to:

My soul mate, my queen, and lifelong companion, my wife, Monya Funderburke, for inspiring me to write this book. Without her I would be lost in a chaotic world. I am forever indebted to her and to our daughter, Nyah.

My mother, "Ma Dukes," for her constant support over the years.

My grandmother, Adell Via, for her knowledge and intellectual insights. She taught me that wisdom can only be obtained from those who have gone before you. Young men and women who learn this early will save themselves a great deal of heartache and pain later in life.

My other family members for their unwavering faith and support.

My teachers from grammar school through college for their insights and expertise. They have been and are underpaid for what they offer and share. Their tenacity is a constant source of inspiration.

My friends who have been there for me and sustained me through the years.

My mentors and coaches throughout my amateur years, including: John Hardiman, Nate Mitchell, Jack Roberts, Fran Anthony, Dan Downing, Bill Chupil, and Dr. Carole Scifres.

Coach Scott Weakley and Coach Chuck Kemper for their patience with me during my teenage years. I have nothing but the greatest respect for them, though I have not always been wise enough to say so.

Coach Bobby "The General" Knight, with whom I haven't spoken since I transferred from Indiana University in 1989. I will always remember the chilling words he spoke as he put his arm around me before practice one fateful day: "Lawrence, just think about those #!#!#!#!#!#!#! back in Columbus who said you wouldn't last this long here . . ." They were right. Almost everyone knows what happened next on that same day. Under Coach Knight's watchful eye and unswerving discipline I did learn to speak my mind. He is truly, an absolute genius of the game (be sure to read Appendix C for the details of this human-interest story and legendary figure).

Coach Randy Ayers for welcoming me home as a transfer student-athlete. I had two opportunities to leave college early for the pros, but his candid advice convinced me to stay and complete my degree. The invaluable lessons and knowledge about the many intricacies of finance have helped me to manage my personal financial affairs. Thanks, too, to Coach Ayers for his in-depth teaching of the game as well.

These men and women not only helped to prepare me for the NBA, but also, and perhaps more important, they helped me to become a better person.

The Sacramento Kings and Maloof Sports and Entertainment for the opportunity to fulfill my lifelong dream to play in the NBA.

The University of Phoenix online program for helping me to cultivate and enhance my writing skills. Although my journey toward an MBA is not yet complete, the program has compelled me to become a more articulate and refined writer.

My fans for their support through the years.

My editors, Joyce Tarpley, Beth Riley, and Shannon Springmeyer.

My literary attorneys, Theodore Scudder and John Ostojic.

Last but certainly not least, my spiritual mentor, Dan Springmeyer, who held me accountable to ensure that my message is gracefully presented.

Foreword

IN *HOOK ME UP, PLAYA!* NBA pro Lawrence Funderburke provides a realistic description of some of the obstacles professional athletes face in establishing their careers. I must admit this book was difficult reading at times because it reminded me of my own experiences. Lawrence is quite correct in his observations about well-compensated professional athletes being easy targets for scams and con artists.

A professional athlete's life seems glamorous. Most people probably believe that between the attention and the fantastic salaries, pro athletes don't have a care in the world. True, many pro athletes have been blessed with remarkable skills that may allow them to earn huge sums of money at a relatively early age. But nothing in life is entirely free. There is a price to be paid. For pro athletes the price is time, privacy, and financial commitments that often surpass their salaries.

Although athletics is what they do best, athletes should remember two things. First, an athlete's career is, as a rule, short. Second, active participation in and an understanding of financial affairs are crucial—more so even than winning or losing.

Athletes are usually taught from an early age to be the best at what they do. Unfortunately, they are often led to believe that education can be left for later on in their lives. While many business opportunities can indeed wait, athletes should learn as much as possible while they are playing. Through education and by exercising extreme care, they can control their own financial destiny regardless of whether they choose to invest now or in the future.

Contrary to what most people think, all athletes are not millionaires. Even those who are do not have unlimited wealth. Helping people who are genuinely in need is commendable. But an athlete who tries to help everyone who has a hand out will end up broke as well as disenchanted with his fellow human beings. Athletes should also remember that helping people does not always mean giving away money. There are dozens of non-monetary ways to be of service.

In *Hook Me Up, Playa!* Lawrence also touches on the increasing problem of parents who obsessively push their children into careers as professional athletes. This is a travesty that is becoming commonplace, whether because of the large salaries some professional athletes command, the media attention they receive, or the pedestal on which they are often (mistakenly) placed by society.

Please don't misunderstand. I have made my living in professional sports and would never condemn it as a career choice. I do, however, condemn pushing a child into a career in sports—or anything else—if the child's interests lie elsewhere. There is a fine line between parental zeal and coercion, and children who are desperate to please unthinking parents often do themselves more harm than good. Gifted athletes who end up resenting parental pressures are not uncommon.

I am inclined to believe (as is discussed in this book) that many parents have come to see their children as investments for the future. Whatever the motivations, parents need to remember that their first and most important job is to provide the love and support their children need. As for career paths, young people themselves should make those decisions. The physical, mental, emotional, and spiritual demands of a career in professional sports are beyond the comprehension of most people. For that reason, no one, not even a parent, has the right to make that choice for another person—not even one's own child.

Most important, parents and youngsters need to remember that the percentage of young athletes who make it to the pros is infinitesimally small. The primary goal of young people and their parents should be a solid education. We need to replace the term "athlete-student" with "student-athlete" so that kids will learn to be students first.

If you decide to pursue a career in professional sports, a realistic assessment of the likelihood of success is critical. If you are fortunate enough to receive an athletic scholarship, use it to earn a potentially lucrative degree, not primarily as a possible springboard to the pros. If you work hard, you can get the degree, whereas you may not get to the pros, no matter how hard you work. That doesn't mean you shouldn't try. It just means you should know what you're up against in the real world—not the fantasy world created by marketing, Madison Avenue, and the media.

Hook Me Up, Playa! is an educational exploration of the other side of the life of the professional athlete. If you're a young person thinking of a career in professional sports, or a parent wondering whether such a career is right for your child, by all means read this book. If you are a die-hard (or only occasional) sports fan, or if you have no interest in sports at all, but are simply fascinated by human behavior, this book is for you as well. One thing is certain: it is much more than a book about sports.

In short, *Hook Me Up, Playa!* is worth your time, whatever your interests.

Best Wishes,
Lou Piniella
Manager of the Tampa Bay Devil Rays

≋≋≋

Originally signed by the Cleveland Indians in 1962, Lou Piniella was drafted by the Washington Senators in 1963 and, in 1964, spent a brief period with the Baltimore Orioles.

He returned to Cleveland as an outfielder in 1968. (It was rumored that he decided to become an outfielder after he was hit by a number of bad pitches as a catcher.)

In 1969, he was drafted by the Seattle Pilots, and then traded to the Kansas City Royals where he garnered honors as American League Rookie of the Year. Three years later, Piniella was traded to the New York Yankees where consistent play and clutch hitting endeared him to fans. During four consecutive years in which the Yankees made it to the World Series, Piniella compiled a lifetime .319 average.

Piniella retired from active play in 1984, and became first a scout, then a batting coach, and finally team manager for the Yankees. No doubt in part because of a predictably stormy relationship with Yankees' owner, George Steinbrenner, Piniella eventually left the Yankees and went on to become manager of the Cincinnati Reds.

In 1990, the Reds became the first National League team to maintain a first place standing throughout the season. The '91 and '92 seasons were less successful, however, and Piniella returned to the American League to manage the then beleaguered Seattle Mariners. That year, the Mariner's finished with a record of 82 and 80. In 1995, they made the playoffs. In 1996, they beat the Boston Red Sox. With that victory, Piniella set a record for the most wins by a manager of any single franchise.

In 2001, the team won 116 games, tying a 95-year-old major league record.

Introduction

The Book

IF YOU ARE AN AVID sports fan, *Hook Me Up, Playa!* is for you. If the extent of your interest in sports is watching the Super Bowl and the last game of the World Series every year, this book is for you, too. If you have no interest whatsoever in sports, but rather an abiding interest in the peculiarities of human nature, this book is for you as well.

Before I tell you what this book is about, it might be a good idea to tell you what it is not about. It is not (in essence) about the sultry advances of groupies, although there are references to them. The underlying premise of this book goes well beyond that kind of interaction.

The image of professional athletes (indeed of celebrities, in general) as arrogant, overpaid whiners with the world (money, fame, and status) at their feet is a prevalent perception, albeit one of debatable accuracy. Whether a person agrees or disagrees with this portrayal, however, it must be noted that high-profile athletes are subject to outrageous requests and demands on their finances and their time, to say nothing of numerous scams, cons, rip-offs, and outright theft. These experiences are not only financially damaging, they also leave emotional and psychological scars that may, in some instances, help the casual observer to understand why professional athletes often seem elusive and aloof to the public.

Whatever the public perception may be, a personal element in the saga of the professional athlete, particularly since the advent of mega-salaries and heightened notoriety, deserves to be explored. Under the near-constant barrage of calculated and often criminal advances, many professional athletes have come to feel betrayed, disillusioned, skeptical, cynical, and openly mistrustful of the motives of almost everyone they meet. The principles and skills a pro athlete must successfully develop to cope with these situations can be useful to anyone dealing with trust, personal finance, and long-term planning.

The stories presented here, in the words of the athletes (and others) involved, are real. No attempt was made to fabricate or exaggerate the incidents in an attempt to gain reader sympathy for past, current, or future athletes. The experiences about which you will read are as much a part of the professional athlete's life as the sport they play, except that in these instances "the opposition" sometimes turned out to be unscrupulous agents and financial advisors, and close acquaintances—those who were counted among an inner circle of people the athlete believed could be trusted. Indeed, much of the anger, pain, and anguish professional athletes experience comes when they make themselves available to others whose ulterior motives do not become apparent until the damage is already done. So, one of this book's goals is to reveal principles of cautious discernment that people from every income stratum can benefit from.

Hook Me Up, Playa! is also a wake-up call for current and future athletes—and their parents, many of whom are paying enormous sums for private training in the hope that their child will be the next Michael Jordan, Tiger Woods, or Roger Clemens. It is my hope that this book will help future athletes and their parents to understand the side of the professional athlete's life that is not visible to the public. To see not just the notoriety, attention, fame, and fortune, but also the tremendous hazards that lie in wait. Everybody, it seems, wants a piece of the professional athlete, figuratively and literally.

To perform effectively in their very public venue, professional athletes must resolve and learn from detrimental private experiences. Many, if not most, succeed and are able to perform at the highest level in their sport. This success is often misconstrued by the public, who tend to think of the professional athlete as a carefree person leading a charmed life. It is my hope that *Hook Me Up, Playa!* will help to alleviate this misconception.

Among other key inside observers of modern-day athletes and the dilemmas they face, a number of current and former high-profile athletes agreed to share their experiences for this book (see "The Author's Friends"). These athletes come from diverse backgrounds and have distinct personalities and opinions.

About now you may be thinking, "Are you telling me that most professional athletes have experienced or are experiencing the difficulties and entanglements described in this book?"

The answer is an unequivocal yes! As you read these stories, substitute the name of your favorite superstar athlete or hometown athletic hero who has made it to the big leagues. Their experiences, if not identical, are similar enough to be startling. Ask any sport's superstar, and ask him about the validity of the assertions made in this book. To a greater or lesser degree, depending on the level of his fame, he has faced the problems and betrayals you will read about here. Using this backdrop, another goal is to provide insights and combative strategies for everyone—athletes and non-athletes alike.

Success is a double-edged sword. The more successful you become, the sharper the downside edge. On the surface, at least, it would seem that the only way to avoid the scam artists and those operating under false pretenses is to avoid human interaction altogether. Realistically, this is not possible, since such an action would necessarily include avoiding close relationships; indeed, all those within the circle of people an athlete deems trustworthy.

Professional athletes are often criticized for not welcoming the public's attention off the court with the same intensity and fervor they portray while playing their games. Although many professional athletes (and other celebrities as well) are, in reality, very private and friendly people, the basis for their seemingly unwelcoming attitude is most often fear: of being conned, tricked, taken advantage of, or publicly disrespected.

Hook Me Up, Playa! is my attempt to tell the other side of the story in an unbiased, uncensored, and honest manner. There is no hidden agenda here. Beyond sensationalized media accounts, the public is unaware of the common predicaments and obstacles that come with the life of a professional athlete, along with the fame and fortune.

As you will see, many of the professional athletes who agreed to speak with me for this book were quite perplexed about the things that have happened to them: the times they've been victimized by scam artists, betrayed by people they believed they could trust, and so on. Their pain is as real as yours would be in similar circumstances. How they cope with betrayal and move forward provides valuable lessons for all of us.

For most people, fame and wealth—especially wealth—seem like the answer to every prayer. Actor Denzel Washington (among others) once said, "Money can't buy happiness, but it can make a heckuva down payment." It would be hard to find anyone who would disagree with that. The flip side is that for many people, celebrities and professional athletes are prime targets for exploitation as an easy way to fulfill their own dreams of wealth. Thus, the attitude becomes, "He's got so much, he won't miss a few thousand." But even if an athlete were willing and able to fulfill the professional, personal, and financial needs of everyone he meets, the question remains: what happens when his money and time commitment run out? Athletes and celebrities may have far more money (and maybe even more time) than the average person, but their time and money are just as finite as yours. There are limits—for all of us.

By no means do I discount the role of fans as the driving force behind the tremendous fame and fortune we professional athletes enjoy. Without tuned-in fans, teams and their players would not have the luxuries that come with lucrative multi-media contracts. This phenomenon has forever changed the landscape of professional sports. With the increased attention and compensation, unfortunately, "hook-me-uppers" (individuals looking for, expecting, demanding, or even illegally taking from, professional athletes), have also become more vocal and problematic.

Does this mean that professional athletes are exempt from responsibility to their fans? Absolutely not! A player may give a fan a high five along with the football he caught to score the winning touchdown at the end of the game. Later, the very same player may seem to ignore the very same fan that waits for him after the game in hopes of having that football autographed. Certainly, the fan is entitled to wonder about this bizarre behavioral transformation. Is it because the players want their space when the game is finished? In some cases, the answer is, understandably, yes. But a large part of the change in demeanor may simply reflect a defensive "what-does-this-person-want-from-me-now?" reaction. Professional athletes are so accustomed to emitting these signals that they may not realize they are doing it.

But this book is not about excuses. It is about helping fans to realize that professional athletes are people, too. Michael Jordan once said that one of the biggest disadvantages to fame is that, as a public figure, you can never be in a bad mood. This is something to which we can all relate independent of our circumstances.

If you are a former or current professional athlete, I hope this book will be a blessing to you. As NBA player Gary Trent notes, our lives are not all glitz and glamour. This is a huge misconception, even though it must be admitted that the advantages usually outweigh the drawbacks.

According to famed television talk show host Dr. Phil, roughly 20 million youths participate in sports each year. It should not come as a surprise then, to find countless numbers of young people (or at the insistence of their parents, anyway) gravitating toward careers in professional sports. Author Melvin Helitzer wrote, "This is the best of times for sports. It is already the 22nd largest industry in the U.S. It ranks ahead of autos, lumber and air transportation. By 1995 total sports revenue had exceeded the $100 billion mark. Those figures may be fly droppings compared with the next 20 years." And pro athletes are reaping generously from revenue calculations, given the fact that the average salary of a Major League Baseball (MLB), National Hockey League (NHL), National Football League (NFL), and National Basketball Association (NBA) player is rapidly climbing, well over a million dollars per year.

To all future and aspiring professional athletes and their parents and guardians who are doing everything within their power to support their children's dreams, *Hook Me Up, Playa!* will give you some insight into the "other side" of a professional athlete's life, not the glamorous lifestyle sensationalized in the media. Hype sells, as you know. My hope is that this book will help prepare your son or daughter if he or she is fortunate enough to travel the professional athlete's road. There are so many things that I would have handled differently if I'd had the right guidance. Relationships, emotional, and financial experiences must be scrupulously examined to avoid debilitating entanglements. Suffice it to say, notoriety plus a mega-salary creates opportunities for swindlers and con artists when an athlete fails to grasp "the game outside of their game."

Federal Reserve Chairman Alan Greenspan, a hero of mine and arguably the most important figure in our world economy, recently touched upon a troubling theme with which you will be acquainted while reading *Hook Me Up, Playa!* Hold these words close to your heart because they'll keep you focused on my intent. He articulated in a *USA Today* interview: "Many [people] appear to have succeeded in a material way by cutting corners and manipulating associates, both in their professional and in their personal lives . . . But material success is possible in this world, and far more satisfying, when it comes without exploiting others."

My prayer is that every young person reading *Hook Me Up, Playa!* will absorb Mr. Greenspan's time-tested advice while establishing their careers, regardless of the chosen field.

One disclaimer: throughout this book I use the pronoun "he" when referring to an athlete. This is not meant in any way to disparage the importance and contribution of women, in the past, present, and future, to professional sports. If anything, the use of "he" is an indication of the inequities that continue to exist for women in professional sports, particularly insofar as salaries are concerned. Fewer statistics appear to be available on the careers of female professional athletes. Rather than run the risk of providing incorrect information, I preferred to err on the side of caution.

Finally, please feel free to contact me to discuss any of the issues raised in this book. I can be reached via the website:

www.hookmeupplaya.com

and I look forward to hearing from you.
Thank you!

The Author

I WAS BORN AND REARED in the Sullivant Gardens Housing Projects in Columbus, Ohio, in a single-parent home. To counteract the effects of our poverty-stricken, crime-ridden environment, my mother, Laura Funderburke, instilled in me at an early age an absolute faith in God and an unswerving desire for academic excellence. With determination, fortitude, love, and support of three older sisters: Adele Gowens, Gina Funderburke, and Tamara Funderburke, I survived the chaos and dangers of the streets.

After graduating with honors from Father Joseph Wherle Memorial High School in 1989, I went on to Indiana University and then transferred to Ohio State University, from which I graduated magna cum laude in 1994 with a degree in business finance. In 1992, I teamed with future NBA star Jimmy Jackson to help Ohio State win the Big Ten Championship.

Drafted by the Sacramento Kings in 1994, I played three seasons overseas before returning to Sacramento, where I played from 1997 to 2004. Nicknamed "Instant Offense," and a member of the famed "Bench Mob," I was a key reserve player for the Kings during my first five years in the NBA. In April 2005, I signed with the Chicago Bulls.

Off the court, I was proud to work with inner city youth and honored to receive the first Hometown Hero of the Month Award in 2001. This award goes to NBA players for their dedication and commitment to the community. I founded the non-profit Lawrence Funderburke Youth Organization (LFYO) to help improve the social, moral, and academic standing of at-risk youth. Our motto is, "Are you a positive one or a negative zero?" We aim to bridge the gap between corporate America and inner city youth (for more information on LFYO, go to www.lfyo.org).

While at Ohio State, I met Monya Fairrow, who would become my wife in 1998. We are Christians and have been blessed with a beautiful daughter, Nyah Ariel. Currently, I am working on an MBA through the University of Phoenix online program. I have many hobbies, but my greatest joy is spending time with my family.

The Author's Friends

Friendship is the hardest thing in the world to explain. It's not something you learn in school. But if you haven't learned the meaning of friendship, you really haven't learned anything.

—Muhammad Ali
Heavyweight Boxing Champion, 1974 and 1978;
Olympic Light Heavyweight Champion, 1960

THIS BOOK WOULD NOT HAVE been possible without the candid, riveting testimonials of my friends and colleagues and their willingness to share their thoughts and feelings on a number of deeply personal issues. I can never thank them enough or praise them enough for their frankness and honesty.

Jeff Blackwell: Lieutenant, Columbus Police Department; sidebar-security expert and mentor for many well-known professional athletes.

Petri Byrd: Better known as "Bailiff Byrd" on the hit television show "Judge Judy."

Kris Draper: Stanley Cup Champion and professional hockey player with the Detroit Red Wings.

Rickey Dudley: Veteran tight end with the Tampa Bay Buccaneers; member of the 2002 Super Bowl team.

Monya Funderburke: Wife of an NBA player—namely, the one who wrote this book. (Monya was a bit apprehensive about speaking on some of the topics covered here, but I felt it was imperative to have the perspective of a wife or significant other because many of them have had some of the same experiences by virtue of their association with the athletes. Certainly, over the years my lovely wife has dealt with many of the issues raised here.)

Charley Hannah: Former NFL pro; starting offensive lineman for the 1984 Super Bowl Champion, Los Angeles Raiders.

Dennis Hopson: Former basketball player; all-time leading scorer at Ohio State University; third overall pick in the 1987 NBA draft; reserve guard on the 1991 Chicago Bulls NBA Championship team.

Barry Katz: Former lead sports anchor for WBNS 10 TV in Columbus, Ohio; more than twenty years in sports as a journalist and broadcaster.

Danny Levitt: Assistant Vice President and financial advisor with Merrill Lynch.

Mark Masser: Associate and summer league sponsor of teams that included NBA players Nick Van Exel, Corrie Blount, and Derek Anderson.

Thad Matta: Men's basketball coach at Ohio State University.

Rick Oliver: Registered and Certified Reflexology Therapist who has worked with several professional athletes.

Steve Sax: Five-time All Star Major League Baseball player with the Los Angeles Dodgers and the New York Yankees; World Series Champion in 1981 and 1988; currently a branch manager and Vice President of Private Client Group Investments at RBC Dain Rauscher, Sacramento, California.

Elie Seckbach: Sports journalist covering the NBA for several newspapers in Los Angeles and Israel; Emmy and Golden Mike Award winner.

Stephen A. Smith: Sportswriter for the *Philadelphia Enquirer* and NBA analyst for ESPN.

Anthony Telford: Sixteen years as a professional baseball player, including six years in the major leagues.

Gary Trent: Nine-year NBA veteran; former college Mid-American Conference (MAC) Player of the Year.

Greg Vaughn: Former Major League Baseball All Star.

Aaron Ward: Stanley Cup Champion, Detroit Red Wings; currently with the Carolina Hurricanes.

Michael Wertheim: Certified Public Accountant (CPA) for many professional athletes.

It was not easy for some of these people to publicly share many of their most painful experiences from years in the limelight. Because of their courage, readers will get a realistic glimpse of life on the other side of fame, and current and future athletes will be more keenly aware of the high stakes at play in the world of the professional athlete. I am grateful for the insights of these professionals, and from the bottom of my heart, I thank them all.

Chapter 1

Hook Me Up? It's A Mind-set

You shall know the truth, and the truth shall make you mad.
—Aldous Huxley

"HOOK ME UP!" WHAT DOES it mean? The closest benign translation is, "Can you do me a favor?" Sad to say, in the world of the professional athlete, "hook me up" is almost never a benign, one-time, request. There are always strings attached, and the hook-me-uppers are often cunning and devious. It is not just a favor they want. What they want is more—more of the athlete's time, more access to his contacts (real or perceived), and most of all, more money. Always, more money.

Of course, one doesn't have to be a professional athlete or a celebrity to be subject to the hook-me-up mind-set. A customer may see an item on a store shelf and, having decided that the price is too high, approach the sales clerk with a pitch such as, "Hey, man. Is this really the price that a struggling brother like me has to pay?" The goal is to obtain the item at a lower price by making the clerk feel guilty about his own status and thus obligated toward the customer, based on some presumed common background they may share. Other hook-me-uppers may be less subtle. "Hey, man. I know you can help a brother out by selling me this for less." The goal is the same: to get a lower price by making the clerk feel guilty or obligated.

I asked my wife, Monya, for her definition of the phrase "hook me up." She thought a moment, then said, "Letting someone in on the goods."

For the record, there is nothing wrong with receiving or asking for help. We all do it. I have helped a great many people and will continue to do so, and I know many other athletes who feel the same way. But there is a tremendous difference between helping someone because you want to and encountering a near-constant barrage of demands for help, as though, by virtue of his success, an athlete is obligated to share the wealth without reservation. This is where many professional athletes have drawn the proverbial line in the sand.

As I was watching game one of the 2004 American League Championship Series (ALCS), it occurred to me with absolute certainty that those players were being subjected to a full-on avalanche of ticket requests. No doubt some of them had to turn off their cell phones to avoid the distractions (although human resolve is such that if someone really wants to reach you, they will find a way).

Every professional athlete is bombarded on a regular basis by people who have elevated the hook-me-up mind-set to an art form. It may be free tickets, personal loans, free vacations, cars, complimentary perks, inflated markups, bogus investment opportunities—the sky's the limit. The hook-me-up mind-set encompasses any scheme that is imaginable.

With that in mind, I confess to some apprehension as I began to approach athletes about being interviewed for this book. Among the fraternity of professional athletes there is an unspoken law to which each of us is bound. Upon entering the fraternity, athletes are sworn to respect the rights and privileges of their fellow athletes by not soliciting hook-me-up ploys, regardless of the nature of the inquiry.

Thus, I was afraid that the people I approached would see my request as a kind of hook-me-up, even though that was never my goal. I wanted nothing more than their insights based on their experiences to add credibility to the book's premise: that the hook-me-up mind-set is real, not a figment of the professional athlete's imagination; that every professional athlete is subject to it; and that the higher he climbs up the ladder of success, the fiercer and more outlandish the hook-me-uppers become. Sharing the lessons learned can be beneficial to individuals in all financial strata of our society, since even retired persons on fixed incomes can get ripped off by sheep in wolves clothing.

To avoid dealing with the hook-me-up encounter, many professional athletes will give someone the cold shoulder by not returning their phone calls, all the while wondering to themselves, "Now, what does this person want?" This is an instinctive reaction ingrained into the psyche of each athlete. It makes them skeptical, not just of fans and strangers, but also of other athletes.

In some ways, an athlete's reaction when confronted by a hook-me-upper is similar to the reaction of a child who is confronted by a bully. The child will either run or stand his ground in spite of the fear that he is about to be beaten up. For the professional athlete, hook-me-up encounters almost always end with him being financially and/or emotionally "beaten up."

To achieve a balanced perspective, I interviewed past and present athletes from four major sports: hockey, basketball, football, and baseball. Do not take this to mean that professional golfers, tennis players, and other high-profile, well-paid athletes, to say nothing of well-known entertainers and other celebrities, are not targeted by hook-me-uppers. People like

Oprah Winfrey, Tiger Woods, Michael Jordan, and Serena Williams, just to name a few, must place numerous barriers between themselves and various inquiries, even though some (like mine, for example) may be well-intended and legitimate.

My two-fold objective in writing *Hook Me Up, Playa!* is first to provide a realistic glimpse of the other side of the world of the professional athlete for fans, current and future athletes, and the general public. Secondly, to convey life lessons, helpful to all, in dealing with life's financial curve balls. This is not about generating sympathy. It is about understanding the effect of the hook-me-up mind-set on professional athletes who must live with it every day. In the future, should you run into one of your heroes who does not seem to welcome your adulation with open arms, perhaps you will remember some of the things you have read here and be less inclined to deride him (or her) for not responding as you would prefer. They are not trying to hurt your feelings. They are trying to protect themselves from what they perceive as the possibility of another hook-me-up encounter of the worst kind.

So, the next time you hear the phrase, "Hook me up!" I hope you will listen with a keener understanding. If you have never heard it, I hope this book will provide you with some understanding just in case you do.

Chapter 2

Show Me the Money!

"Money is honey. Money is honey."
—from *The Producers*

The Main Hookup

WITHOUT QUESTION, THE MAIN THING the hook-me-uppers want from professional athletes is "borrowed" money: money to either get them out of a bind, pad risky investments, pay off a mortgage, or put somebody's child through college. You name it. Some close acquaintances, and even complete strangers—want money from professional athletes, who are often viewed as the perennial cash cows. On the other hand, it's an absolute joy to help close loved ones (or strangers) in their time of need. Most professional athletes feel the same way.

Once the hook-me-uppers get what they want, they often get a bad case of amnesia when it comes to the said "loan(s)." Many of the athletes I interviewed for this book said that they were less bothered by the so-called loan than by the hook-me-upper's unwillingness to at least acknowledge the debt. A simple phone call would be enough: "I haven't forgotten about what I owe you, but things are still a little tight, so I can't pay you right now. If you can just be patient with me a little longer, I should be able to pay you back in a few months." Here, at least, the athlete is not left with the feeling that he is being taken for granted. More to the point, it shows at least a modicum of courtesy, which goes a long way with most people—not just professional athletes. Borrowing money with no intention of returning it is bad enough. Not bothering to acknowledge the debt, particularly if you will be back in the future for another "withdrawal," makes the athlete feel like even more of a chump. It also makes him angry and much less likely to open his wallet the next time.

An integral part of the hook-me-up mind-set is the erroneous assumption that the professional athlete earns so much that he will not miss the paltry sums (as the hook-me-upper sees it) he hands out. It never seems to occur to them that a thank-you might grease the path to our wallets a bit more for the next request. You see, the hook-me-upper almost never strikes just once. There will always be another "crisis": another expense that comes due, another loan payment (to somebody else, of course) due, a new investment that "can't fail."

Some acquaintances come to me for a loan (it is always a "loan," even though they often have no intention of paying it back), and then disappear from my life for months, even years. That is, until the next financial crisis hits, at which point they come back to the First National Bank of Funderburke. I might add that almost all of those "loans" (some of which range into the thousands of dollars) remain outstanding.

"You're the only one I can turn to," is a common approach—the professional athlete as a life preserver. There is nothing like guilt for accomplishing what might not be achieved otherwise. In truth, the hook-me-uppers come to the professional athlete because no one else would be inclined to lend them money, even grudgingly.

Petri Byrd noted, and I agree, that people who are hurting for money borrow from athletes because they (sometimes mistakenly) believe that an athlete is the only one who has it readily available.

Also, many times the professional athlete is closely connected with the borrower, and subsequently, he or she may find it easier to borrow from the athlete than from a total stranger. There may even be no underlying intent not to pay back the loan. It's simply that the person is in a jam and they may think that if for some reason they are unable to pay back the loan, the professional athlete is (in their mind) the one who is in the best position to absorb the financial loss. Quite often the same person may approach an athlete for a loan more than once. Although the person may be too ashamed to come right out and ask for money the second time, they still find ways to make it clear that they are in financial trouble—again—and count on the athlete to feel sorry for them and bail them out—again. As my wife, Monya, noted, "Be prepared for more phone calls and requests, because you can never help some people enough. You do it because you care about people, but they take your kindness and your money for granted."

The holy passion of friendship is so sweet and steady and loyal and enduring in nature that it will last through a whole lifetime, if not asked to lend money.

—Mark Twain

Professional athletes learn quickly that the first casualty of a loan to a friend is often the friendship itself. In fact, money can become an obstacle in any relationship, especially if the lender feels that his money is being squandered rather than put to good use. Suppose, for example, you loan money to a friend because he or she is behind in mortgage payments, and later you learn that the money was spent at the track? Care to guess what your attitude will be if (make that *when*) that friend comes back for more? Care to guess what your friend's attitude will be when (make that *if*) you say no?

Too many experiences like this can leave an athlete with a bad taste in his mouth. After having been burned a few times, Dennis Hopson is emphatic: "If a friend comes to you to borrow some money, eight out of ten times you are not going to get it back. So don't expect it."

Athletes, being human just like the rest of us, can easily be persuaded to feel sorry for people. A former teammate, who claimed that his wife had cancer and that he could not afford the treatment she needed, once asked Steve Sax for $10,000 to help with the medical costs. Sax was all set to help until he found out that the man's wife didn't have cancer. Although this happened some time ago, Sax still feels disheartened by the experience and shares Hopson's feelings on the matter, that if you loan money, the chances are you will not get it back.

If an athlete is big-hearted and wants to share, very soon it's open season for some "distant folk hook-me-uppers" to come out of the woodwork. As Gary Trent noted, "One cousin will ask for $500. Another asks for $200. Another asks for $500, and another, and another. Pretty soon you're out two or three thousand dollars. They keep coming back, too. Some of them think they are the only ones who have been hooked up. Others figure, 'Well, he's got so much that he will never miss it.'"

Valuing money should be the same whether you're rich or poor.

—L. Funderburke

How does an athlete convince someone that lending $500 isn't insignificant, especially when that person has just seen his annual salary in *USA Today*? It's a hard sell, to say the least, especially to the "homies," the guys who were your "runnin' buddies back in the 'hood." They're the least likely to be convinced, and if they walk away empty-handed, they're most likely to be angry. Valuing money should be the same whether you're rich or poor.

Some players view loans (small ones, anyway) in religious terms. For example, the Bible instructs that you forgive the debts of others, particularly if they cannot pay back the money borrowed. Anthony Telford summed up his philosophy this way: "If I am willing to lend money in a particular situation, then I'm willing not to have it paid back. I go into the situation knowing that."

Religious precepts aside, many athletes do expect to be paid back if they loan money. The most infuriating situation is when the hook-me-upper refuses to pay back the loan even when he or she has reached a position where it is possible to do so. As Greg Vaughn says, "I think they forget that we have feelings just like they have feelings."

Then, too, the hook-me-uppers often fail to recognize that, unlike other professions, most athletic careers are comparatively short. Thus, an athlete has only so much time to secure a financial future for himself and his family. As NHL professional Kris Draper put it, "Basically, I have between six and eight years (left in my career) to set myself and my family up in order not to have to work again, whereas, everyone else I know is going to be working in their sixties and will be earning a living for a long time. I have to make as much money as I can in a short span of time. I've worked hard to put myself in this situation, and I don't want people, especially my friends, to take advantage of my hard work and success."

Another factor, with which the professional athlete has to contend daily, is the implied promise of financial help. Someone asks me for a loan and, instead of saying no plainly, I may say:

"I am not promising you anything—because right now I am not sure I can help you—but I will see what I can do later," or

"I might be able to, but then again, I might not," or

"If you call back next week I will let you know, but not now," or

"I would be lying if I said that I couldn't help, but now is not a good time," or

"I don't think I can do anything for you at the present moment, but next week or next month might be a different story."

My wife has warned me a million times not to leave that door open (and she is usually right!). Yet with every one of these responses I am leaving the door open as it relates to their inquiry. There is no way the hook-me-upper will forget it. If I say, however casually, "maybe next week," I can count on hearing from the hook-me-upper the following week, right on the dot.

Nor does it matter how long the "door" was left open. Countless acquaintances have approached me about fulfilling (usually expensive) promises that I supposedly made years ago, perhaps purely in jest. Hook-me-uppers are like elephants: they never forget.

Most hook-me-uppers will not persist if an athlete says no, unless he has said no in the past, then later given in when pushed a little further, usually by comments intended to induce guilt. The assumption is always the same: that he will never miss the money requested.

Then, too, there is the unspoken expectation that once you have "made it," right away you are available to take care of old friends and their families— even the neighborhood. Steve Sax recalls overhearing a conversation about himself. The speaker was berating Sax for not having refurbished the town's Little League field, though as it turned out, he had.

"A lot of times people just assume that you're going to be the savior for [the community]," Sax noted.

Even promises made in jest can come back to haunt an athlete. Anthony Telford remembers, "A guy I knew in college said, 'Whoever makes a million dollars first has to buy the other one a Porsche.' I said, 'Okay, you're on.' We both knew it was a joke. As it happens, he made a million before I did, but my salary was published in the paper. We still kid each other about it. 'Man, how's my Porsche? Have you got it ordered yet?' But I've seen it happen in a very real sense to other teammates, who find themselves being pursued by legions of childhood friends, each one expecting the now-successful athlete to literally take care of him. It's amazing, the mind-set. People, some of whom you barely know at all, completely take you and your success for granted. Recently, at my twentieth high school reunion, I ran into two guys with whom I played Little League as a child. They suggested that we get together for a game of golf. I made the mistake of telling them to pick the place. Well, you can guess the rest. They picked the most expensive club in town on the assumption that I was going to pay. It never fails."

Some athletes have developed artful ways of dodging loan requests. For a while, Gary Trent tried some variation on this as a standard reply to hook-me-uppers: "I have to call my accountants because I went over my budget last month and they've been screaming about how I spent too much. So right now I can't help."

He admits it didn't always work. Sometimes the hook-me-upper comes back the next month. Still, it was better than trying to convince them that he didn't have the money to give. Hook-me-uppers will never believe that, regardless of how true it may be. Although Trent says he will always be available to help a real friend who is going through a genuinely rough time, for the most part he just says no.

I Scratched Your Back . . .

WHEN I WAS in college, I used to bum a ride with a friend of mine, who also bought me food once in awhile. Mistakenly, as it turns out, I thought he was doing these things out of the goodness of his heart. Years later, when I ran into him, I discovered I was wrong. He made it clear that I "owed" him for those kindnesses and that he was ready to be rewarded. Like many forward-thinking hook-me-uppers, he had planted the seeds (a little pocket money, a pair of shoes, a meal here and there) years ago, with the idea of reaping a handsome Return On Investment (ROI) later if and when I became a successful pro.

The truth is, many high school and college athletes with promising careers are broke in the beginning, and most did not come from a privileged background. They are grateful for any gifts or offers of help, and it almost never occurs to them that they may be mortgaging away their future if they accept illegal stipends. Hook-me-uppers instinctively sense this need and exploit it to the fullest. It is a kind of "street venture capitalism." The hook-me-uppers' view is that if they do a few favors to help a young athlete make it, then they (the hook-me-uppers) are entitled to a deferred payment in the future. The mind-set is, "I helped you out when you were getting started. Now it's your turn to help me. It's the least you can do."

Several years ago it was reported that sports agent "Tank" Black had provided several star players with cash and other perks while they competed at the collegiate level. At the time, Black and his agency represented several professional athletes as well. Black has since been sued by several of his former clients, and the Securities and Exchange Commission (SEC) brought money laundering and racketeering charges against him.

Some cash-strapped college athletes would be tempted by such enticing overtures (cars, money, etc.), even though the ensuing backlash can be enormous.

Black's out-of-pocket expenses for such advances were probably quite high, but he knew that his deferred ROI was just around the corner. Shelling out $10,000 in exchange for a possible $1 million (or more) future return is a whopping thousand-percent gain. That is enough incentive for nearly every unscrupulous financial advisor in America to lay down some immediate cash.

To avoid this hook-me-up trap, an athlete had best become a good judge of character, something Kris Draper says his parents instilled in him from an early age. "I've learned that no matter what somebody gives you, they always expect something back. They may give you a little here or there, but one day they are going to ask for something. I've really tried to distance myself from those types of situations."

Even in retirement, an athlete is not immune. "I still run into people who expect me to help them out financially," laments Dennis Hopson. "It's as though they believe that money—your money, that is—never runs out. They can't seem to grasp the idea that although your salary may be bigger, you have responsibilities—bills to pay, things to take care of—just as they do."

Any association, no matter how tenuous, is grounds for an attempted hook-up. (No, I did not say "hold up." We'll get to that later.) As Steve Sax notes, "They usually approach you with something like 'Hey, you know, uh, my cousin knows your uncle's aunt's best friend's nephew. Let's do dinner.' I don't have to tell you who's picking up the tab. But it's not just about the money. It's about your time, as well. They don't seem to realize that you might want to spend your off-time with your wife and family, just like normal people."

One of the biggest prices of fame is the sense it gives to people that you owe them simply because you knew them at some point in your life. Once you've climbed the ladder of success, you are somehow obligated to share the wealth. Gary Trent notes, "I have cousins who are always being told, 'Man, your cousin plays in the NBA! You should be driving this type of car!' or, 'Man, your cousin is in the NBA. You should be wearing this!' I tell them to stop listening to what they hear on the streets. After my NBA draft party, one of my relatives said, 'I'm glad you made it. Don't forget the house you promised me!' It's hard to believe that people even have the nerve to approach you in that way."

Believe it. As a hard-working athlete (or a hard-working anybody), you might be inclined to wonder about people who seem to prefer to spend their lives looking for handouts and financial support.

This is not to say that any one of us can't find ourselves facing some tough financial times once in awhile. But the hook-me-uppers seem to be in a constant state of need, which makes them think of athletes as walking ATM machines. Put in the right number (or message), and the money is automatically dispensed for credit card bills, bank notes, school tuition, clothes, or cars. Bottom line? The hook-me-uppers think that all athletes are rich. But as Gary Trent says, "Rich is when you don't have a budget. I have a budget, so I am not rich."

Promises, Promises

As a summer league sponsor whose teams included several NBA players (Nick Van Exel, Corrie Blount, and Derek Anderson, just to name a few), Mark Masser has shared some especially telling thoughts on the "street venture capitalists" and how they identify and latch onto gifted young athletes. College athletes are the primary targets, though talented sixth- and seventh-graders are not immune. Some (though certainly not all) coaches and so-called advisors see talented young people as walking gravy trains of the future. "They're latching on to them by giving them things and then trying to ride the boat [so] that when the kid turns pro, they can recoup it all plus a hundred times more," Masser says.

If a child with tremendous athletic potential happens to come from a single-parent home, the street venture capitalists will provide a kind of parenting, as well. If only one out of twenty young athletes make it to the pros, then the coaches and advisors will be amply rewarded for their investment. What happens to the kid who buys into all the promises, but in the end doesn't make it? He's quickly forgotten, and the coaches and advisors are off in pursuit of fresh talent to groom.

Ohio State basketball coach Thad Matta has also seen what can happen when people approach kids who have a better-than-average chance of making it to the pros.

"The people who approach these kids are often those who are close to them. It could be a family member or an AAU (Amateur Athletic Union) coach," Coach Matta says. The AAU circuit usually occurs in the summer where the top middle and high school athletes compete on the state or national level to gain exposure.

"Recently the shoe industry (Nike, Adidas, and Reebok) has become a major player in terms of influencing kids to attend a certain school. When (if) the kid turns pro, he is expected to sign with the shoe company as a professional. Whatever benefits the young prospect receives come back to the shoe company a hundredfold through commercials and product endorsements.

"College athletes are given nothing less than 'star' status in college athletics in general, and college basketball in particular. The National Collegiate Athletic Association (NCAA) basketball tournament is the single biggest money-generating event for CBS Sports every year. The money that conferences and schools make for advancing in the tournament is staggering," says Coach Matta. "Small wonder that the push to win, and win big, has created a monster in intercollegiate athletics, and the student-athlete is in the belly of the monster."

True, some people want nothing in return for the benefits they provide to college athletes. Their ROI is often a simple ego boost: pride in knowing or at least feeling as if they are part of the program. Coach Matta notes, "A booster who provides money to an athlete on the side (without the knowledge of the school/staff) can strut around at alumni or booster functions and events and boast that they have a 'relationship' with the quarterback or the school's power forward."

Still, the punishments for an athlete who accepts illegal gifts can range from suspension for a game or games, to dismissal from the team, or a loss of eligibility, since college athletics are considered amateur sports. Acceptance of cash and other benefits puts an athlete in violation of that status.

Coach Matta believes that the same sort of "scouting" (for lack of a better word) that occurs on college campuses happens at the high school level as well. Again, the shoe industry is aggressive in this area, especially given their ability to outfit a high school team with practice and game gear (such as shoes, caps, or parkas). According to Coach Matta, some high schools are fully fitted by major shoe companies.

"Any school that has a rising athletic phenom can expect to receive an offer from a shoe company to set that school up with gear," Matta states. "This not only makes the prospect feel good, but the school feels good about the shoe company, and the company itself gets free advertising because it knows that prospect will get major attention on a national level.

"A shoe company will outfit an Amateur Athletic Union (AAU) team for the same reasons. The difference is that the AAU program/coach will often push the pro prospect toward a particular school that has been outfitted by the same shoe company. For example, an AAU team that wears Nike will often have kids attending Division I schools that also wear Nike gear. If a kid happens to be a 'can't miss' pro, not only will he never finish college, but he will be wearing Nike gear as a pro, too."

So when the next thirteen-year-old kid is already a highly rated player on a national level, you can bet that the "Big Three" of sports gear will know about that kid.

You're in Good Hands—*Not!*

SOME YEARS AGO a former acquaintance, with whom I'd had no contact for quite some time, asked me if he could borrow $90,000, which he would pay back over a period of thirty years just like a conventional mortgage! Contract and pen in hand, he came to my home expecting me to sign on the dotted line at once. Before answering, I went to look in a mirror, thinking that perhaps someone had painted the word "Stupid" on my forehead unbeknownst to me. When I told my wife about the request, she looked at me as though she were trying to decide if I was being funny or was having an end-of-season clearout in the cranial department. It was a preposterous request, and I confess to being surprised that he even had the nerve to ask.

Another time a gentleman who had once done me a great favor in the past tried to interest my wife and me in a real estate investment opportunity. Since neither he nor his partner (I will call them "Mike" and "Tony") was putting up any of their own money, one might have been forgiven for wondering, "opportunity" for whom? In a nutshell, they wanted to use our money to make money for themselves. Mike's job was to bring the high-end investors to Tony, who would "manage" the real estate ventures through his own company. Each would receive a handsome fee for having invested nothing other than their so-called expertise.

For the record, we declined their offer. Apart from the fact that neither Mike nor Tony was investing their money, what they proposed was, at best, a speculative venture. Moreover, the deal seemed unusually confusing even to me, with my background in finance. Finally, and perhaps most importantly, the investment they wanted from us would have totaled several hundred thousand dollars!

In fairness, I have no proof that Mike and Tony were engaged in some type of swindle. I do know that Mike made several attempts to contact other athletes about the same deal.

Sadly, professional athletes (and people in general) are often victimized in this way. "A" will bring high-net-worth athletes to "B," the so-called brains behind the project, ostensibly to facilitate a partnership among all parties involved. For the scheme to work, "A" will usually have met the athlete before (at a game or a nightclub, for example). The friend-of-a-friend strategy is also quite successful. If "A" really is a personal friend of the athlete's, so much the better. That makes "A" seem even more trustworthy.

For the professional athlete, dubious investment opportunities abound, though not always because of an athlete's "rolling-the-dice" financial attitude. More than likely they have been deceived into believing in an absurdly high and immediate ROI. It's usually trusted associates who bring these deals to the table. No matter how many times we remind ourselves of the adage, "if it seems too good to be true, it probably is," each of us wants to believe that certain people in our lives can always be trusted. These people know that athletes will listen to what they have to say, and more often than not, hand over the cash.

So an athlete should never dismiss an instinctive skepticism about a deal regardless of the emotional pull of the person who is putting forth the so-called opportunity. The worst deals for athletes usually come from those in their inner circle. Vast amounts of money have been lost in this way. Several years ago, I lost roughly $100,000 on an investment deal that I was assured (by a trusted individual) couldn't possibly lose. I was upset, of course, but I also learned a lesson. Now I only invest in less risky ventures. The returns may be lower, but they are usually more reliable.

As any good financial advisor will tell you, however, checks and balances among all parties involved can go a long way toward ensuring financial integrity and, most important, rooting out a scam before the damage is done.

Guaranteed claims of unbelievable investment returns and success are almost always exaggerated. There are no guarantees in any aspect of life—least of all in terms of investments and business. Yet it is often the "can't miss" venture that attracts athletes the most, particularly if other athletes are already on board.

In Lorraine Hansberry's timeless play *A Raisin in the Sun,* a young black man loses his father's life insurance benefits when he invests in a deal to become a partner in a bar. Pressured by two or three of his friends, who have already put their money down, the young man succumbs only to learn later that both his money and the friend who first brought the deal to his attention are gone, and that at least one of his other "friends" was in on the scam. (In 1961 *A Raisin in the Sun* was produced as a film and starred actor/director Sidney Poitier as the hapless Walter Lee Younger. In one of the most riveting scenes, he slowly begins to realize that he has been bilked out of the only real money his family ever had. It is no joke to say that you feel his pain.)

Which brings us to the issue of "due diligence": the process of checking the accuracy of information contained in a company's public statement, such as a prospectus, before recommending that company to others; also, the act of one company's investigating another before buying its shares.

In plain English, *Never get involved in any deal, project, business venture, whatsoever without first checking it out thoroughly—in detail.* If you have to spend money to have the deal investigated *by an independent party,* do it! But don't put one dime on the table until you know where that dime is going, what it will be used for, how long it will be there, when it's coming back, and how many of its friends will be coming back with it.

A scam can be so cleverly designed that it actually makes sense—on the surface (infomercials are based on this principle, and they make millions every year). To the scammer this is half the battle, getting his proposed investment project on paper and in front of an athlete. The other half is finding as many other athletes as possible to hook into the deal.

Some have suggested that athletes are particularly vulnerable because they live in a fantasy world where everything somehow magically works out for the better. It's a lovely idea, but it only works in the imagination. The starship *Enterprise*, on "Star Trek: Next Generation," featured a neat recreational venue called the Holodeck. You set it for whatever fantasy place, time, person, or event you wanted, and when you walked in, bingo! There it was: love, fame, fortune, success, happiness, spiritual enlightenment, you name it. On the Holodeck anything was possible. It also wasn't real. In real life, fantasies backfire, and you find yourself back on the bridge heading for a black hole at Warp 9.5.

Undeniably, some professional athletes do get caught up in a fantasy world. Nor can you really blame them, since so many things are available to them literally at the snap of a finger. Small wonder that even if an athlete asks an unscrupulous financial advisor whether there are any risks associated with an investment, the scammer is going to say, "Absolutely not." That's what the athlete wants to hear—it's what athletes are accustomed to hearing.

In the movie version of *The Producers*, greedy con man Max Bialystock seduces the bookish accountant Leo Bloom into participating in a fraudulent scheme by painting a vivid verbal picture of what the money will mean to their lives: "This is freedom from want forever! This is a house in the country!! This is a Rolls Royce and a Bentley!!! This is Wine, Women, and Song!!!! And *Women*!!!!!!" Poor Leo is hooked like a starving catfish.

So a word of warning: The minute a deal starts to sound so unbelievably good that you feel your fingers itching to reach for your checkbook, run for the nearest exit and don't stop running until you're at home and the doors are triple-locked behind you. Just five more minutes in that spider's web, and you will be a dead fly.

But back to due diligence, and how you go about checking on an investment proposition, particularly one that has no prior history. Of course, if the financial advisor's track record is iffy, that's a good sign that you should pass on the deal. Also, many athletes get caught up in a sort of numbers game where the odds of success are presented to them as so high that they "just can't lose." Athletes, better than most people, know how to manipulate circumstances in their favor on the court or in the field. Scam artists know this, and they use that knowledge to entice them into a playing-and-beating-the-odds strategy.

For example, the odds against any one becoming a professional athlete—that is, making it to the NFL, NBA, or NHL—are astronomical. As business tycoon Stedman Graham points out in his book *Move Without The Ball*, "Only 5 percent of high school athletes go on to become college athletes, and only 1 percent get to play at the Division I level. Also, only about 1 in 10,000 [young] athletes go on to become professional athletes."

Yet here we are. We have beaten the odds. Indeed, winning and losing are an intricate part of our everyday professional landscape. The odds that one team will triumph over another depend on a great many factors, including: the skill level of players, the strategy of coaches, the morale of the team, whether the team is playing in a friendly or hostile environment, the strength of the schedule, the collective desire to succeed, and overall mastery of game.

Of course, the odds in favor of a victory go up exponentially with the presence of a Michael Jordan, John Elway, Joe Montana, Nolan Ryan, or a Wayne Gretzky. Yet even with all these things in place, as the great NFL coach Joe Gibbs once observed, "On any given Sunday afternoon, any team in the NFL can beat any other team regardless of which one has the best record." It's all about odds—and good fortune.

Knowing the significance of playing the odds in the life of an athlete, a clever scam artist can easily convince you that if you have beaten the long odds against achieving your current level of professional success, "Why shouldn't the odds be in your favor in a particular business venture? After all, you must have the 'golden touch,' right?" It is a surprisingly easy sell, especially if the scam artist has a reputation as a financial trendsetter or "guru to the stars." Confronted in this manner, the unwary athlete is a mere lamb among wolves.

It is also critical to remember that wives, girlfriends, family members, agents/financial advisors, trusted confidants, acquaintances—in fact, all those who are within an athlete's inner circle of companions—are vulnerable to the advances of financial predators.

For a clever con man (or woman), it can on occasion be remarkably easy to pierce the wall around an athlete and penetrate his inner circle. All it takes is an inside tip or just careful observation. In the world of scam artists, this is the equivalent of due diligence. They will learn as much about an athlete as possible before they make the approach.

The best con artists, of course, appear on the surface to be legitimate and beyond reproach. Gaining your confidence is their agenda. My wife, Monya, is amazingly good at seeing through the sheep's clothing to the wolf underneath. (In fact, a lot of women are good at this. At the risk of being considered a traitor to my gender, they probably get a lot of practice separating the real men from the jive artists and losers.)

Sometimes the initial contact for a scam will come from a third party, a liaison or a runner, who may be working with the scammer or an independent operator with his own deal going on. Whatever the case may be, they will do whatever is necessary to reach the athlete.

Among the most vulnerable are high school and college athletes from impoverished neighborhoods and backgrounds. For these young people, money can seem like a distant dream. When parents have no money to send an athletically-gifted child to college, the temptation of a (seemingly) guaranteed career in the pros and a salary higher than anyone in the home has ever seen is often and understandably irresistible. What teenager doesn't want to drive the finest cars, wear the best clothes, and show off for the homies in the 'hood? Unscrupulous agents, as well as agenda-minded AAU coaches and advance men know this. All manner of predators know this.

It has been reported through various media outlets that star college athletes across the country have accepted gifts from complete strangers. With lucrative licensing arrangements, universities make millions off these amateurs, some of whom don't have two cents to call their own. Knowing, as they do, that everyone else is already making a profit off their talent, they can be overwhelmed by the temptation to accept gifts, in spite of any consequences, especially since the deferred payday for these athletes may still be a few years away. The con artists and scammers know that to a young person, a year can seem like an eternity.

So the star collegiate athlete is a sitting duck, and once he takes the bait, be it money and/or other perks, the people behind those gifts know they have, in effect, set themselves up for a huge payday sometime in the future. Whatever they have spent enticing the young athlete, they will get back—sometimes ten- or twenty-fold.

Of course, once scammers are "in," the athlete will usually feel compelled to reciprocate the seemingly generosity of his newfound "friends." He may also feel compelled to reciprocate this newfound generosity by signing a contract or reimbursing "Santa's helpers" when his pro paychecks start rolling into his bank account. Or else the giver will threaten him with some type of repercussion, perhaps a lawsuit or a word to the NCAA about how they helped Mr. Big-Time College Athlete while his university "parents" ignored these illegal perks.

This is a huge problem that the NCAA must overcome. The NCAA's legislative branch can't police college campuses, nor can a school's athletic program. Why should the burden fall solely on the players' shoulders? Mind you, I am not encouraging college athletes to accept the perks offered. I am just attempting to explain why they might do so. Illegal (or simply unethical) gifts will inevitably prove detrimental to an athlete's eligibility on the collegiate level. I believe this threat could be minimized by a joint effort among universities, coaches, and sports leagues to sell the benefits of an education as much, if not more, than they sell sports.

Whether you are a college athlete or a pro, in fact, regardless of the profession, we all must be on guard against those who seem to be offering us something for nothing. Back in the day, a group called, prophetically, Undisputed Truth, recorded a song called "Smiling Faces Sometimes," which includes the lines, "Beware, beware of the handshake that hides a snake. I'm telling you, beware. Beware of the pat on the back. It just might hold you back."

As a professional athlete's wife, Monya, I'm sure, has had more experience in this arena than she would have preferred.

"A lot of people go out of their way to be extra nice to me, because I think they feel that we have such a close bond that if they get in good with me, then they have a better chance of getting what they need from Lawrence," she said. "They are either 'extra' pleasant, bring me gifts, or being super-nice on the phone. Perhaps some of it is common courtesy, but in most cases the objective is to get to Lawrence to ask for something—money, a favor, etc. They think that going through me gives them a better chance of getting what they want from him.

"I can't speak for other wives, of course, but I'm sure they must get tired of people taking advantage of their husbands and their position. To counteract the hook-me-uppers, a lot of wives probably come across as somewhat distant and snobbish, even at times when they might prefer to be friendlier. For better or worse, we become suspicious of everyone's motives. Unfortunately, our suspicion is usually justified.

"Let's face it: how many people know someone with ready access to millions of dollars, or who they believe has such access? In a way, it stands to reason that you would go to that person if you needed financial help. But that doesn't make it any easier on him or his family.

"Up to now, at least, no one has ever asked me outright to ask Lawrence for financial help. Still, it could happen, and I probably wouldn't be surprised."

Small wonder that professional athletes and celebrities change their cell numbers quite often. As Mark Masser noted, "Once somebody has a professional player's number, they want to meet him to try to sell him insurance, financial planning, clothing, jewelry, etc. Soon the number has been passed around, and he is inundated with calls day and night and often forced to change his phone numbers. What else is there to do?"

I asked Mark if he, as a team associate, summer league sponsor, and a member of the "inner circle" of many well-known athletes, had ever been personally approached to relay messages back to athletes.

"Yes," he said. "I have been approached by other people, such as, again, financial advisors, who want to market their services, so they approach me to try and make a contact for them. I've become sort of a screener for the professional players that I've met."

Because an endorsement from a professional athlete is almost guaranteed to attract other investors, hook-me-uppers looking for business funding will often use an athlete's family and friends as a means to make contact.

Petri Byrd remembers working for a firm that specialized in direct and multi-level marketing plans: "There are always people who assume, because of an athlete's reported salary, that he must have money to invest."

It is not unreasonable to suppose that at least some of the hundreds of investment opportunities that athletes receive are quite legitimate. That said, however, there is no such thing as easy money. "You just have to be discerning about what is legit and what isn't," Byrd advises.

The same holds true for endorsements. An athlete may be the first to be approached to endorse the efforts of a particular nonprofit charitable organization simply because somebody in the organization knows somebody who knows somebody who met him once on some social occasion. Although the organization may be legitimate, it is just as possible that the person who approaches him is just a hook-me-upper in disguise looking for a way to make a fast buck.

"An athlete had better do his homework before agreeing to endorse a particular endeavor," Byrd says. "It may turn out that the best answer is 'thanks, but no thanks.'"

Another common investment opportunity offered to many athletes involves backing a new club, restaurant, independent retail outfit, or other small business. If the athlete is expected to put up all or most of the money for the operation, he should probably pass, or else risk being the primary (or only) loser if the business fails. All parties involved should have capital at risk, to ensure that they fight for success in a tough business environment.

Steve Sax still gets hook-me-up investment requests by mail, prompting him to wonder, "Do they realistically expect me to write a check and send it in the mail to people I don't even know?" Limited partnerships were big in the early to mid-'80s, and Sax remembers being bombarded with investment opportunities in condominiums, apartments, a turbo charge company, and chicken restaurants. He credits the fact that he is now in business—finance—with the precipitous drop in the number of these so-called investment opportunities.

"The hook-me-uppers seem to know that I'm no longer a good candidate for a snow job," he says. "I've lost money on investments before, way back when. Anybody in investing knows the word you can't use is 'guarantee.' You can never guarantee anybody anything. I can guarantee I'll try hard, but I can't guarantee you a return."

Like all athletes, Steve has been approached by hook-me-uppers who openly display an attitude of, "What's $20,000 to him? He makes $5 million a year?" They should know better.

"I hate that," says Steve. "I mean, who decides? How do other people know what you and I need or don't need? Or how we feel about our money? Or whether we've made a lot or lost it all? How can people presume to decide that for you and me? I just don't like it."

Apartment buildings, car lots, dubious real estate deals, you name it, the professional athlete is a prime target for those looking for unwary investors.

It's like somebody robbing you with a pen, instead of a gun.

—Gary Trent

Anthony Telford, who now lives in Florida, got his real estate license when he retired after sixteen years in baseball. He's comfortable with real estate, but pretty much distrustful of other ventures.

"A representative from an Internet company contacted me looking for a huge investment," he says. "They had a contract with American Airlines to provide onboard wireless ISP service, and they were about to take the company public. All the numbers, even the ROI for me, looked good. But I turned it down. Something about it just didn't seem right. You have to be so careful."

Telford recalls even being approached in church on a number of occasions by people looking for investors: "A girl had this idea for a special sharpener for eyeliner pencils. She brought me the whole prospectus and said she needed just $10,000 to get started. It doesn't matter where we go.

"Surprisingly, or perhaps not so surprisingly, people in church are often quicker to approach you than people in other places. They assume, often with good reason, that an athlete will be less likely to distrust someone in church. Also, people in church often feel that they don't need to give as much as they normally might because you're there and your contribution will be large enough to cover theirs and the contributions of several others. It's an amazing mind-set, but it's common. Everybody, wherever you go, has an angle.

"I personally have been very, very conservative. I lost money in the market around the same time everyone else did, but that's about it. I have seen guys make poor decisions—'My buddy started me in an Internet company. My friend has this invention'—and giving them $10,000, $20,000, $30,000, $50,000, $100,000 and losing it, and then wondering why."

Telford continues, "I have a pro athlete friend who passed up a deal in a pre-construction condo because his brother-in-law was starting something on the Internet, and the condo he passed up ended up making about $300,000. So it could have been bought for a price and then resold for $300,000 over what he would have invested. Instead, he ended up losing money on the Internet deal.

"Another time someone called my father in California to get my number for a business proposition. I didn't know that person, but the person knew my father. When my Dad called me I said, 'Absolutely not.' People have called my wife, Christine, to say, 'What do you think Anthony would think of this?' It's common; we've all seen that."

Greg Vaughn agrees. "I've had people offer me collateral—'I'll give you my car note. I'll sign over my house note'—when they know they already have two or three liens on the house and the car isn't paid for! Whether it's gyms, subdivisions, bars, or restaurants, I am not going to invest money to support a business in which I am not personally involved. I'm talking about hands-on involvement."

Athletes know (or should know) that everyone's ears perk up when the press starts talking about which pro is pulling in six or seven figures annually. Clubs, parties, churches, and locker rooms soon become fertile ground for the hook-me-uppers.

Kris Draper remembers being approached by someone who wanted to open a restaurant in his name. Others have come to him about starting a trademark line of clothing. Although clothing lines can be lucrative, Draper has known teammates who invested heavily, only to have the product line disappear from the shelves in a year or two.

"Carrying a clothing line is not easy," Draper says. "Michael Jordan, Tiger Woods, and some few other very high-profile athletes can do it. But it's easy for an athlete to get sucked in, too. After all, it's a real ego boost when someone wants to use your name or number on a product. But athletes have to realize that what these people really want is to use them, and what they do to make money for themselves. It's tough. Basically, I tend to stick with blue-chip companies."

As Charley Hannah noted, quite correctly, there will always be people asking athletes to invest in different things.

"After I got out of football, I unfortunately took part in some bad investments," he admits. "Sometimes those involved are people you thought were friends. That's part of the dilemma. Athletes, like everyone else, in a sense, need to feel that they are dealing with someone they can trust. Also, scammers are more sophisticated in a lot of ways. The same old rule still applies, though: *If something sounds too good to be true, it probably is. A slow, steady, disciplined approach to things is best over the long haul.*

"Regardless of the profession, everyone needs to weigh the risks and rewards of investments carefully. Ask yourself how much you are willing to risk for the potential reward. Ask lots of questions before you invest. It's a good idea to assume the worst: i.e., that a deal won't pay off until or if you get evidence to the contrary.

"Also, as hard as they are to find, you have to have knowledgeable people around you whom you can trust. That's critical."

Dennis Hopson recalls an unpleasant experience.

"A con artist, posing as a financial expert, stole $100,000 from me. He even had his own television show in Chicago, but he was running under a fake name and a fake Social Security number. So he bilked a whole bunch of people. They caught him, and he served eighteen months. Of course, that didn't get my $100,000 back.

"The scam involved a stock market investment. You give him the money and basically he showed you statements, which turned out to be fake. If I had to give advice to any new athlete, I would tell you to keep your money. You probably put it in a bank. Put it into something that is as close to being a sure thing as you can find. Don't try branching out into different things. If I had to do it all over again I would never ever do that.

"Somebody is always trying to reach me about some so-called opportunity. All the time. My parents are listed in the phone book, so that's a big avenue for hook-me-uppers, along with 'mutual friends.' People I've never met in my life sometimes call my parents and ask for 'Dennis' and leave a message. I think that is a bit outrageous. But it's happened before. It happened when I was playing pro ball, too. Hook-me-uppers will go to great lengths to get what they want."

Gary Trent admits to having made a few ill-considered financial decisions.

"I lost some on a small detail shop, and in trying to restore cars. Thankfully, they weren't major losses, but they were part of the learning process for me. You never invest in something that will seriously hurt you if it doesn't pan out.

"Certainly, hook-me-uppers will go to any lengths. They'll call your family and harass them. I've had people call the basketball office and leave messages. One guy told my dad that he was my cousin, and he didn't even recognize my dad! Another guy told me he went to school with my dad: 'We played a little ball together.' In the first place, my dad has never played ball, and in the second place, he was standing right next to me, and the guy didn't recognize him. That shows you how ignorant some of these people really are.

"I've had people leave urgent messages—ASAP. But after so many years with dealing with so much, you learn how to fizzle a lot of that out. I don't have the same headaches now because I've been around too long.

"If the conversation starts with, 'You know I ain't even want to come at you like that,' or, 'Man, I don't even really know how to say this to you,' right away you know they have their hand out. Not that everyone is out to steal from you. Some people really are in trouble, and if you help them out they will pay you back. I appreciate that because there have been so many people who haven't. It's the fact of someone not taking your money and your time for granted that makes so much difference."

Kris Draper recalled similar experiences.

"People have asked me to invest in restaurants, lines of clothing, and things like that. It's always something that 'can't miss.' People will do everything they can to get in touch with you. Sometimes if you're out with friends or something, people will hand you business cards. I take the card and I try to be as polite as possible, but most of the time I don't call them back."

Greg Vaughn comments.

"When I first started, everybody was trying to buy up land. A lot of players lost a lot. Regardless of what it is, though, everybody is still trying to make a quick buck. I really don't know too many players that made a ton of money on various projects. I don't know too many players that have made a whole lot of money unless it was in investments, as far as stocks, bonds, or whatever. Do you?"

No, I don't.

Friend or Foe—Building Distrust

SHAQ DIESEL-THROWING ONE down on your head for a monstrous dunk? Nope. A Roger Clemens fastball passing inches away from your dome? Psych!

How about Ray Lewis busting you in your gut while making a catch after jumping high in the air and you know what's coming? Please.

For professional athletes, the most feared foe is not on the court or in the field. It's the old friend, the homie with whom you grew up in the projects, or a pal from college. I am but a small cog in the celebrity wheel of athletic notoriety, but for all the hook-me-uppers I hear from, I might be mistaken for the sheik of a wealthy oil-producing nation.

The truth is that a great many athletes are quite generous in their philanthropic and family commitments. This is often publicized unbeknownst to them. Some NBA candidates will tell you that they turned pro because their families needed the money. They take seriously their duty to care for their parents, siblings, and others. Alas, once the reason behind the decision to turn pro becomes public knowledge, an athlete will be amazed at how many "friends" feel entitled to the same financial care and protection he affords to his family. To paraphrase the late Tennessee Ernie Ford, if they were with you while you were eatin' down around the hocks, they feel they have a right to be there when you're eatin' higher off the hog.

Heaven protect the athlete who is perceived to have turned his back on his roots. The air around him will be filled with cries of "Man, that cat did me wrong. He promised me such and such, and he acted like he didn't know what I was talking about when I brought it up with him."

Back in our college days, a friend of mine and I shared a mutual love for a high-end luxury automobile. In jest (I thought), I promised him that one day I'd buy him one. Years later, I heard through mutual friends that he had "dissed" me heartily on more than one occasion for failing to live up to my "promise."

My friend and I are cool now, I'm glad to report. Sadly, for many athletes the outcome is not so positive. That tight bond of brotherhood that was so prevalent "back in the day" has been subordinated to inflated expectations of open-ended monetary support. Many athletes have lost friends when a request for money was denied. Friendship turns bitter in a heartbeat when the former friend walks away empty-handed and fuming, "I can't believe he didn't hook me up!"

There is a saying among athletes that probably holds true for any highly-paid profession: "A friend can turn foe, if you say no."

It is, of course, arguable that anyone who would cease to be your friend because you refused to give him money could not have been much of a friend to start with. As the old adage goes, "With friends like these, you don't need enemies."

Still, there is no point in an athlete's pretending that it doesn't sting when someone whom you thought was a friend, someone who you thought "had your back" no matter what, turns out to have the same sort of secret agenda as the regular hook-me-uppers. In a perfect world, friendship, loyalty, and trustworthiness would not be for sale. But as we know, this isn't a perfect world.

For the professional athlete or celebrity, finding someone who is truly trustworthy is like striking oil or discovering a gold mine in his back yard. Surrounded, as he is daily, by people with a multiplicity of hidden agendas, that one friend to whom he can turn, with whom he needs to be nothing more than himself, is a true gift from God.

Above and beyond the constant requests for money, the hook-me-uppers fuel an athlete's basic distrust of people. The tendency to question the motives of everyone he meets is strong, particularly if he has been burned in the past. Small wonder that athletes keep their defenses up at all times. They have learned from bitter experience not to trust anyone too quickly or too easily.

Dennis Hopson admits that he has lost friends because of their failure to pay back money they'd borrowed from him. "Money can ruin things. When you start making a little more money, you soon find out who is true, and who is not. People stop calling just to see how you are. Seven times out of ten if they call, it's because they want something."

A sad realization, to be sure, but one with which most pro athletes and celebrities are likely to agree.

Nor does the change in friendships become apparent only when an athlete gets yet another request for money. If an athlete goes out to dinner with friends, when the check comes they will automatically push it in his direction or else wait for him to reach for it. Steve Sax notes, "Even if they asked you out, you're still expected to pick up the check!"

If all of this is beginning to sound like a treatise against making a better-than-average living, nothing could be further from my intent. As Woody Allen once observed, "Money is better than poverty, if only for financial reasons." Moreover, it can hardly be denied that money changes people, sometimes for the better, sometimes for worse. Most athletes will tell you that their friends, people whom they have known for years, believe they changed when they started earning enormous salaries. The funny thing is, their friends are often right, though not in the way that they think.

Yes, money does give some athletes (also bankers, lawyers, and accountants) an overinflated opinion of themselves. But just as often, the more money an athlete makes, the more value he places on family and real friends. Money breeds insecurity in terms of not knowing who can be trusted and who is just out to make a fast buck. As Sax says, "An athlete, possibly more than most people, really clings to the things that are most dear to him, and that's family and close friends."

Gary Trent recalls an incident when he flew a cousin out to see him during a road trip. Only later did he learn that the cousin had contacted Trent's agent and arranged for a second ticket, at a cost of $1,000, for his girlfriend. Trent remembers feeling as though he'd been robbed, not by a street criminal, but by a family member.

The more successful an athlete becomes, the more he can expect some basic, even lifelong relationships to change. It is not unusual for an athlete to encounter outright animosity from close acquaintances as he moves up in the sport.

Anthony Telford recalls two friends he'd known since childhood and with whom he has tried to keep in touch over the years. "In their eyes we can never be as close as we once were simply because I made it and they did not," says Telford. "They blame me because they made some poor choices and their lives didn't turn out the way they wanted, and then they tell me I've changed and that now I act as though I'm too good to hang out with them. They look at my house, my lifestyle, and the fact that I now eat in places that I couldn't afford in the past, and think, 'Well, he doesn't have time for us any more.' But friendship is supposed to be deeper than that. Real friendship is not about who has what and who doesn't and who is driving what and who isn't. They don't seem to realize that you would value their friendship now more than ever."

Greg Vaughn says that his real friends, the people he talks to daily, have never asked him for anything.

Kris Draper considers himself to be fortunate to have maintained friendships with guys he has known for more than thirty years from elementary school and from his minor league hockey days. "I still go back to Toronto in the summer and hang out with those guys. They hung with me when I was slugging it out in the minors and not making a lot of money. They are my friends because of who I am, not what I am or what I have."

Many professional athletes are far less fortunate and have lost friends who expected them to literally take care of them once they became successful. If an athlete refuses to honor that so-called obligation, friendship quickly sours. Draper advises athletes to weed out these types of "friends" as quickly as possible. "They are the guys you don't want in your life," he says. "You don't want them around your real friends or around your family. Just accept the fact that you made a bad choice when you chose to call these people your friends, and move on."

Charley Hannah is equally blunt. "If someone is asking for things, assuming that you are going to do things, riding on your coattails, and taking and taking because you have the ability to give, that person is not your friend."

An athlete's true friends are the people who are willing to contribute as much to the friendship as he is. It's not about money. It's about caring and support and being there when you are needed, not just for your money.

"I've got friends (on both coasts) that I haven't seen in five years," Hannah says. "But if one of them called me in the middle of the night and said he needed to see me, I'd go. My faith in them and in our friendship is that absolute.

"Another good friend, a guy with whom I roomed when I was a rookie and who now runs his own successful business, once told me that he divides his clients into givers and takers, and that he only does business with the givers. He and I are as different as night and day in many ways. Still, he's the kind of guy you want to talk with when you need to renew your faith, both in people and God."

He who loses money loses much; the athlete who loses a friend loses much more; the athlete who loses faith loses all.

—Variation on a quotation from Sir Francis Bacon

Last, but certainly not least in the pantheon of hook-me-uppers are the groupies, most of whom are fairly well-educated women—a fact that will surprise many people. The reasons why women become groupies are as varied as the women themselves. Some simply want to get close to a person who has been on television. Some want to be able to tell their friends that they had sex with a professional athlete. More basically, some just want money, jewelry, and expensive gifts of which they are willing to exchange intimacy for. Whatever their reasons for doing what they do, groupies are a fixed part of the subculture of professional sports.

Maturity has more to do with what types of experiences you've had and what you've learned from them and less to do with how many birthdays you've celebrated.

—Unknown

Players, especially rookies, often find groupies overwhelming and may be unaware of the trouble that can come with such associations. Veteran players know—some from bitter experience.

When a player wakes up "the morning after" to find that his acquaintance has disappeared—along with his watches, jewelry, cash, one may ask: Was it a hookup? Or a holdup? The answer is—both.

Nor are groupies always a comparatively benign threat. Carloads of groupies have been known to pursue professional athletes, many of whom understandably find the attention more frightening than enticing.

Whoever is behind the hookup, for whatever reason, professional athletes need to exercise common sense and maturity.

The Tax Man Cometh

ALTHOUGH I'VE NEVER met my Uncle Sam, I hook him up every payday without fail. Uncle Sam gets his cut of my income, just as he does of yours, no matter what.

When I was a child, I always wondered who this tall, thin dude in the white hat and the red, white, and blue suit was, and what he had to do with me. People called him Uncle Sam, but I knew we weren't related, so there had to be something else going on.

Some of you may be curious to know just how much athletes and other high-income individuals pay this federal relation. Well, Uncle Sam gets hooked up with well over 30 percent from each athlete. His nieces and nephews (otherwise known as the states) get their piece of the pie as well, depending on where an athlete lives and plays. There's an extra kicker, though.

It's called the jock tax. If you've never heard of it, that's not surprising. Most people haven't.

What is the jock tax?

It is a law that requires traveling professional athletes and other team employees to pay income taxes in every state where games are played. Thus, a professional athlete is required to file a tax return and pay taxes in the state where a game is played as well as in his home state. Even if an athlete resides in a state where there is no state income tax, he must still pay taxes in the other states where his team plays.

Sportswriter Mark Brown of the *Chicago Sun Tribune* believes that the jock tax started in 1991 after the Chicago Bulls beat the Los Angeles Lakers to win the NBA Championship. The state of California taxed the NBA champions in a move that many considered to be unprecedented as well as retaliatory. Other states soon followed California's example.

In an online *Business Week* article, writer Mark Hyman called the jock tax "the dirty little secret of the tax world." It is hardly surprising that athletes themselves are by and large the only ones who object to this double standard of taxation. State officials may claim that nonresident tax codes are not biased according to profession. Professional athletes find this difficult to believe.

In a *Budget & Tax News* article, Scott Hodge, president of the Tax Foundation, noted that, in addition to its capricious nature, the jock tax often means that people must file more than a dozen state income tax returns. These people include not only the athletes, but also trainers, scouts, and support staff whose income may, in fact, be quite moderate.

Certainly, professional athletes can be taxed without fear of political pressure. Moreover, as an independent monopoly, each league decides when and where its employees will work. No player would (seriously) consider demanding that management schedule games based on which states have the lowest tax rates. For better (if you are a state) or worse (if you are a player), an athlete's movements and salary are, alas, public information. Thus, the jock tax can easily become an integral part of any state or even city budget.

Not surprisingly, those athletes whom I interviewed for this book were very vocal on this topic.

Dennis Hopson remembers, "When I played we only had three [states] to deal with. Now it's twenty or more. True, if you are a professional athlete, the system pays you well. But then they turn around and take most of it back. So, in the end, it isn't only your family, friends, and people you don't even know who are trying to get money from you. An athlete who signs a contract for $30 million or $40 million can consider himself fortunate if he gets half."

I know what you're thinking. "I'd 'settle' for half of $30 million any day of the week!" You're right. Half—even a quarter—of that kind of money would be a gold mine to the average working person.

But this is not about a bunch of highly-paid pro athletes expecting sympathy from the public. It's about a group of people who are unfairly singled out by state and city tax systems because of what they do for a living.

The jock tax is an integral part of many state and city budgets. For example, it is reported that the city of Pittsburgh has financed a new sports stadium in part with the cash flow generated by the jock tax.

With the exception of those few states that do not levy state income taxes, we all pay taxes in the state in which we reside. But think about what it would mean to you if, in addition to state tax, you had to pay taxes for every state in which you do business in a given year. What would that mean to your personal finances and lifestyle?

Greg Vaughn remembers the tax situation when he began playing professionally in the late 1980s.

"My first year, there wasn't anything like [the jock tax]. Ohio was one of the first places that I had to start filing, and then, all of a sudden, here comes New York, and now it's all of them. They can track us, just like the players' association was saying. When a businessman flies in two or three days, usually they're working for a company and they get an out-of-state tax break. But we don't get that break. We are an easy fix so everyone can fix their deficit. It's crazy."

Anthony Telford comments, "As for the jock tax, itself, I think it's brutal. I think that they're getting enough tax [revenue] from the guys who live in the states and cities."

This is an issue both here in the United States and across our northern border. Kris Draper, who is a Canadian citizen, noted that in some Canadian provinces professional athletes are taxed if they are in the province for more than five days and they have a game during that time.

"It builds up, especially on our team, which has had the highest salary in the NHL for the past couple of years," Draper says. "So when we are coming into any city or province in Canada, they (city officials) have their calculators out and are already crunching the numbers to see what the income will be."

My wife oversees record keeping and tax information for our family. This is a difficult, draining, and time-consuming task, so, understandably, she becomes a bit more agitated than usual at the beginning of each year. Potential write-offs from the previous year are gathered, along with W2 forms and other relevant documents. For us, as for most families, maximizing write-offs while minimizing tax liability (legally, of course), is the preferred method when dealing with Uncle Sam.

Accountants and savvy advisors to professional athletes prepare for the onslaught of states that demand payment of taxes as well. States and municipalities know, to the exact penny, what each player will owe. They know how many times a professional team is coming to their respective cities or states. They know who is on that team, including coaches, equipment managers, and trainers, and what amount of revenue they can expect to collect when tax time rolls around.

My accountant, who handles all of my tax concerns, lives in Louisville, Kentucky. One year the state somehow mistook my CPA (Certified Public Accountant) firm's address in Louisville to mean that I, too, was a Kentucky state resident. As much as I love the Bluegrass State (that derby pie is delicious!), I live in Florida, where there is no state income tax. Nevertheless, I received an overdue tax bill from the Commonwealth of Kentucky for a small fortune. I was amused—and confused, since there are no professional NBA teams in Kentucky.

At this point you may be wondering why I introduced the subject of taxes. My goal is to drive home the point that an enormous salary (or what may seem to the public to be one) does not automatically translate into a free ride with lots left over to give free rides to anyone and everyone who asks to get on board. Upcoming professional athletes need to know this.

"I'm up near the 34 percent federal tax bracket," Petri Byrd says. "If you throw in 10 percent for state income tax, that puts me not far from 50 percent. People think I make a lot, and maybe I do. But half of a lot is a lot! Still, Jesus said, 'Render unto Caesar the things that are Caesar's.' So I give Uncle Sam what's due, and I don't cheat or look for false deductions. Even so, I cry a little every time I see how much 'Caesar' jacks every year."

Tangentially, Byrd also suggests that if parents really want to give their children some respect for what it takes to earn a dollar, they should have the children sit with them when they are paying the bills—including taxes. At least the kids will have some sense of what it takes to maintain the lifestyle to which they would like to remain accustomed.

But it's not just the children who are unaware of the complicated tax regulations and tremendous penalties, particularly for professional athletes. Did you know, for example, that an athlete may have to pay taxes based on the number of days he played in a particular state *or* on the number of days he was merely present in that state? It depends on what the state's rules are for a particular team. Thus, when an athlete gets off a plane, plays a game the following day, and then leaves, for tax purposes the state may tax him for two days—one for the game played and one for just being in the state!

Michael A. Wertheim, a CPA who works with professional athletes, was kind enough to speak with me on the subject of athletes and taxes. I confess that even I was a little shocked by some of the things I learned.

"States regulate professional athletic teams in different ways," Wertheim says. "For example, the state of New York makes each professional team that plays in that state give them an active roster, including coaches, equipment managers, and whoever is working with the team. How many days they were in that state, etc. That alerts the state of New York to look for tax returns from those individuals.

"Depending on the state, you are either taxed based on the days you are physically in the state or the number of games you played in relation to the schedule. To make matters worse, the total schedule could include pre- and post-season play or games played. To show the discrepancy, in football you have a sixteen game season, meaning that if you play in a state using the games played method of taxation you will be required to pay taxes on one-sixteenth of your compensation. Conversely if that state uses the duty day method and you spend two days in that particular state, then you would be required to pay approximately one-sixtieth of your compensation (assuming 120 days for the season).

"When professional athletes receive a salary, a W-2 Form is issued. Most players are in the highest federal rate of 35 percent based on 2005 rates. A player's state tax liability can reach as high as 12 percent depending on the state. To complicate matters, different states have reciprocal agreements affecting how the taxes are collected. By the way, athletes may also be subject to municipality and local taxes. Don't forget about the burden of social security and medicare taxes. If that wasn't enough, most players customarily pay out of pocket expenditures such as union dues, disability insurance, agent fees, legal fees, accountant's fees, travel expenses, etc."

Whew! Think maybe Wertheim's words on taxes should be required reading for every college kid who is thinking of making the jump to the pros *before* graduation?

Gary Trent recalls, "When I was living in Ohio, I was paying federal tax, Ohio state income tax, Columbus city tax, Gahanna tax [Gahanna is a suburb of Columbus], and New Albany tax. Every jurisdiction wants a piece of the pie."

People see an athlete sign a $30 million contract and somehow believe that he is making a full $30 million a year. They don't understand how much his salary will be reduced from tax deductions alone. This misconception is undoubtedly one reason why hook-me-uppers have no remorse or hesitation about asking an athlete for money. They see those huge numbers and figure that the athlete will always be making that much and, therefore, will never run out of money. So the actual $30 million is coming way down, but they don't look at that.

Enormous tax inequities are one reason why Steve Sax favors a flat tax. "With a flat tax, basically everyone is going to pay their fair percentage. Being in the 34 and 35 percent tax bracket, rich people (or people who are considered rich) are already paying more than their fair share. Then, too, there are some people who work and don't pay taxes. You can't give a tax break to someone who isn't paying taxes. It doesn't make sense."

There is a certain psychology involved

A rich man is nothing but a in this issue, too. Call it envy, jealousy,
poor man with money. greed, whatever—but rich people are, as
—*W.C. Fields* a group, fairly unpopular, and the richer
they are, the more unpopular they are
likely to be with the masses. Nor do we waste a lot of sympathy on rich people. Have you ever heard somebody say they felt sorry for Bill Gates? He may have just as many problems as the rest of us, but as far as we're concerned, one of them isn't money. This is why a politician can almost never go wrong by attacking the rich for getting too many tax breaks. As voters, we don't really know for sure what kind of tax breaks the rich get. But the thought of how much money they have, compared to how much we don't have, sticks in the public craw so much that we are willing—even anxious— to believe that the rich are getting more breaks than they deserve.

Steve Sax remembers how he and Bo Jackson laughed one day when they compared paychecks. Neither had ever thought they would reach a point in their lives where they were being paid so well. Then they looked at the column of deductions. Let Sax tell it: "Back then, I was making well over $3 million a year, and I was giving $1.5 million to Uncle Sam. That's just ridiculous. I'm not bitter about it, but it does seem ridiculous. I've donated more money than I can ever count to charitable organizations, and done so gladly. At least in those cases I know where the money is going."

Still, when you talk about what an athlete takes home versus what he makes, just in terms of basic math the numbers are mind-boggling. An athlete who signs a contract for $1 million may actually see a little more or less than half of that amount depending on where he plays. Play in Texas, and he may clear $600,000 to $625,000. Play in Toronto, and he may see anywhere from $400,000 to $450,000.

Although I deliberately did not raise politics as a major issue in this book, I think it's important to note that many people assume that professional athletes favor and endorse representatives who appease their interests, for example, a political candidate advocating a lower tax base for high-income earners. This is not necessarily true. An athlete may have as many different reasons for choosing a certain candidate as any other citizen has. Some athletes do "vote their wallet," without apologies. "I see nothing wrong in voting for a candidate whose policies would seem beneficial to my financial security," says Gary Trent. "Some cities base a significant part of their budget on which teams will be playing in their jurisdiction. They may say, 'We're going to make $2 million off the NBA players this year, so we can allocate $500,000 for new school buses and another $500,000 for computers, etc.' Now that team schedules are available on the Internet, every city mayor and city official can plan their budgets in advance around the NFL, NHL, or Major League Baseball players."

Anthony Telford remembers paying more than $300,000 just to the Canadian government one year because there were no write-offs. Even if he'd been due a refund from the Canadian government, the refund would have been in Canadian dollars, which at that time would have been about sixty cents per dollar in American money.

"People don't understand that when they see your salary published in *USA Today*, you can immediately cut it down by 50 percent," Telford says. "That still doesn't cover things like clubhouse dues, tipping, and other expenses. In 2000, my salary was $1,150,000. At the end of the season, we had $200,000 in the bank. We paid $600,000 in taxes! We were stunned. I'm retired now and, praise God, we have no bills. I stayed well under the radar during my career and sheltered enough money so that we could enjoy a better-than-average retirement. Still, there are times when it feels like we are penalized for being successful at what we do."

To some of you, this may sound like a bunch of bitter, overpaid athletes sitting around feeling sorry for themselves. Nothing could be further from the truth. To a man, every one of these athletes will tell you that he has been truly blessed to have more than he ever thought would be possible in his life. Nothing in the book should be interpreted as a plea for pity, sympathy, or anything like that. It is an attempt to help the public understand the other side of the coin of fame and fortune, and to see that what an athlete has to do to ensure a future for himself and his family is not as easy as it sometimes seems from the outside.

Not by a long shot!

Chapter 3

You *Can* Cheat an Honest Man

*Integrity is not a ninety percent thing, not a ninety-five percent thing;
either you have it or you don't.*

—Peter Scotese

Player Beware

OXNARD, CALIFORNIA, FINANCIAL ADVISOR Donald Lukens was a high roller
with the money and lifestyle to match. In an article for the *Ventura County
Star*, T.J. Sullivan notes that someone once said Lukens "looked like a
televangelist."

In fact, Lukens was a con man that specialized in fraudulent investments
for the rich and powerful, particularly rookie athletes with promising
careers. In 2001, the IRS caught up with Lukens pursuant to collecting
well over a million dollars in unpaid taxes. At about the same time the FBI
and the SEC also began investigations into Lukens' activities. Whether any
of the people whom he swindled will ever get any of their money back is
anybody's guess.

W.C. Fields starred in a film called *You Can't Cheat an Honest Man*.
Fields played a con man whose swindling schemes worked only on people
who were as greedy and dishonest as he was. It was a great movie, albeit
based on a demonstrably false premise—just ask any professional athlete
or high-profile celebrity who has been swindled by honest naiveté.

Financial representatives, agents, attorneys, accountants: the more a
professional athlete earns, the more he will need to rely on these business
professionals. Without their services, athletes and celebrities would be lost
in impenetrable financial darkness.

It is important to state at the outset that the majority of the men and
women who provide these services are competent, hard-working, fair, and
honest. Their first priority is their client's financial well-being now and in
the future. To paraphrase Paul Newman in the classic film *Hud*, we don't
want to shoot all the dogs just because a few have fleas.

Sadly, it is also a fact that trusted representatives and associates are
ripping off many professional athletes every year. It is remarkably easy to
do. All that is necessary is for the player to allow his paychecks to be sent

directly to his agent or financial represen- ***It is an equal failing to trust***
tative, who then deposits these checks in ***everybody and to trust no-***
an account to which only that agent and ***body.***
his staff have access, effectively excluding ***—An Old English***
the player from access to his own money. ***Proverb***
The agent or representative may then bill
the player for bogus expenses, which the player may not question, or may
simply withdraw the money at random without giving the player any supporting documentation. The player, preoccupied as he is likely to be with
the season, may never be aware of what is happening. It's a sleight-of-hand
trick that would be the envy of every magician.

Then, too, some rookies and even veteran players are not disciplined
enough to handle their own money. Charley Hannah believes, "This attitude
is part laziness and part fear of being thought ignorant." Whatever the
reasons, athletes who give total control of their financial future to others are
prime targets for dishonest agents and crooked financial representatives.

Let's do a little math. If a representative "appropriates" $5,000 to
$10,000 from each paycheck he receives over a twelve-paycheck period,
this amounts to roughly $60,000 to $120,000 per year—even if he is *not*
earning a seven-figure overall salary. If the representative is bilking other
clients, even at incrementally lower amounts, the cumulative total for a
given year is staggering.

Some billing mistakes are inadvertent, and some are intentional. No doubt
I have saved myself quite a lot of money by following my momma's childhood
advice: "Boy, you better ask questions when you don't understand." Many people
think they will ruffle some feathers by asking about billing and accounting
discrepancies, but one need not be confrontational to be diligent.

CPA Mike Wertheim believes it is
important that there be as many checks ***It is the very backbone of wis-***
and balances as possible with a profes- ***dom not to trust too hastily.***
sional athlete's financial advisors. Checks ***—Latin Proverb***
and balances help address issues such
as conflicts of interest or the potential
problems when one individual has too much control over an athlete's
finances. It is also important that athletes have a good professional person
behind them, whether it is an attorney or a CPA. Wertheim adds, "If you
need an insurance guy, get an insurance guy. If you need an investment guy,
you get an investment guy. If you need an accountant, you need to get an
accountant. If you need a lawyer, you get a lawyer. Together they can help
him build a proper foundation for his family and himself as well. The idea
is to look at both long-range and short-range planning."

For their own protection, young athletes (and young people in general)
should have, or take steps to acquire, a basic understanding of business. Greg
Vaughn comments: "I've met guys that were twenty-one or twenty-two

that have never written a check before. Right away you know they don't know how to read a financial statement. Yet they are giving someone else control of their earnings and financial future."

Simple things such as knowing how to write a check, balance a checkbook, read a bank or financial statement, and read the stock pages can give an athlete a certain peace of mind. Some young athletes about to make the jump to the pros have never seen a tax return and know nothing about income taxes. They need to learn. Wertheim suggests that athletes use some of the time they spend on planes reading up on business basics or perhaps reviewing financial material they may have recently received and making notes about possible questions. Fifteen minutes or a half-hour spent going over financial material can make a world of difference. The more an athlete knows about his personal financial picture, the less vulnerable he is to unscrupulous financial planners, advisors, and accountants, who make their money by bamboozling the ill-informed.

There are different ways for each professional athlete to take care of his financial affairs. Many hire firms for this purpose. Others prefer to handle their own finances. (This is my approach, because if something goes awry, I know who to contact: my lovely wife.) Still others allow a firm to gather information and prepare checks and invoices, which are then forwarded to them for their signature. This is a good way for an athlete to be sure where his money is going.

It sounds extraordinary, but it's a fact that balance sheets can make fascinating reading.

—Mary Archer

If an athlete decides to hire an individual or a firm to handle his finances, the most important, and often most difficult, task will be finding someone he can trust. Danny Levitt, Assistant Vice President and financial advisor with Merrill Lynch, says, "The most important aspect of our client relationship is trust. Most major financial service firms have a similar menu of products and services; however, it is the fashion in which they are delivered and executed that adds the underlying value to the relationship. This process starts with trust. I don't ever want a client to question whether a recommendation is in my best interest or theirs, and this is particularly relevant in the case of the professional athlete. They must have advisors whom they can trust."

The peak earning period for a professional athlete is finite. Because the money he earns during that time is not automatically replaceable, it must be invested with care and managed with a high level of diligence. Today's investment products are highly sophisticated, and professional athletes, even those with some financial knowledge, may not have a full understanding of their own investments—all the more reason that an athlete's financial advisors must be trustworthy and beyond reproach.

Once an athlete has identified a qualified individual advisor or team of advisors, the next issue is planning. *"Those who plan are ruled by reason. Those who don't are ruled by emotion,"* Levitt says. "Going back to the fact that professional athletes have relatively short careers, it is even more important that planning be incorporated into their investment strategy. Most athletes have grown accustomed to a certain lifestyle during their playing career, and our job as financial advisors is to help preserve this lifestyle after their playing days are over."

Planning should encompass every aspect of an athlete's financial life, from educating his children to financing a house, as well as planning ahead to ensure that assets pass to his heirs as tax-efficiently as possible. Athletes may not see the importance of these things during their playing days because of their level of income; however, it is the job of the financial advisor to make them aware of the importance of planning. An athlete must ask himself, "How much money will my family and I need to live on each year after I retire? How much risk am I willing to take?" An athlete with enough assets to sustain his current lifestyle after retirement should be concerned with making sure that money is working for him.

Athletes can create wealth by virtue of what they do. The right financial advisor will help them sustain that wealth for the future.

Financial mismanagement and outright theft are enormous problems for professional athletes. Dennis Hopson recalls that it took him many years to assemble a trusted team of lawyers and financial management people: "I've hired and fired so many different people because they didn't have my best interest at heart or because their primary interest was short-term profits for themselves rather than long-term financial security for me and my family."

In the late '80s and early '90s, financial mismanagement and shady investment deals involving professional athletes became quite common. In the worst cases, athletes lost millions simply because they trusted the wrong people to handle their money and they allowed themselves to be led rather than taking proactive responsibility for their financial affairs. "Four out of ten professional athletes will probably end up broke because of bad planning, bad financial management, trusting the wrong people, and not staying on top of their own finances," Hopson notes. "In the end, an athlete should always be responsible for his own finances. Always."

Steve Sax remembers being victimized by a crooked financial advisor.

"He put me into insurance products that I didn't need so he could generate his $40,000 to $50,000 in commission up front. He put my money in the bank, where it was drawing less than 1 percent interest, when real interest rates were at 18 percent. Without telling me, he wrote checks out of my account to pay taxes for other players and then put the money back at the end of the month. It was fraud, pure and simple. Giving complete control over your finances to an advisor is like giving an eighteen-year-old kid a keg of beer and the keys to a car. It's a recipe for disaster."

Contrary to popular stereotype, athletes are not dumb. They are, however, for the most part, unschooled in financial matters. It's like asking a heart surgeon to go out and change the brakes on his car. He's a bright guy, but he's not a mechanic. The principle is the same.

Sax noted that fewer than two percent of the people he interviewed for a book he is working on knew the difference between a stock and a bond. (What are the odds that more than 2 percent of the entire population knows the difference?) It's a simple matter of taking the time to learn; and for professional athletes in particular, financial knowledge is critical. His advice to athletes? "Never give full financial discretion to anybody, and pay your own bills."

Every professional athlete is his own business. This is sometimes hard for them to conceptualize. An athlete needs to find objective opinions on different aspects of his financial life, and it is difficult to find people to whom he can entrust his money. For better or worse, everybody is out to make a dollar.

Anthony Telford believes the biggest mistakes players make are giving power of attorney to their attorneys and entrusting all of their financial dealings to one person.

"Let's say that all of an athlete's checks go into his bank by direct deposit, and let's say he has an agent who then gives him and his family an 'allowance,'" Telford says. "If they needed to buy a car, they had to call their agent. It's ridiculous. The athlete is leaving himself wide open to being robbed blind. A lot of athletes simply don't want to be bothered with sitting down and paying their own bills. So all the bills go to an agent. A friend of mine, after being in the NFL for eight years, found out that his agent had spent $200,000 on a project and never told him about it. He trusted the wrong person, and he trusted that person with everything he had. Not a good idea."

As ill-advised as it seems, one can see the attraction for an athlete of having one person handle all his finances. An athlete is on the road almost constantly. A lot of statements come at the first of the month, but suppose an athlete is in the middle of a ten-day road trip? He may not even see the bills before the fifteenth. His first instinct is to hire someone to take care of the bills—to write the checks.

Then there's the seasonal possibility of being traded to another team in another area. There can be times when an athlete simply has no fixed address where bills can be delivered. He may have to get a change of address every time he moves from one apartment or house to another. Again, it's a great temptation to put all of his financial matters in the hands of one person in one place.

Even so, it's a high-risk gamble. As Telford says, "Giving someone the power to pay your bills means you are also giving them the power to take your money. If an athlete is making $90,000 to $100,000 or more a week, an enormous amount of money can disappear in a short period of time. An athlete may find that his advisor is paying himself 'fees' even while he is losing money on investments the advisor selected!"

Then there is the issue of the sheer volume of money involved for a professional athlete. How do you go about managing an annual salary of $25 million when you are playing eighty-two games a year and trying to find time to spend with your family as well? An athlete receives a monthly bank statement listing all of the checks that went to his account as direct deposits. But with the right kind of software, an unscrupulous accountant could print a bogus bank statement for the athlete who, if the figures were correct, would be unable to tell that the statement itself was a fraud. In this way, the accountant could withdraw money from the athlete's account, make profitable investments for himself, and then return the money—all without the athlete's knowledge. It's theft, albeit of a sophisticated nature.

None of this is new, of course. There have always been, and will always be, people who make their living taking advantage of other people. That said, however, it's not impossible to find honest, reliable people to provide the kind of financial assistance an athlete needs. The younger the athlete, the more he needs the help. As Charley Hannah says, "At twenty-two years old, how is a guy going to manage millions of dollars? He's not! But if you can get him to put even a fraction of the effort it took to get him into the pros, where he could earn a fortune, into looking for a reliable advisor to help him invest that money wisely, the outcome would be very different."

Young athletes in particular need someone to help them spot the hook-me-uppers—the guys in the flashy clothes and the flashier cars. "These guys live from chump to chump much in the same way that an NFL player may live from paycheck to paycheck," Hannah notes. "It's hard for a young athlete to resist the aura and the trappings of success, the instant gratification of every wish. They won't know until it's too late that the short-term pleasure of a frivolous lifestyle will not make up, in the long run, for being taken to the cleaners by a scam artist."

Gary Trent believes that one way to at least cut down on the possible rip-offs is to deal with established agents and companies. "You have to figure that if a company has been around for thirty or forty years, they haven't lasted that long doing bogus deals. Besides, why steal a million from me if the company is worth billions? Why would they risk their reputation? It's not a hundred percent infallible, but I think going with an established firm with a long-standing reputation for excellence and for being conservative in their investment recommendations is one way to reduce the risk of being cheated."

Greg Vaughn remembers a friend who was bilked out of two or three million dollars during several months while playing overseas. His financial advisor, who remained in the states, made a number of bad investment decisions and never bothered to consult him. "It just proves that old adage," Vaughn says. "Separate friends and business. An athlete needs someone to help him invest responsibly and manage his money wisely. But he should always control the purse strings himself."

For the athlete, as for anyone else, it all comes back to surrounding himself with the right people. If he finds himself wondering where his paycheck is going every two weeks or whether his money is being allocated the way he wants it to be, then the odds are that he needs to find an advisor or a team of advisors in whom he can have more confidence.

The athlete should be particularly careful when choosing an agent. "When an athlete chooses an agent, it should be with the idea that he is creating a long-term relationship," says Kris Draper. "It's not just about finding somebody to negotiate your first contract. A good athlete/agent relationship should last fifteen or twenty years."

Charley Hannah has been stung more than once. "A guy I knew talked me into a real estate deal that turned out to be financially devastating. Another time, on the advice of a family member, I invested in a shelter system limited partnership. When the LP got audited, I ended up owing the IRS a tremendous amount. In fact, that coincided with another deceptive real estate deal that ultimately went sour."

Financial misfortunes aside, being cheated by friends and family can take an equally devastating psychological toll. "I was real depressed," Hannah admits. "With the support of some good people and a lot of hard work, I dug myself out. For the past eighteen years I've been in business for myself, and I'm financially secure. What's funny is that everybody thinks my money was made from football, when the truth is the football money is gone twice over."

Limited partnership scams (such as wind energy tax credits, or cattle feeding and breeding operations) with inflated profit guarantees were common back in the '80s. Now, as then, a clever financial advisor with unlimited access to an athlete's financial resources can easily involve an unsuspecting client in schemes that could leave him broke, and the advisor personally wealthy.

Hannah also remembers a tech stock scam artist back in the '80s who collected hundreds of thousands of dollars from a number of athletes over a period of several seasons. When the house of cards finally tumbled, they discovered he had been doing nothing more than taking their money and producing reports.

Any investment has a certain amount of risk, of course. Hannah advises, "If you get scammed, don't feel sorry for yourself after the fact. Learn from the experience. Take more responsibility for your investments, and next time, check your advisor's credentials more thoroughly."

Hannah also suggests that athletes look at the dynamics of any deal before investing. He recalls an incident in which several athletes pooled their money to buy property that was to be turned into developments. "The dynamics were that they bought this property. Somebody else assembled the money and probably made a commission for it. Somebody else bought a piece of property and got a commission when that property was sold. Somebody else managed the property and received a fee for that. When the property was finally sold, even though it was not making a profit, somebody received a commission on the sale. Nearly every party involved in this scheme came away with a profit—except the athletes who put up the money in the first place. It's sad, but this kind of thing is not uncommon."

Of all the stories I heard in preparing this book, Aaron Ward's experience was in many ways the most mind-boggling and the most telling, in terms of lessons to be learned. Here is his story, in his own words:

"The thing I learned is that nothing is free, and that old saying 'If it sounds too good to be true, it probably is.' As an athlete, people are always coming to you about investing in the newest, latest, greatest idea. The pitch usually involves how much your name, notoriety, and influence will bring to the project in terms of the kind of marketing campaign that can really put the deal over the top. Your name (and your money) are your passports to success in the venture. You don't really have to do a whole lot. Basically, they just want to use your name and fame.

"Lesson One: You cannot do business with people that are not in the same realm as you are in terms of finances and life experiences. They don't understand the sacrifices you have made, especially if you have been playing a sport since you were a child. Preparing yourself to perform, as an athlete, has been your primary focus.

"They come to you for an investment in the business because you are good at what you do. At first it's great, and your part in the project seems easy. Your name gets you in the door. As an athlete you have the potential to quickly attract other investors, so the partnership grows faster. But that gets lost as time passes, and you begin to experience some resentment once the contacts are established and you have served your purpose, so to speak. You are an athlete first, and a businessman second. That is your understanding, but there comes a time when your partners may lose their sense of that, at which point the 'agreement' starts to change, and you begin to sense a sort of 'what have you done for us lately?' attitude. Have they forgotten that they used your name and fame to build the foundation—to attract other investors—for the venture? It begins to seem as though they have, and your resentment begins to grow.

"Up to this point, it may not have occurred to you that you should have protected yourself legally. You are in business with people who know business, whereas you do not. Legalese is a language of lawyers. Most people never become fluent. As the non-business-minded partner, you won't always be there to second-guess possibly illegal decisions, even though your name is on the company. Maybe you run into a clause in the contract stipulating that 'in the event that A decides to leave the business, the athlete agrees to pay this much as a buy-out.' A lawyer would have spotted that clause right away. You didn't.

"Suddenly you realize how far out of your depth you really are as an athlete in a complex business with many parameters that you may be unable to fathom. As the business goes on, you begin to recognize, too late perhaps, the importance of protecting yourself. Things can change at the office when you're not there. 'Well, he's on the road and he makes hundreds of thousands of dollars,' your partners may say, or 'We're paying him this much, so let's give ourselves a larger share of the profits.' But wait a minute. The agreement was that you would split the profits three ways. Of course, that agreement was based on a handshake among friends. It was never put in writing.

"Lesson Two: Be aware how your name is being used and where you stand in the company as a legal participant in the decision-making process. That was the biggest lesson for me. Know the people with whom you are going into business and how they plan to use your affiliation. To this day, my name is still being used in certain places even though I left the company in question long ago.

"Lesson Three: Catch them off-guard. The next time a business offer comes your way, be prepared to ask questions. 'What's my liability if this turns sour?' There are complications in every business, and as an investor, and particularly as a partner, you need to know what those complications may be and how they will be handled. They'll be surprised because they won't expect you to be at all knowledgeable."

Knowledge is power. Aristotle said that, though he may not have been the only one to say it. Doesn't matter. It's true. Ask Aaron Ward.

If what you have read thus far seems mind-boggling, be aware that you haven't yet heard the worst.

Though the vast majority of companies are quite legitimate, some companies in business to provide a service automatically inflate their prices once they learn that the potential client is a professional athlete. A company based in Columbus, Ohio, once gave me an estimate of $10,000 to clean my house. We turned them down, of course. It was clear that they knew who I was and how much money I made. If they thought we would pay that outrageously inflated price, however, they didn't know us very well. Another company offered to do the same job for $700. In the end, we did the job ourselves with some help from family members in about five hours.

In a separate incident, an independent contractor whom I thought I knew and could trust over-billed us for bogus additional labor hours of two workers, with the secret intention of paying them their actual hours and pocketing the difference. I detected the scam when I compared the contractor's invoice to that of one of his workers. "We can back Lawrence into a corner and get even more money out of him," he supposedly said. Later, after returning my deposit in full, he begged me to keep him "in the loop" for future contracting jobs. Even though I refused (emphatically), I learned later that he was using my name as a reference for other contracting jobs, some for other professional athletes. As peculiar as it sounds, this same contractor even tried to interest me in going into business with him!

When discussing the price for a particular service, I am at once suspicious if the company representative asks me, "How much do you think is fair?" It's a dead giveaway for a rip-off. The clear implication is that all customers are not charged at the same rate. This person is counting on the fact that many customers may not be familiar with the standard, going rate for their services. Thus, they can attempt to bill the customer at their "ceiling" profit margin.

Dennis Hopson understands the inflation that comes with being well-known: "If I am on the telephone discussing business or getting something done, I never say my last name because I know the minute they hear it, the price goes up, sometimes as much as $200. It happens all the time." (Interestingly enough, the same thing happens when you live in certain zip codes. So if they ask for your address and it ends with 81611 or 33480 or 20815 or one of several others, expect the price of the service to go up.)

"They know you probably don't know what's considered a reasonable price to pay for something," Hopson says. "But once they have your check, don't expect somebody to say, 'Look, I charged you too much. Let me give you this back.' It's not going to happen. Here is where they have an opportunity to establish a long-term relationship with you, but instead they opt for a quick buck."

Steve Sax remembers going in to buy a car and getting a quote that was $4,000 over the invoice! "After a while I started sending a friend of mine out first to get an estimate because I knew if I went in person they would jack up the price. Another time a company tried to charge me $50,000 for a $15,000 patio job at my house in Manhattan Beach," Sax says.

At least Jesse James used a gun when committing highway robbery.

I invited my wife, Monya, to provide some insight as to how these issues apply to the wives of athletes.

"I have noticed that if a salesperson is with a customer before I walk in a store, they will sometimes put that person aside to tend to me," she said. "They make sure that the fitting room is set up for me. They ask me if I want something to eat or drink. They are totally attentive because of the possibility of a large sale and, for them, a huge commission. The theory is that I'm married to a professional athlete, so that must mean I have money. Even when I shopped in different NBA cities, people would recognize me if I went back to the same store more than once."

Monya recalls a scenario in a high-end boutique in an NBA city.

"I wasn't dressed very nicely, and at first no one would give me the time of day. Then I happened to start talking to a sales associate who asked me what I was doing there. When it came out that I was traveling with my husband—my husband the professional athlete—they pulled out all the stops. Every high-end garment in the place was suddenly available for my personal viewing. Once it became known that one of my favorite designers is Dolce & Gabana, whenever something new and expensive came in they made sure I got a call, and they would reserve a fitting room for me and hold my size so that I could try things on. I've made some pretty bad decisions a couple of times because of that. I am going to get myself in trouble now. [Note from author: you were in trouble about three sentences ago!]

"Still, it upsets me that my appearance and who I am determines what kind of service I receive in certain stores. Sometimes I react to it, 'Okay, you don't think I can afford to be here. Give me that, that, that, and that.' After that, when they realize that I can indeed afford to shop there, I suddenly become their best client. But I've learned to walk out of stores like that. By shopping there, all I am doing is helping the sales associates increase their commission."

To paraphrase Richard Gere in the film *Pretty Woman*, "Stores don't like people. They like credit cards." He might have added, and big-name customers who seem to have money to burn.

Taking advantage of professional athletes (and their families) is nothing new, of course. Although there are many managers and businesspeople who treat all their customers the same way, including athletes or other high-earning individuals, some have a different modus operandi.

A source that wished to remain anonymous said car brokers may be the best example. The source explained, "As a rule, when a player signs his first big contract, the first thing he wants is a shiny new car to let everybody (particularly his homies) know that he has made it. Sticker prices for these young players can be inflated by $10,000 or more. Often an athlete has been hooked up by someone who pretends to be getting him a good deal, but who in reality is getting paid under the table for bringing a star athlete into the dealership. It's good publicity for them as well to be able to say that so-and-so bought a car there. They may even get a couple of autographs to put in the display case. That can go a long way. From that point on, people in the industry will use the vehicle as a hookup and an excuse to overcharge other customers. Of course, the athlete never sees the receipts from the companies that put in the stereos, TV's, wheels, custom upholstery, or Gucci/Louis Vuitton seats. That's all part of the hookup. There is no warranty on any of that stuff. If something breaks, the hook-me-upper offers to 'take care of it.' Sometimes they do, sometimes they don't.

"In general, the markup on merchandise for an athlete is three or four times the retail cost for ordinary customers, and if you consider all the under-the-table money that changes hands, he is being taken to the cleaners," the anonymous source said. "The hook-me-upper will even polish the car, shine the wheels, and deliver it to the camp or the stadium, always just in time for his teammates and friends to see him and the car, and to be suitably impressed by the service. With any luck, someone will ask him, 'Who hooked you up?' It's a vicious cycle that goes on and on.

"Indeed, most athletes don't have time to get two or three estimates for a purchase or a service. Since money isn't [or doesn't seem to be] an object, they can afford to ask for what they want and arrange to get it right away. Then, too, athletes [including yours truly] are, by and large, impatient. So they may ask a dealer, 'Can you get that for me by tomorrow?' and the dealer may say, 'I might be able to get it, but I'll have to charge you a bit more.' For the sake of convenience, he will probably say yes—a perfect setup for those who wish to take financial advantage.

"It's a double-edged sword. At the end of his career, with nothing much to look back on besides a great deal of frivolous spending, an athlete may wonder where his money went, and regret sinking $50,000 into a car, when $20,000 would have bought one that was equally serviceable, only with a lot less flash.

"In the meantime, an athlete can save some money on products and services by flying under the radar, so to speak. Take your registration and any other forms of ID out of the glove box when you drop your car off to have work done. [Given the increasing prevalence of identity theft, this is good advice regardless!] Take off any identification, other than the tag, and use a pseudonym on any paperwork. Prices go up anyway when a fine car rolls in. Why give the company an excuse to jack up the price even further?"

Basically, it all comes back to trust. Athletes, perhaps more than most people, have to be careful about whom they trust with their money, their cars, or anything else of value.

Anthony Telford recalls an incident in which he needed an estimate for brick paving alongside his house.

"We called two legitimate, bonded contractors, neither of whom knew us. They came out, and after inspecting the job, gave us quotes that were fairly close—within $200. Then I called one of my friends from church. His quote was $1,700 higher. A quote from another general contractor was almost $2,000 more. I had to laugh. Wouldn't you think a friend might give you a little break? Even if the quote had still been a little more, I might have said, 'Okay. I'd rather have someone I know do it.' But it never happens that way. It's like companies have two lists: one for everyday people and one for athletes and celebrities. So the minute they hear your name, they turn to the other list and start giving you quotes that you know are way out of line."

No matter where an athlete goes, if he is recognized, he is likely to run into the same problem.

Gary Trent remembers a day at the Ohio State Fair. The first parking lot attendant with whom he spoke said it would cost six dollars to park. Around the corner, a second parking lot attendant, who recognized Trent, said, "Six dollars, but you can go on and give me ten, man." When Trent asked why, the guy said, "Man, you got a big truck." Understandably, Trent was steamed. "Okay, yeah, I got a big truck, but if I pull out of this parking spot, it will still only hold one other car. I'm not taking up two spaces. If everybody else around here paid six dollars, I'll pay six dollars. I don't have a problem paying ten dollars if everybody else is paying ten dollars. But you are not going to make me pay ten dollars because I'm Gary Trent. If I walk in the grocery store and green beans are a dollar, the grocer doesn't raise the price to two dollars just because of who I am.'"

Of course, this is another sword that cuts both ways. For example, a professional athlete with some business know-how may be able to help a friend or family member get a better deal on a new or used car because he is likely to be in a better financial position to negotiate. As Trent notes, "It's a lot of catch-22s. Our whole lives seem to revolve around catch-22 situations."

To paraphrase the late Ann Landers, trust in God, but watch your wallet.

"I Need Two on the 50-Yard Line!"

IT WOULD BE reasonable to assume that professional athletes look forward to games scheduled in their hometowns. It's a chance to relax a little and spend some time catching up with close acquaintances.

It would be reasonable, but to a large degree, it would also be incorrect. Many professional athletes actually dread playing close to home because of the distraction and interruption caused by people looking for free tickets to the games. On a Saturday afternoon edition of the CBS pre-game show "NFL Today," one former All Pro tight end and future Hall of Famer said that he enjoyed playing on the road during playoff games because he knew he didn't have to worry about the distraction of getting additional tickets for people.

Ticket hookups are just about every professional athlete's first, if not worst, nightmare. Nor do the hook-me-uppers have any idea how much of a distraction their requests create.

Ticket requests from close acquaintances are one of the biggest headaches an athlete faces. More important than the sheer inconvenience and the financial outlay, they can distract an athlete from what should be his primary focus: performing on the court (or field or ice). The more important the game (the seventh game of the NBA Finals, the World Series, the Super Bowl, or the Stanley Cup Finals), the more intense the demand for tickets and the angrier people become if they don't get theirs.

The added pressure never seems to cross anyone's mind. A former teammate of mine once bought tickets from a scalper just to satisfy all of the requests he had received!

Although some athletes leave ticket requests to ball boys or locker room caretakers, many do not.

I cannot speak for the other major sports, but NBA players receive four complimentary tickets during home games and two complimentary tickets on the road. That's all. Regular season or playoffs, the policy remains the same. Thus, to meet ticket demands beyond what are allowed by organization policy, athletes must pay out of pocket. (I know several big-time players who bought a hundred tickets or more for various games, usually on the road.)

If an athlete had a nickel for every time someone has said, "I'll pay you for them, just let me know how much I owe you," he would be set for life financially!

Athletes dread playing in or near their hometown in part because of the endless ticket requests. Another player, who grew up in the Bay area, used to say, "I hate coming back here."

Every athlete can relate to his frustration. It's not that we don't enjoy seeing close acquaintances, but we know we will never be able to satisfy all of the ticket requests.

It's not just free tickets. They want complimentary guest passes to meet and greet the athletes after the game as well. With a pass, the hook-me-upper gets access to free food before, during, and after the game, inside information on the whereabouts of athletes after the game, autographs, phone numbers, networking opportunities, and a host of other perks. Small wonder that complimentary passes are just as hard for an athlete to get as the tickets.

Another point is that some attendees don't seem to realize how relieved a player is when the game is over. We just want to get out and go home. So our level of frustration doubles when, as it happens quite often, someone for whom we got tickets confronts us after the game with, "I appreciate the tickets, but you could have gotten me some a little better." I get them free tickets and they complain they aren't courtside?! Trust me: this is *not* the way to an athlete's heart. It's also not the way to ensure that an athlete will hook you up in the future either.

"People don't understand that when you [are] playing on the road you get two tickets," says Dennis Hopson. "Any more than that you had to buy on your own, unless your teammates or coaches were willing to give them to you, which is not likely."

Nor do the hook-me-uppers seem to understand or respect the fact that on game day an athlete's full concentration must be on the game. Phone calls asking for tickets, autographs, or personal appearances distract an athlete from his primary job, which is to put in his best effort on the court or the field or the ice.

Steve Sax remembers acquiring a whole new cadre of friends during the World Series: "I played in two World Series, '81 and '88. I got calls from people I didn't know—all wanting tickets. Some were associates from television shows that I was on, radio interviews, people that I used to go to school with. Baseball players used to get six free tickets. We got two in the family section and four scattered around the stadium. On the road I think it was two and two. But that was all."

It's not that athletes are not generous, because most are quite generous.

"I have to be honest," says Anthony Telford. "Sometimes I gave passes just because I wanted to. But when a guy asks for fifteen or twenty passes and tickets? They don't seem to realize that tickets cost a lot of money. We are given an allotment of tickets for free. You get the family section, which is usually two, and then you have four tickets somewhere else in the park. I remember once in San Francisco having to go out of pocket because somebody else on my team lived in the Bay area and he needed a lot of passes and tickets. I don't remember the exact number, but it was somewhere around 150 tickets total that we got."

An athlete who says no to ticket requests is not going to win any popularity contests, but sometimes that's a chance he has to take, especially since the ticket requests may turn out to be a scam. Greg Vaughn remembers an incident in Seattle.

"This was back in 1988. A guy I knew had a friend, and we gave him tickets. Turns out he didn't use them himself. We found out later that he was scalping them! Security got in touch with us, and of course, we never gave him any more tickets."

Kris Draper says, "In the NHL, we get two tickets at home and none on the road. All our comp tickets basically go to coaches or management. I'm from Toronto, but I am real glad we only go there once a year. Everybody wants to come to the game. Everybody wants to see you play. They don't realize how much it costs to get everyone there. Toronto is one of the most expensive ticket markets for the NHL, and I have to get anywhere from twelve to sixteen tickets. Of course, I would never expect any family members to pay for any tickets, and when I get a chance I get tickets for my buddies as well. But it does add up. It's a tough situation."

Charley Hannah agrees.

"People seemed to think I printed the tickets! After a couple of times I realized that I could get ticket-poor real fast. Playing in the Super Bowl, we were able to buy some extras. I think I bought about thirty-six tickets to the Super Bowl."

Indeed, the costs of those "free" tickets for the hook-me-uppers can add up. Aaron Ward did a little math.

"For two consecutive years, I tallied the total amounts I spent on tickets. It came to several thousand dollars. Now when people ask me for tickets I tell them, 'Give me a credit card. I can get them ordered and leave them at will-call.' That leaves the ball in their court, because I'm not paying for them."

There's a psychology at work here, too. The hook-me-uppers expect athletes to be so embarrassed by their exorbitant salaries that they feel compelled to hand out tickets as a way of apologizing for making more money than most people. But as Ward says, "You have to get past the embarrassment of making a ton of money."

Crimes Up!

FEW PROFESSIONAL ATHLETES will admit to feeling threatened by street crime. It doesn't fit their tough, macho image. Besides, the size and splendid physical condition of the average professional athlete should be enough to deter would-be thieves and muggers, right?

Wrong! As strange as it may seem to most people, professional athletes are often the victims of street crime. In particular, and predictably, they are prime targets for theft because of their wealth and high profile.

There is a slang expression—bling bling—that means wearing the most eye-appealing jewelry imaginable or driving a high-end car (such as a Benz, Ferrari, or Bentley).

Everything about an athlete's attire and lifestyle screams "mucho dinero." Music videos flaunt it. Teenagers gawk over it, and celebrity athletes display it. Small wonder that athletes attract criminals. A frugally-inclined, conservatively-attired athlete seems almost out of touch.

So, like mice walking through an alley full of starving cats, athletes display their wares while thieves watch and wait for the opportunity to relieve the athlete of his car, jewelry, wallet, and cash. It's the Great Athlete Robbery.

While there are no statistics on crimes committed against professional athletes, anecdotal evidence abounds:

- Two armed robbers forced an NFL defensive back into his home, while his wife and children were sleeping. The athlete, however, was able to break free from his attackers, who then fled the premises.
- Three armed robbers attacked an NFL player, leaving him and his significant other tied up inside his home, and locking their infant daughter in a closet.
- Another NFL player was assaulted, had gasoline poured on him, and robbed when he returned to his home.

Crimes against professional athletes receive very little media attention. But even if that were not true, it is doubtful that such crimes would engender much sympathy from the public. So, like millions of other citizens who feel that they have been left to protect themselves, some athletes do own guns. By some estimates, as many as 50 percent of NFL players own firearms.

Before you start firing emails at me for being pro- (or anti-) guns, let me say that these statements do not represent a bias in either direction. My goal here is simply to underscore a point, namely, that physical strength and excellent conditioning do not convey immunity to crime on anyone—be it an athlete or any other professional.

In inner city neighborhoods, the professional athlete is a particularly ripe target, his image shouting, "Look! I'm really making it!" Robbing a high-profile professional athlete can enhance the reputation of a thief among his peers.

Often the athlete finds himself between the proverbial rock and the hard place. Make it big and don't visit your old neighborhood, and you run the risk of being branded a sellout.

Professional athletes are often criticized for "forgetting where they came from," especially when they move from the ghetto to the suburbs. Cries of, "He ain't done nothing for the 'hood since he left here" are common. Those athletes for whom this is a particularly sore subject may try to appease their critics with gifts and donations.

On the other hand, if you make it big and roll through the 'hood in a pimped-out ride, fancy clothes, and expensive jewelry, you may end up as a crime statistic.

So the athlete has to ask himself, "Do I want to be a sellout or sucker?" Basically, it comes down to three choices: leave the fancy stuff back at your new crib, have some of your homeboys look out for you, or hire security to watch your back.

Of course, the media shines a spotlight on athletes and their possessions. People watch the news, "SportsCenter," and the games, and they see it all. It's almost as though an athlete is being set up before he even encounters the street criminal.

Lieutenant Jeff Blackwell, of the Columbus Police Department, is also a side-bar security expert and mentor for many well-known professional athletes. Lieutenant Blackwell's experiences speak volumes about the issue of athletes and street crime.

"One time Mike Bird [not his real name] and I were in Tampa at the Super Bowl between the Ravens and the Giants. At these high-profile events you get a lot of people who are there for only one purpose: to rob a high-profile athlete. They figure he is likely to be wearing a $10,000 watch, maybe $20,000 earrings, and several necklaces. He'll probably be driving a really nice car and maybe carrying a lot of cash. He will be vulnerable because thugs know that an athlete is not likely to risk his life getting involved in some altercation on the street.

"So Mike and I were in front of this club in Tampa, and it was really late. There were several thousand people inside the bar. I was watching Mike, and I had another officer with me who was bringing the car around. I spotted two guys who were pacing Mike—checking him out. While Mike was talking to someone, I overheard the two guys talking about robbing Mike. Specifically, they wanted his earrings, which were about five and a half to six carats each. Fortunately, I stepped in and got their attention to let them know that I was watching them and I was armed. Basically, I defused the situation before it had a chance to escalate. As far as I know, Mike was never aware of what had almost happened. The point is, this was a potentially tragic scenario. Not only would Mike have been robbed, but he would very likely have been seriously hurt in the struggle, since one of the thieves would certainly have tried to take Mike's earrings off."

Lieutenant Blackwell went on to note that situations like the one he described are a no-win for an athlete because of the possibility that the athlete may be hurt—or killed. The thugs know that although you're an athlete, you're probably not a fighter. Your instincts aren't on that level; you are not in that game. You're not scanning the room when you come in looking for the guy who is watching you. Sadly, perhaps surprisingly to many people, athletes are considered a soft target.

Even if an athlete manages to get the upper hand in a scuffle, there's always the possibility that the situation will be turned around in the press to make him look like the aggressor, to say that he was intoxicated or involved in some illegal activity. The athlete is left having to defend his innocence, indeed his character, to a public that is already inclined toward being suspicious of athletes. Either way, the cards are stacked against him.

"Of course, the best advice is to avoid those situations," says Blackwell. "But if you have to be out there, have someone around that has your back, that has your best interest in mind, and who is professionally trained to handle these types of altercations. Old friends or your homies from the neighborhood are not good enough. In fact, they are more likely to get an athlete in trouble because he then must be responsible for his own actions as well as their actions on his behalf.

"Again, there is a certain psychology at work here as well. Most athletes are surrounded by people who flatter them, who tell them they are the greatest people on the planet, who idolize them and want to be seen with them. They want to go out on the town [with the athlete picking up the tab, of course]. They want to be there when he attracts women, and glamour, and more attention. With any luck, they hope to ride his coattails to success. It's a tremendous ego boost, as far as it goes. But the truth is, most of these hangers-on have an angle to play. They may see a well-paid pro athlete as their personal ticket to financial and professional security."

Lieutenant Blackwell thinks it's also about validation: "What better way to validate themselves in other people's eyes than to hang out with superstar athletes? So when they wear expensive clothes and jewelry, or drive high-end, high-priced cars, they become known as the guy that hangs out with Lawrence Funderburke, or some other big name. Then they can use this so-called relationship to contact other people in key positions of power. Sometimes the athlete has no idea of the real motives in play, nor of the very real possibility that his name could be used in some illegal transaction, drugs maybe, without his knowledge. If that is the case, it will cost him a bundle in attorney's fees to disentangle and dissociate himself from the people and the situation, not to mention the negative effect on his marketability and reputation, which he may never be able to restore.

"Then, of course, there's women. A fine woman is the Achilles' heel for most athletes. Somebody who wants to set an athlete up won't use a girl from the 'hood, who wouldn't have a chance of getting close to him. They will use a woman who looks like a Bengalette or a Lakerette cheerleader. She is going to be a hammer. She is going to be a ten, but she is going to have an association. She is going to be a setup person just to get him to a certain location where the robbery will take place.

"Bottom line? In a nightclub, on the street, wherever, an athlete is a prime target. If the bad guys are using knives and pistols, then the situation can really get ugly. The athlete must make a quick decision: walk away and be thought a punk, or mix it up with the bad guys and risk going to the penitentiary and throwing his whole life away."

Steve Sax can speak to this issue from firsthand experience. "I got robbed one time. I'd just been called up to the big leagues as a Dodger. I was at a celebrity event, and this guy said he was related to some movie star, and my buddy was hanging out with him. Later a bunch of us, my friends, were having a get-together at my house, and this guy asked me where the bathroom was. I wondered why he went toward the master bathroom off the bedroom. Then he stole a couple of thousand dollars I had hidden in my closet. It was stupid on my part, but it also could have been worse.

"Kirk Gibson was followed home one night, and some guy with a gun robbed him. They can easily follow you from the parking lot. Athletes are such targets. A couple of years ago in Florida, Morgan Ensberg [Houston Astros] and Mike Rose [Oakland A's] were held up at gunpoint in a hotel room. Luckily, no one was killed."

Anthony Telford believes athletes are easy targets because of the high-end automobiles they tend to drive, flashy clothing, and jewelry they tend to wear.

"A guy that I played with in Montreal was walking in West Palm Beach with his wife when somebody stuck a shotgun in his mouth. Why? Because his wife had on a four-carat diamond ring and he was wearing a solid gold Rolex with diamonds. Crooks also know that athletes are not going to risk their lives over possessions. It's too easy to replace them. Why bother?"

"They're not going to pawn your jewelry, anyway. They'll wear it around the 'hood as a crown," says Gary Trent. "It's more of a street fame thing than anything else. The stuff is too easy to trace if they try to pawn it, unless they're dealing with a fence."

There is an old saying: "If you've got it, flaunt it." Most athletes are flashy by nature.

"I've seen guys wearing watches that cost as much as a Hummer," Telford notes.

So if a street thief is looking for someone to rob, guess who he's more likely to pick on? It's not rocket science. The bank robber Willy Sutton said it best: "I rob banks because that's where the money is."

Of course, theft is not confined to the streets. Anthony Telford comments: "Many athletes are careless about where they put their valuables in the clubhouse, particularly if it's a big league outfit. So a guy may just throw his wallet on the shelf in his locker. But the truth is, you never know who is going to be in the clubhouse during the game. Theft during games is very common. Ken Griffy, Jr., used to travel with his own lock boxes on the plane to keep his things separate and safe."

I can attest to the truth of what Anthony said about theft in the locker room. In Sacramento our equipment manager was responsible for making sure players taped up their wallets and secured jewelry and other valuables to ensure that nothing was stolen. Things did mysteriously disappear from the lockers of certain players, so the necessary steps had to be taken to ensure that this didn't happen again. It's amazing how many highly sought-after items are stolen out of players' lockers in every sport, especially the superstars. Why? eBay, baby! There is big money to be made on the latest memorabilia, and some people will resort to just about anything to make a few bucks.

Anthony remembers having four autographed baseballs worth at least a thousand dollars stolen from his bag.

"Another time I sent a baseball to a friend in Boston who got all of the Red Sox players to autograph it," he said. "I was going to auction it off on eBay and give the proceeds to the church. I told my friend, and he made sure all the other guys knew where the money was going from the sale. Well, it turned out there was so much memorabilia for sale on eBay that I couldn't sell the ball, not even to benefit a church. You have to wonder where people are getting all this stuff. A friend of mine told me he got one of my bats—a bat I had in my locker—off eBay. I know I didn't give it away. So go figure."

An athlete who has work done on his home may be opening himself up to a robbery just by virtue of what contractors and workers are able to observe while they are on site. "A guy is looking around and thinks to himself, 'This guy Trent might have a wall safe. Somebody told me they saw it when they were cleaning the house,'" says Gary Trent. "Now, even if you have a safe, you may not have a single thing in it. But if he thinks there's money or jewelry in that safe, right away your home and your family could be at risk. It's just rough like that."

Athletes are also easy targets because they are so recognizable. Basketball players and football players especially are likely to be much bigger and much taller than the average person. They literally stand out in a crowd, as Gary Trent points out.

"I remember once in Hollywood, I was sitting on a couch in a nightclub with some of my teammates when three guys confronted me. One of them was standing over me with a shiny chrome gun. He had it up against his thigh. I think he was hoping that just by flashing the gun I would freeze, which the average person would. Me, I lunged and grabbed his wrist so that he couldn't raise the gun. The two other guys start to grab me, but I dipped my shoulder into the gunman's chest and knocked him backwards. Then I took off running back toward the dance floor. They ran out the exit. I called security, and we (my cousin was with us) ran down the street toward the parking lot after them. When we caught up with them, they were walking along calmly as though nothing had happened. When I confronted them, they pulled out their guns, and we ducked. There was a tow truck nearby and I yelled for him to block the crooks in so they couldn't get away, but there was another car backing out, so the tow truck couldn't get in position, so they got away anyhow. Now I don't wear jewelry when I go out in L.A. Depending on where I am, I may hire security to go out with me. Of course, if they're just off-duty police officers out of uniform, the thugs might mistake them for regular guys, and you could end up in a shoot-out anyway.

"That incident in L.A. stayed with me for a long time, but it was a wake-up call, too. Now I know it can happen to me as well as the next guy. . . . It was good that it happened to me 'cause it was like a wake-up call to let me know that no matter how far you go up the ladder, you still ain't but one step. You can go a hundred steps up the ladder, but you're not but one step from falling back to the street and being a victim, and I was victimized."

Greg Vaughn believes that some players use their possessions as a way to promote themselves, a kind of self-advertisement. Even so, athletes rarely feel safe in their old neighborhoods, and if they can't feel safe, there is little point in going there.

"I've been fortunate enough to win three Stanley Cups, and the rings are beautiful, with lots of diamonds, and they generate a lot of attention," notes Kris Draper. "So I don't wear them too often, usually just to weddings or on other special occasions. They just attract too much attention."

In the end, athletes are just very high-profile people, and high-profile people generate a great deal of greed, envy, and jealousy. For some, that can translate easily into crime. They think to themselves, "He's got plenty. So what's he going to miss? Look what I got for free."

They who are on their guard and appear ready to receive their adversaries are in much less danger of being attacked than the supine, secure, and negligent.

—Benjamin Franklin

Chapter 4

"I Don't Get No Respect!"

The words of the late, great comedian Rodney Dangerfield must ring in the ears of nearly every professional athlete and celebrity.

Crossing the Line

THIS SECTION IS ABOUT SPORTSWRITERS. I will say up front and for the record that the majority of sportswriters are hard-working, talented professionals who do their best to be fair and impartial in their coverage and reporting while maintaining the interest of their readers, who are also (in most cases) our fans. Indeed, sportswriters are often more knowledgeable than we professional athletes give them credit for.

If you are going to be an athlete (or a public figure of any kind), one of the most important things you must learn is to take the jeers with the cheers. I have had my share of bad press, whether it was a sportswriter blasting me for signing with and then transferring from Indiana University (IU) and the enigmatic coach Bobby Knight, or for going 0 for 5 from the field in a close ball game. Occasional bad press comes with the territory of being a professional athlete. When Harry Truman said, "If you can't stand the heat, stay out of the kitchen," he wasn't just talking about the presidency. I have always had a cordial and exemplary relationship with sportswriters as a professional athlete, because it is expected from me and all my colleagues.

There is a line, however, and when bad press becomes personal and/or antagonistic, the writer has crossed that line. A personal vendetta can never be confused with objective reporting. Nor can it be successfully presented in the guise of constructive criticism. Professional athletes not only can play between the lines, but most can read between them as well.

Those outside the world of sports are less apt to be attuned to the times when bad press crosses the line into something vicious and ugly. Surprisingly small things can trigger a change in the attitude of the press. Perhaps a sportswriter felt that an athlete was disrespectful to him or her in the locker room. Perhaps the athlete failed to speak or acknowledge the sportswriter's greeting on some occasion. Some sportswriters feel themselves to be intellectually superior because the athlete's job is (or appears to be) primarily physical (the psychological rigor necessary to successfully compete as a professional athlete is often overlooked and underappreciated).

For sportswriters, the competitive pressures and demands of their work may sometimes compel them to emphasize the tabloid angle of a story to increase daily readership.

Deadlines and nerve-wracking sessions in front of a computer trying to write a riveting story may also tempt a sportswriter to cross the line and blame an uncooperative athlete for frustration and writer's block.

Then, too, sometimes it's just a case of bad chemistry. We've all met people to whom we took an instant dislike for no apparent reason. It doesn't make sense, but that is often the nature of human nature, so to speak.

It could also be a simple case of jealousy, envy, or some other hang-up that causes a sportswriter to bring out the poison pen.

To illustrate my point, let's look at a hypothetical scenario. Sam Sportswriter goes to a game and does what he normally does before the game begins: he kicks it around with the other sportswriters and maybe some of the athletes in the locker room. However, Sam notices that Alan Athlete, whom he has been waiting to interview, is not around. In fact, Alan has been giving Sam the cold shoulder for some time, relaying numerous messages through batboys. Indeed, the interview has been scheduled for days, and the team's public relations director has briefed Alan on several occasions. Still, Alan refuses to cooperate, perhaps thinking to himself, "This guy shows up five minutes before game time, and he expects me to drop my daily routine and talk to him. I ain't doing it!"

Now, Sam has promised his editor a blockbuster article, including the interview, and the deadline is fast approaching. In the locker room, he is needled by the other players and his fellow sportswriters for his inability to complete his assignment. It is obvious to everyone present that Alan is deliberately avoiding Sam. Having failed to get his story, Sam steams out of the locker room feeling humiliated. Normally one of the best sportswriters in the business, this time Sam is truly ticked off.

So he stays up late that night writing an article that flays the arrogant Alan alive: "Mr. Hot Shot went 0 for 4 from the plate tonight, and is only 3 for 20 for his last 5 ball games," Sam thinks to himself. "This is just what I need. When I think of how many times I've covered for him in interviews, making him sound at least halfway literate, trying to keep the public from finding out the truth, that he's just a big, dumb, jock, I could kick myself. Well, no more. I'll teach him not to disrespect me!"

Perhaps the original article was going to include coverage of Alan's charitable work in the community. Not now, though. Instead, the article portrays Alan as a game-choking, gun-toting gangsta more concerned with brandishing his Smith and Wesson at a nightclub than with his commitment to the game. In the end, while there is some element of truth in the article, much of the information presented is pure conjecture. Because readers prefer controversial articles and subjects, most can't wait to discuss Sam's article the next morning at the water cooler.

Needless to say, Alan is angry, and he promises himself that he will never talk to Sam again. So begins a feud that is destined to run long and hot for many seasons. Readers will look forward every morning to reading what Sam has to say about Alan—true or false.

It is important to note that readers create a buzz that attracts other readers, thus guaranteeing the paper a bigger audience. Who ends up as the big loser in this scenario? The athlete.

Some sportswriters seem to feel that the power of the pen guarantees them the respect of professional athletes. For the most part sportswriters are respected, but there is a fine line between respect that is earned and fear thinly disguised as respect. When I was in Sacramento there was a reporter who desperately tried to get some of the players, including me, to speak critically about one of our teammates whom the reporter personally disliked. That sort of behavior is not likely to win respect. On the other hand, I have known some big-time athletes who go out of their way to befriend reporters just to avoid unfavorable articles. This must be pretty gratifying for some writers, especially when they know that these same athletes wouldn't give some people the time of day. This is not to say that all sportswriters are ruled by emotion rather than reason (because most of them are not); as an author, I definitely have a heightened respect for what they do, especially in terms of intellectual insights.

"The media will either make you or break you," Dennis Hopson notes. "So when you are asked to do an interview, you better know exactly what you are saying and how you are saying it. You never say anything the reporter can twist or turn around to mean something else. In fact, I sometimes think that it's not really a bad thing if an athlete doesn't talk to the media. Of course, if you don't, the media will still make you out to be a bad person. I don't know. Maybe that's just part of the baggage that comes with being in the limelight."

Steve Sax remembers a face-to-face confrontation with a writer: "I felt that was the best approach. The guy had written a horrible piece about me that was totally untrue. Among other things, he'd called me a punk kid with braces on my teeth, and said that at twenty-two, I had no business hanging around a team of veterans. I just didn't feel that I should allow myself to be personally denigrated in that way. If a writer wants to talk about my performance as a player, that's fine, but don't talk about my character. The day after I confronted him, he apologized and said he respected me for coming to him man to man.

"There was a press conference when I signed with the Yankees, and I remember telling them that I knew they had a job to do and that I would cooperate with them fully, but that I had a job to do as well, and if anyone slandered me or wrote anything that was not true, I would not talk to them even if I got the winning hit in the seventh game of the World Series. I never had a problem with the press in New York, and I think it's because I was straight with them from the outset."

Then, too, for a lot of writers, reporting on a particular athlete can become very personal if a player "disses them." Barry Bonds received a good bit of negative press prior to the steroid allegations, but the people who know him see him differently. "I know Barry pretty well," Sax says. "I've seen him with his family. He plays hard, for sure. But off the field he's a nice guy."

To get a view from the other side of the fence, I spoke with Barry Katz, the former lead sports anchor for WBNS 10 TV in Columbus, Ohio, for many years, and a veteran journalist and broadcaster with more than twenty years in the business. His remarks were candid and revealing.

"I got into television because I couldn't be an athlete. Or maybe I should say, I got into the medium because I couldn't be an athlete. I love sports, and I just kind of wanted to be there. But there was no agenda on my part. I never said to myself, 'I'm going to report on these guys and show them that I'm just as good as them.' I just enjoyed being around sports and talking to people. Are some journalists just frustrated athletes? Probably. Some of them probably feel that intelligence should trump athleticism, which it doesn't, certainly not in terms of wage earnings. Maybe their frustration comes out because of that. But that shouldn't be [an athlete's] problem. That's the journalist's problem. They made a choice in life that this is what they wanted to be. I made a choice in life of what I wanted to be, and if it didn't work out I'm not blaming Lawrence Funderburke or some other athlete. I made my own choice. I'm not going to take it out on them because my life didn't go the way I wanted it to.

"I've had discussions with writers, and many of them will say that if the athlete at least shows some courtesy, it's easier to report favorably on him. On the other hand, some writers can't be friends with an athlete because if he messes up during a game, the reporter has to be able to report about that fairly. Some reporters do cross the line. So do some athletes. Yes, there is a lot of envy involved on the part of the sportswriters. You've got guys who have been covering sports for twenty years making fifty times less than what the guy who just joined the pros is making. As a friend of mine used to say, 'Everybody wants you to do well, but not as well as they are doing.'

"But it's not just envy over the disparity in wages between the athlete and the media guy. Sportswriters are also competing with radio, television, cable, and the Internet. Print journalists can be very envious when they see a television guy breeze in, ask three questions, and leave. The television guy seems to have instant access because of the glamour of his medium. He also gets, or seems to get, more respect. Plus, he's making more money, and he's probably better-looking!

"I was a print journalist when I started out, but I got out of it because it seemed too negative for my personality. I was an upbeat, happy-go-lucky, not a care in the world kind of guy. I enjoy life, and some writers never seemed to enjoy their lives. Maybe it was the wages or the fact that television seems more player-friendly. Still, if you're a print journalist you have to fill your column. That's the nature of the beast."

Katz went on to note that back in the early days of sports—the days of Babe Ruth, Jack Dempsey, and Jim Thorpe—there were only two ways people could see athletes: in movie newsreels and in person. Television hadn't been invented yet. (In fact, television is still comparatively young. It didn't become part of virtually every household until the '60s.)

Today, with satellite, cable, the Internet, and other high-tech media, print journalism is becoming less and less important. Readership has fallen off dramatically. It's not that people don't read any more. It's simply that they have less time for reading. That explains why the readership for *USA Today* is higher than for the *New York Times*. People don't have time (or don't want to take the time) to sift through volumes of newsprint. *USA Today* condenses stories into five paragraphs as opposed to a page and a half.

Katz believes that 99 percent of conflicts between sportswriters and athletes could be settled if the parties involved sat down and talked it out in a non-confrontational manner. I agreed, though I wondered if that wouldn't give some sportswriters bragging rights with their peers: "Look at me. I got Mr. Hot Shot Athlete to acknowledge me."

"When I went to journalism school they always taught you how to be unbiased," Katz continued. "But the truth is, there's bias in everything you do, no matter how fair and just you try to be. There is bias in the way the front page of the *Columbus Dispatch* is laid out. They're biased in the way they report everything. Everybody's got an agenda. It's just human nature, and there's no other way to explain it than that. People always have a bias."

Katz raised some interesting points. Although I was aware of the competition between print and other media, I did not realize the extent to which that competition could affect the public's opinion of and feeling toward athletes. Nor was I aware of the huge increase in the number of people who get their sports news (as well as other news) from television, cable, and the Internet rather than newspapers and magazines.

"Print and TV just don't get along," Mr. Katz noted. "They're not bedfellows. Here's the thing that always got me though: print journalists would always criticize or denigrate television or radio journalists, but if a print guy gets a chance to make the leap to radio or television, he'll be gone at a moment's notice. Yet how often do you see a radio or television journalist writing a column? Almost never. Why is that?"

> *One of the things that makes the grass look greener on the other side is money.*
> *—Unknown*

Maybe it's because many print journalists, like a lot of other people, want to lead the "Lifestyles of the Rich and Famous."

For another perspective, I spoke with Emmy and Golden Mike Award-winner Elie Seckbach, who covers the NBA for several newspapers in

Los Angeles and Israel. His comments shed light on some limitations of sports writing.

"Sportswriters experience the life of professional athletes up close and personal, being part of an inner circle to which very few people will ever have access," Seckbach said. "One would think they'd be happy-go-lucky people enjoying a life for which millions of outsiders would give anything. Instead, you meet so many sportswriters who have become bitter, angry, resentful, and mean-spirited. Many come into the locker room with an agenda.

"If they don't like a particular athlete, they will find every opportunity to throw dirt. It's easy to do. There's an old saying that if a white board has a small dot, everyone will focus on the dot. They know what they're looking for, much like the shark circling the swimmer. They want the blood, the headline, and the controversy. If it's not there, they'll create it. For instance, they may try asking the coach and/or an athlete's teammates a question that is deliberately phrased to be negative. 'Why is such and such taking so many shots every game? Should that change?' No matter what the answers, they can then go to the player and tell him what others think of him. It doesn't take much to provoke someone until you get the quote you're looking for. Ask the same question in fifteen or twenty different ways, and pretty soon you get the quote you're after. Now imagine having thirty reporters like that around you day in and day out."

Seckbach added that some sportswriters believe that players are one-dimensional, that they have no life outside of sports. Most fans want to know more than the X's and O's, but the sportswriter's view of the world may limit what the fans can learn. For one thing, being a talented basketball (or football or hockey) player doesn't automatically indicate a lack of intelligence or interest in other things.

"I've never heard a reporter ask a player, 'Please tell me about your nonprofit organization and the work you do within the community,'" Seckbach noted. "Shaq O'Neal has a heart of gold, but nobody writes about the many things he does off the court. He once bought a $150,000 van for a ten-year-old amputee who lost both of his arms and legs to meningitis. But a lot of reporters would rather focus on going after Shaq day in and day out, questioning his character. At seven-foot-one, he is an easy target. People are always surprised when I tell them how nice Shaq is. He is what we call in Yiddish a 'mensch,' a well-mannered person. But you will not read that anytime soon, not as long as the same people write for the same papers. I'm certainly not saying that all sportswriters are like that. Most of them are not. But there are more than a few. Then, of course, there's the money angle. Every time a player gets a new contract I hear some writers complaining."

Finally, I asked Seckbach to comment on sportswriters and respect from professional athletes. "As odd as it sounds, small-minded reporters with inflated egos will sometimes try to gain a player's respect and attention by trashing them. I've seen this happen. If a player is being attacked day in and day out, he may start being nicer to the reporter, hoping to stop the negative campaign. It usually works, at least for a while. Within a few months, the attacks start up again. What the player may not know is that particular approach is the personality and style of the writer. Be nice to him or ignore him, the response will be the same. The negative shower will keep coming down."

As Greg Vaughn noted, good sportswriters (and most of them are) treat athletes with respect because they know how difficult an athlete's life can be regardless of how it may appear to the public.

Although there are some markets where players are never exempt from personal strikes, in most cases as long as a team is winning, there isn't a lot of leeway for media attacks and open antagonism. But, as Kris Draper stated, "When things don't work out for an athlete, you will see the story over and over and over in every paper on every sports newscast from one end of the country to the other."

"Another thing people need to remember is that when you are in the locker room, that's your place," Draper added. "You spend so much time in the locker room, and the one thing that guys have learned over the years or over a career is that when the media is in there, even if

> *Be careful what you say and how you say it, just in case your words come back to haunt you.*
> —*L. Funderburke*

you are not talking to them you've got to be careful with what you are saying because they're listening too, and sometimes recording, every word. If there is one thing I have learned, it's to be careful when the media is around."

For still another perspective on the relationship between sportswriters and athletes, I spoke with veteran sportswriter and NBA analyst Stephen A. Smith. Articulate, colorful, and insightful, Smith is a columnist for the *Philadelphia Inquirer* as well as an analyst for ESPN. In a world where equivocation can seem like the norm, Smith is known for saying what he means and meaning what he says.

I began by asking him if he thought sportswriters take advantage of their influential positions when covering professional athletes.

"Clearly sportswriters have significant power, more so than most would like to think," he said. "Regardless of the influence television and radio wields, on most occasions they're relying on information that was printed in the newspaper. What people don't realize is that in television and radio, on most occasions you're required to be in studio. Therefore, you're . . . a bit detached from the athletes or subjects you're talking about in most instances, simply because you're not around that often. Whereas with newspaper guys, it's their job to be around you, in your face, attaching a face to the names [the public] may hear. Hence, it breeds credibility, making that newspaper person somewhat of an authority on a particular subject. Newspaper people know this, and sometimes, a few of them even take advantage of it. But I'd like to believe most don't abuse that power/privilege because when all is said and done, it is unethical to have personal agendas when it comes to the athletes they cover.

"As to whether some sportswriters are frustrated athletes, absolutely! Not all of them, of course. But there isn't a sportswriter in this business that doesn't wish he was in better shape or that he had the skills most of these athletes possess.

"Of course what frustrates some even more is the money these athletes make. Newspaper folks not only earn less than athletes, but they also earn less than television or radio folks in most cases. So when they sense a lack of appreciation by the athletes for the opportunities that have been bestowed on them, it's offensive to society at large.

"For better or worse, newspaper people are no different than anyone else. There's always occasional jealousy and—yes—racism, too. Out of more than 4,000 general sports columnists in this nation, less than twenty-five are African American, covering sports like basketball and football, which are predominantly black. While I don't believe it's as prevalent as some would claim, anyone who denies racism occasionally factors into the equation of covering these athletes is a flat-out liar or one of the most ignorant people on earth."

I asked Smith if he felt that, given the competitive pressure from media such as the Internet, "SportsCenter," and *USA Today*, sportswriters tend to lean toward the controversial when covering professional athletes.

"Yes!" he said. "Controversy definitely sells, and the newspaper business is a business. However, I truly believe on most occasions, people are simply speaking what they feel. I know I do."

Finally, I asked Smith to address the question of respect between sportswriters and athletes, and specifically whether sportswriters sometimes demand respect based on the power of the pen.

"I don't believe sportswriters ever coerce pro athletes into giving them respect because I don't think they're stupid enough to think they can get away with it. The one thing about athletes is that they can smell phonies from a mile away most of the time. They see the wolves in sheep's clothing. Newspaper people are around these guys enough to know better. So I don't believe that, although I do believe they wish they could."

(For additional insights on the relationship between pro athletes and sportswriters, see famed journalist Bryan Burwell's outstanding commentary in the Summary Observations.)

Old Ties That Bind

THOMAS WOLFE ONCE SAID, "You can't go home again." The truth is you can go, but you probably can't stay very long, particularly not if you are a successful athlete. It's all right to reminisce about the 'hood, but an athlete can never be all things to all the people there.

Athletes sometimes don't know how to react when they see someone with whom they were friends back in the day, but who hasn't changed since that time. More often than not, they feel that their sphere of friends and acquaintances shouldn't change either, including athletes now turned celebrity friends.

Most athletes feel guilty about their inability to communicate with old friends on the same level they once enjoyed. Still, in their heart of hearts they know such communication is impossible. They have been separated from old friends not only by miles and perhaps by years, but also by different worlds of experience.

Sometimes it's even hard to know how to greet old friends. Would they be offended if you said, "What up! How you been? I'll see you later. Stay up now"? Such a greeting might not sound genuine in the way that it once did, even though your affection for them as friends may still be strong.

Then there are the inevitable hookup attempts. "Man, how can I get a hold of you?" You don't want to think this is the prelude to a request for money, but somewhere in the recesses of your mind, you know it is. So you wonder if giving your phone number is wise, even to old friends. Even without your number, some will try to reach you through your team's office or some affiliated philanthropic or business organization.

Athletes know that if they give out their numbers (home, cell, or otherwise), they might as well prepare to be inundated with sob stories (some quite legitimate), financial emergencies, "investment opportunities," and speaking engagement requests.

To avoid this, many athletes try turning the tables with, "How can I get a hold of you?" or "Give me your number, and I will holler at you when I get a minute." That minute may or may not come, but at least this shields them (albeit perhaps temporarily) from the inevitable hookup. In my experience over the years, requests seem to come to the surface at some point in the conversation. They almost always wanted money. Nor is my experience unique among athletes, sad to say. This is one reason why athletes and high-profile celebrities make it as difficult as possible for people to contact them. Some athletes hire personal assistants to handle their day-to-day inquiries and activities.

Anthony Telford remembers, "In San Francisco, I'd have thirty or forty passes. I mean, because that's where I was from, San Jose. I love my family, but they never seemed to understand how important it was for me to maintain my routine when I had a game. So they would show up to the game, stay late at the hotel, and be there early in the morning. It would completely disrupt my schedule. Of course, some of them didn't have time to drop by and say hello, although they did have time to ask me for tickets to the game. It's something you just have to deal with."

Dennis Hopson remembers, too. "Once they find out where you are playing, you can go up to that office to make a phone call or talk to the

GM [General Manager], and the secretary will hand you a ton of messages. 'Dennis, such-and-such called and he wants you to return his phone call at such-and-such.' Half the time you're looking at these things and thinking, 'Now where do I know this guy from?'

"People call my parents all the time: 'Can you have Dennis give me a phone call?' just because they are listed in the phone book, and I don't mean just people around Columbus. I mean people all over the place. I have basketball cards in my mailbox every night. I played with Michael Jordan, and people still ask me if I run into Michael could I get something signed for them.

"Athletes change their phone numbers often because they are so bombarded, and 90 percent of the calls are from people—friends, family, etc.—who want something: money, your time, whatever. Changing your phone number often is the only way you can get any peace."

Once I called two pro athletes only to find out that their numbers had been changed. When one of them finally got back to me, I asked, "Who's been bothering you and wearing your phone number out?" I didn't have to guess what was going on. (In case of emergencies and because I get calls from people who do need to get in touch with me and people with whom I need to speak, I don't change my number very often. In contrast, I had a teammate who changed his number every year.)

Steve Sax understands the impulse behind such drastic measures. "You run into people you haven't seen in years and with whom you no longer have anything in common really, and right away they want your number. Give it to them, and you know the phone will be ringing day and night until they get you. You also know they want something. It's sad to feel that way, but you know it. You know there's always an angle. Also, people don't understand (or want to understand) that athletes have personal lives, too. We have personal obligations—wife, children, community activities, etc. You don't want to blow somebody off, but sometimes it's either that or neglect your own personal life, to which you are just as entitled as the next person."

I asked Steve if people who try and fail to contact him by phone have tried other avenues of getting in touch with him.

"A lot of times they'd call and leave messages at the stadium. Sometimes they would even call my mom to get her to relay a message to me. Sometimes I'd get a FedEx. Sometimes they'd just show up at the stadium and yell at me from the dugout. Or they'd send somebody who knew me to relay a message to me. On one occasion a message was relayed to me through my coach, Tommy Lasorda: 'Hey this guy's been trying to get a hold of you.' Nine times out of ten it's because they want something. I hate to say it, but it's true."

There is a school of thought that holds true that if you choose a profession that may thrust you into the limelight, then part of the price you should expect to pay is a certain loss of privacy. It's a point of view that is not without merit, but it's also one that is very easy to express from outside the limelight.

In his book *Iacocca: An Autobiography*, Lee Iacocca, the chief force behind the success of the Ford Mustang, recalls being confronted by "Mustang mania" from car owners eager to speak with him via short-wave-radio! It was a Sunday morning and the famous Ford executive was napping while en route to Europe, flying over some remote corner of the globe.

No matter what your profession, if your name becomes a household word, you can expect to be treated as though you belong to the world and not to yourself. That isn't always a bad thing, especially when you are given the opportunity to make a difference in the lives of those who truly need your help.

But what happens when you want to take back your life, even briefly? I asked Gary Trent to comment on this.

"I always tell people, 'If I give you my number, don't give it to nobody, because anybody that's supposed to have my number already has it. If they don't have it, it's because I don't want them to have it.'

"There are times when I just don't want to be found. Anyway, 99 percent of the time, the people who are trying to find me just want something. They want to come to games, but they want me to fly them out in the best seats on the plane. They want me to put them up in a hotel and pay for their meals. They want to get into certain clubs, maybe get hooked up with some girls. It gets crazy.

"It's not that I don't appreciate their wanting to come out and support me. I do. So I might be able to get them a discount on a ticket and maybe a better price on a hotel room. But people are so out of touch, they don't understand. I can run into a guy on the street, and the first thing he says is, 'I want to come to some games. Mail me some tickets.' Now, why would I mail him tickets to a Los Angeles Lakers game when he's in Columbus, Ohio, unless I was planning to send him some plane tickets as well, which is probably what he's angling for. That's how far people are out of touch with reality.

"That's why I don't have voicemail either. They might say, 'I know you got my message,' or, 'Hey, man. Didn't you get my message last week?' Finally, I had the phone company come out and put in a separate phone line with a phone number that just rings. There's no answering machine, no phone plugged in to it. It just rings. It's my Internet number and fax number. Sad to say it, but this kind of game is what it has come down to."

Ah, the price and the problems of fame and fortune. Still, as the lyrics to an old song attest, most of us would "rather be rich, rather be sittin' on [our] money bags, than be digging a ditch, pulling a switch."

Find me ten—or even five—ordinary working people who wouldn't agree with those sentiments. For proof, I refer you to the millions upon millions of lottery tickets that are sold every day.

Ironically, the only people who might not wholeheartedly agree are the people with the money, and who have had the experiences, good and bad, that come with having money.

Gary Trent continues: "I never understood what people were saying when they talk about what it's like to have money. That's an experience you won't understand until you are going through it. For me, it's been about growing pains, and it has cost me a lot emotionally and financially. Sometimes you learn too late, 'I shouldn't have given him $100,000,' or, 'I knew I shouldn't have given him that car because he wrecked it and doesn't have any insurance.'

"The truth is that a lot of the people who are trying to get to you to ask for money have a distorted view of what money can and cannot do. This probably explains why people you know will sometimes say it's hard for them to find you a present you will like for your birthday or Christmas. After all, what can they give you that you don't already have? Since they can't afford to give you the things that now befit your standard of living, they don't know what to do and they don't understand you or your situation. Professional athletes want the same things that everyone wants. We want to be appreciated, respected, and loved, and if people show us those things by their actions, then a lot of times that's all the gifts we need. Then these are the people you will bend over backwards to help when their car breaks down or something else happens where a little extra money, which you have and they don't, can get them over a rough patch."

Somebody once said, "Money, you should pardon the expression, is like manure. It isn't worth a darn unless it's spread around encouraging little things to grow."

A great many people with considerable fortunes seem to agree. While they (understandably) resent being treated like walking bank machines by some people who are close to them, and sometimes perfect strangers, they are generous in their support of people, community groups, and grassroots organizations that are trying to make a difference in a community and in the world at large. In short, the rich tend to be believers in the adage, give a man a fish and he will eat for a day; teach a man to fish, and he can feed himself for a lifetime.

Again, Gary Trent: "Money gives you freedom, but it's not the solution to every problem. For some people, there could never be enough money. It doesn't matter how much you give them, they'll still end up broke. In fact, money can make situations worse. If an alcoholic wins the lottery, he will just become a rich alcoholic with the money to buy as much alcohol as he can consume until the money runs out or he dies, whichever comes first. Money will not, in and of itself, make you smart. You can be brilliant and still not have a dime. Money will bring out the best or the worst in you.

Money is not the solution to every problem. Sometimes it just makes a bad situation worse.

—Gary Trent

"Of course, I would rather have money and deal with the headaches that come with it. Not having money is a headache. In a way, it's all relative. There are some people who make $100,000 a year and are much happier than somebody making $5 million a year. The truth is, you can have the biggest cars, the finest homes, and all the trappings of real wealth and still be empty inside, especially if there is no one to share it with. There is some truth to that old saying about it being lonely at the top. One reason young athletes are so quick to loan money to their friends is loneliness. Good fortune is no fun unless you can share it with loved ones. So young athletes end up buying their friends clothes and plane tickets and cars and getting them into certain clubs. If he has to go on the road, he doesn't want to go alone, so he pays the cost of bringing his friends along. But then one day he looks around, and it's ten or fifteen years later and he's still supporting the same friends, who still don't have jobs or prospects. They've gotten used to living off him.

"Money can solve a lot of problems, but it's not the key to a full, rich life, or to being at peace with yourself. It's amazing how many people don't understand that."

There is another issue for Gary, which will resonate with other athletes and celebrities, but which might at first glance seem trivial to others.

Consider this question. How many people do you meet every day? I'm not talking about the people you know already, like family members and co-workers. I mean strangers, people with whom you may have contact for only a few minutes at the drug store or the grocery store or when you take your car through a car wash. If you stop to think about it, you probably have a dozen or so of these types of casual encounters every day.

Now suppose, for a moment, that every person you met, no matter how briefly, expected you to remember them and even got a little upset if you didn't. Ridiculous, right? You couldn't possibly remember each and every person you meet on a daily basis in all the places you may be. Moreover, you would think they were a little light in the cranium if they expected you to remember them.

Now multiply by fifty or a hundred the number of people you meet every day. Suddenly you have hundreds, if not thousands, of strangers, each expecting you to remember them, even if you only met them once for fewer than five minutes.

Welcome to the world of the high-profile professional athlete or celebrity. Gary Trent adds: "I see people in the streets, and it's, 'Hey Gary, you don't remember me man, you ran into me at such and such?' Most of the time I just don't remember these people. They take it personally, even though I'm not trying to hurt their feelings. Every year I travel to forty or fifty cities. I have a family. I have business to take care of. Is it my fault if I can't remember somebody who says we ran into each other in 1999, and this is 2005? For me to remember a person, the situation has to have had an impact on me. Maybe that person's name and picture were in the paper in connection with a charity I'm interested in. Or maybe you delivered pizzas to some community event for neighborhood kids. Outside of things like that, I just cannot remember every single person I meet. In the first place, even if I wanted to, I meet too many people for that to be possible. In the second place, it's a safe bet that the ones who so badly want to be remembered are just looking for a hookup of some kind."

My wife, Monya, laughingly admits that often when I get a phone call she suspects it's a hook-me-upper.

"It's sad, I guess, to be so skeptical," she says. "But that's just the way I feel. I mean, not everybody, of course, but I honestly think most of the people who call have some kind of angle, whether it's some type of business opportunity, business venture, a loan, or something along these lines, tickets, whatever. It's always something."

It's not unusual for athletes to suddenly hear from people they haven't seen in years. For most people, it could be just an old friend who hasn't touched base with you in a while. But if you are an athlete, you can bet the person wants something, and they will usually go out of their way to reach you to try and get it.

Anthony Telford remembers one such incident among dozens.

"One year when I was in San Diego, a girl called me in the visiting clubhouse. I vaguely remembered her name, but not much else. She said that she and I had gone to school together and that her son's Little League team was in town and really wanted to meet me after the game. I asked her to talk to me about our high school days and she gave me all the right answers. Obviously, she was in school around the same time I was. So I agreed to meet the kids. I chose a place away from the team hotel. When she got there and I saw her and I realized that I'd never hung around with her or her friends in high school, even though she insisted I had. Her name was familiar only because I'd seen her picture in the school yearbook. I got tickets for the kids to see the game anyway, but really, the phone call was just a ploy, a roundabout way to get me to hook her up with some tickets. Isn't it funny how they never think about getting in touch 'for old times' sake' when you're in the minor leagues? Like that rap record says, 'I wasn't that cute when I didn't have no loot,' or access or contacts or whatever the hook-me-uppers are looking for."

As Telford's experience shows, many adults are not above using children as part of the hookup to get to an athlete because they know most athletes will respond positively to kids. Many an athlete has signed a poster or a ball for a child not realizing that the child's parents plan to sell the item on eBay. So focused are they on getting something for nothing from him that it never dawns on them the lesson they are teaching their kids about how to get along in the world: that you can get what you want if you're willing to lie, cheat, mislead, and misrepresent yourself. (In the Introduction to *Hook Me Up, Playa!* Federal Reserve Chairman Alan Greenspan was quoted as basically saying these exact words.)

Another issue raised by Telford's story is privacy. How was the woman able to convince security to let her speak directly to him in the locker room? What kind of urgency did she fake? Did she pretend to the security guard that she was one of Telford's old girlfriends, and then, once he was on the phone, switch stories to become an old and close friend from high school days? Had she really been a friend, perhaps she would have realized that interrupting a player's routine just before a game is the worst kind of distraction and prevents him from concentrating on the business at hand: playing his best and helping his team win.

Of course, hook-me-uppers always have a story, and it has to sound pretty convincing if it will get them past the wide buffer zone of people with whom athletes and celebrities understandably surround themselves.

Telford continues. "If they can get your number, the next thing they need is a story. Everybody has a story or some kind of gambit by which to introduce themselves to you. They know they only have a few minutes to get you to let your guard down. So the story or the intro has to be a good one. As an athlete you deal with so much of this that you begin to wonder if anybody will ever again call you just to see how you and your family are getting along. At that, they'd probably have trouble convincing you that they really didn't want anything else—that all they wanted was to touch base and see how you are. Even after you hung up, you'd still be wondering when the other shoe was going to drop. Were they going to call back in ten minutes and pretend they forgot to ask you something? Of course, the other side of it is, if the person calling is actually an old friend, [the athlete] immediately thinks to himself, 'You call me now that I'm playing pro ball. Why didn't I hear from you when I was just starting out?' Not knowing whom to trust, you end up trusting no one, which is sad. Still, in your mind, you're always thinking to yourself, 'Here it comes. Here comes the pitch. What do they want?' It always comes out. Sooner or later, it always comes out."

Greg Vaughn agrees. "You hate giving out your phone number because everybody wants something. That's a sad way to think, but who wants to call somebody back just to find out that person is looking for a hookup of some kind? It happens all the time. Friends, cousins, everybody, they call the stadium just to ask for things. Or someone will leave a message with my mom, and she calls me, 'So-and-so has been trying to get a hold of you.' But I know that person is just using my mom to get to me."

Calls to the stadium or the locker room are particularly distracting and aggravating.

"People don't understand," says Kris Draper. "On game day you have a routine that you need to stick to. I always have a two-hour nap before games. The last thing I need is phone calls: 'Hey, listen, you got any extra tickets? I would love to come to the game tonight.' Or, 'I have tickets, but can you get me some guest passes so I can see you after the game?' These kinds of interruptions can really throw you off. Of course, if you're playing in your hometown, it gets even harder. The problem is, interruptions or no interruptions, you still have a game and you have to show up and play your best. So you don't want any distractions."

I asked Charley Hannah if he'd had experiences with old acquaintances or friends with whom he hasn't spoken in many years suddenly trying to make contact with him after he made it to the pros.

"Of course. They always claim to have been your best friend. 'Ah man, it's great. I haven't seen you in so long. Let's get together. I need to talk to you about something.' It's like you're wearing a bull's-eye on your back. They need something, and you're the target for getting it. It's a shame because sometimes I really didn't want to blow them off."

Kris Draper shared similar experiences.

"It usually starts out with a little small talk, then they take it to the next level, which is, 'Why don't you give me your number? Let's stay in touch.' A guy you haven't seen in ten or twelve years suddenly wants to be your best buddy? Right away your guard goes up. Let's face it. If this guy was such a good friend, the chances are you would have stayed in touch with him over the years regardless of what either of you has been doing professionally. And of course every athlete runs into people who say, 'Hey remember me, remember me?' Right away you're in a tough situation because, given the number of people you meet every day, there is no way you're going to remember them all. You don't want to be rude, and you don't want to hurt their feelings, but the truth is you're not going to remember them.

"As for giving out your phone number, it all comes down to being careful and being sure that you surround yourself with the right people: that is, people who have proven to you that they can be trusted. Some guy shows up whom you haven't seen in years and asks for your phone number? Right away you have to be suspicious of his motives.

"Most athletes, especially the really high-profile players, have restricted cell phone numbers. It's a safeguard against unwanted calls. Obviously there are people to whom you have to give your number, though you can always use a callback number. Still, you never know. Even if the person calling you is someone you contacted for a service or to buy something, the minute the guy says, 'Hey, you play for the Detroit Red Wings,' you know they have your cell phone number, and you have no idea what they will do with it. That's why some athletes change their numbers often. If your number gets into the wrong hands, it could be a disaster."

I Need It, You Don't

AT THE BEGINNING of a television talk show host's new season, each person in the studio audience was presented with a new car. It was, to say the least, a mind-boggling gesture. Several weeks later,

Nothing is more honorable than a grateful heart.
—Roman Seneca

there was a rumor circulating that some of the guests had complained. Why? Because they had to pay the taxes on the car! Apparently, it wasn't enough that they were given a new car; they expected the taxes to be paid on the car as well.

Somebody *gives* you a brand new car—no strings attached, except that you have to pay the taxes on it—and instead of being glad that you were in the right place at the incredibly right time, you complain because you have to pay the taxes on it!

There is a prevailing attitude among the hook-me-uppers when it comes to asking athletes for money: "He's got so much; he's not going to miss it. What I'm askin' for is no biggie to somebody with that much money."

Responses vary when and if an athlete fails to come across with the cash, though anger is certainly high on the list. They may not say a word, but body language and general signs of agitation will tell the story. Often the physical manifestations of anger, urgency, and disappointment are a tactical ploy designed to make the athlete feel guilty for his refusal to help out. Over time, the hook-me-uppers hope to wear him down to the point where he will give them money just to get rid of them (which, of course, never happens—they always come back).

If the athlete says no and sticks to it, the hook-me-uppers will make sure that others hear about (sometimes even read about) his appalling lack of "generosity."

Over the years, in addition to the usual nickel-and-dime (make that $50 and $100) requests, I've been asked to "invest" in:

- Pizza parlors
- Restaurants
- Real estate
- Junk stocks
- A construction company

- A cleaning business
- Loan arrangements
- Nonprofit ventures
- A barber shop
- A movie (still in the first stages of planning)
- Clothing businesses, and
- Drug breakthroughs.

The scenario usually plays out something like this:

Athlete meets an old acquaintance. After a few pleasantries, the pitch comes.

"Say, can you hook me up with $2,000? I ran into some financial problems that have set me back a bit."

"Look," the athlete says, "I've helped you out many times before, but right now I might have to pass on kickin' you that loot."

"You make mad loot every year, and you telling me you can't give me a stinking $2,000? What's up with that?"

The acquaintance is now clearly frustrated, but so is the athlete.

"First of all, why am I always bailing you out? I know you know how much money I make every year, but if I tell you no, does that make me a bad—."

The acquaintance interrupts.

"I just can't believe it. You got all that dough and you can't give me a little something just to help me out of a jam. All the money you got, it's not like you gonna miss it!"

So the acquaintance storms off to tell everyone about the greedy, selfish athlete so lacking in compassion that he wouldn't even help a person out, even though it wasn't that much money. Of course, the acquaintance conveniently forgets to mention all the other times when the athlete came through for him. So the people who hear only the hook-me-upper's sad story are left with the impression that the athlete really is greedy, selfish, arrogant, and uncaring.

I asked Dennis Hopson about his experiences in this regard.

"Happens all the time. I mean, it could be something as small as a dinner. Somebody asks me out to dinner, maybe to talk about an investment or something, and when the check comes they expect me to pay, even though they asked me out! Of course, that happens almost all the time if you are out to dinner. When the bill comes, if there is an athlete or a celebrity or entertainer at the table, everybody just looks at it. Nobody touches it. Basically they are waiting for you to pick it up and pay it, and if you don't, the bill just sits there. It's almost funny."

I asked Dennis how he could tell when someone is angry with him for refusing to give them money if they don't actually say anything.

"You can tell by their body language. If you're on the telephone, you can tell by their tone of voice. It's as though they can't take no from you because you are making so much money. From other people, they can accept it, but not from you, as though you have nothing else to do with your money other than make it available to anyone who needs something. They rationalize, 'What's $5,000 (or $10,000, or $20,000, etc.) to you?' It does no good to explain to them that you have little things like a house with a mortgage, bills, children, and expenses. They can't see it, or they won't. The only thing you can count on is, if they leave empty-handed, your name will be mud to everyone they meet, and eventually the story will probably get back to you, about what a mean, selfish person you are."

Steve Sax agreed: "People often preface their requests with, 'I know this is asking a lot, but do you think you could do this or this or this?' You get the impression that they feel that approach might work better than another. The point is, they wouldn't even consider asking other people because they know the resources aren't there."

I asked Anthony Telford whether, in his experience, people seemed to expect him to fund their ideas, no matter how bizarre.

"I lost one friend over something like that. He had an idea that needed financing, but I just didn't believe it would work. I was right, and he hasn't called me once since. But a lot of people think that you don't have a right to an opinion about the investment. They want your money, and then you're supposed to let them do the thinking. So they act as though they can't believe it when you tell them you don't think their idea will work.

"Worse still, they think you are obligated, because of your salary, to help them because they haven't yet achieved the level of success they want. Their idea will be the breakthrough for them. It's their ticket to success, and they can't believe that you don't share their vision and aren't willing to help them achieve their goals. Most of the time, they haven't tried any of the ordinary avenues for financing a venture. You are their first, and usually last, resort, the theory being that if the idea goes up in flames, you can absorb the financial loss without even thinking about it. It's crazy, but that's the way they think.

"Another time I met a young woman who had what I thought was a pretty neat idea. But she got angry when I insisted that, if I were going to invest in it, we would need to have a contract drawn up. I don't do business without a contract. Neither does anyone else, if they're smart. Like all the other hook-me-uppers, she

Never be afraid or ashamed to say no if something doesn't feel right or if someone asks for more than you have to give.

—L. Funderburke

wanted to use my money to finance her idea, and then keep all the profits for herself. After all, why should I want a share of the profits? I make so much money I don't need a return on my investment. Again, it's insanity."

Gary Trent's comments echo Telford's: "They seem to feel your money is unlimited, especially if you're in your first or second year of a six-year deal.

Then it's, 'Man, you can give me $10,000. You got four more years coming.' Sometimes I think the hook-me-uppers count your money more than you do. 'Man, he got $4 million coming in for the next four years. That's $16 million. He can give me $10,000 for a car, it's not going to hurt him.' They may not say it out loud, but that's the way they think. You know they've played that scenario in their minds. Otherwise, they wouldn't have the gall to come to you and ask for some astronomical amount of money. They think because you make so much money, you don't put the same value on it that people in different professions do. As clever as the hook-me-uppers can be thinking of ways to separate you from your money, in other ways they show very little common sense and a lot of flat-out ignorance.

"It's probably a little sad, but I think that's why so many athletes end up limiting their friends to mostly other professional athletes in the fraternity. Nine times out of ten, you won't have to worry about them trying to borrow money from you. They know the situation because they're in it themselves."

Here is what Greg Vaughn had to say.

"When someone asks me for $200,000, $300,000, $700,000 to build something and I say no, I'm automatically the bad guy. I know it from their body language and tone of voice. And I usually hear about it later because the person I turned down has spread the word. But not one of those people ever drove me to practice, or helped me do my homework, or gave me a pat on the back and a hug when I was little and crying when I needed something.

"The people that have always been there for me are still in my life. Of my closest friends, the people that actually supported me when I didn't have anything, when I was in the minor leagues struggling, not one has ever asked me for anything."

I asked Kris Draper about the hook-me-uppers' mind-set.

"People don't realize that, at least for hockey players, the season now lasts the entire year. After the playoffs, I take two weeks off to vacation with my family. Then I'm back in the gym working out two, three, four hours a day. I've worked hard to get to where I am. That means I'm not going to part with my money just because someone asks for it, regardless of what his reason is. I try to be polite, of course. But, basically, the answer is going to be no."

Charley Hannah recalls the experience of a player who tried to live up to his parents' highest expectations, which turned out to be too high.

"There is a perception, especially among young players, that once they make it to the pros and get the big contract, the financial world will open up and the world will, literally, be at their feet forever. And it's worse for him if his family and friends feel the same way. There are parents who have stopped working and prefer to depend on their son to support them. That's what happened to one athlete I know. The dream, being drafted into the NFL, was realized, but the realization was not the panacea he and his family had thought it would be. He made a good living, but he wasn't offered the $10 or $20 million contracts they, or he, expected. What with taxes, the cost of living, and the impact of other things that most people don't take into consideration, he soon realized that there would be a limit to how much he could do to take care of his parents, which he felt obligated to do because they had been supportive of him. Once he got into the NFL, however, his parents and others in the family began to view him as an open checkbook. He did what he could for everyone, but without the lucrative contracts, he simply could not support his parents and everyone else for the rest of their lives. He tried, but I'm not sure it was something his family ever really understood, and I don't think the scars ever healed."

I don't know the key to success, but the key to failure is trying to please everybody.
—Bill Cosby

Aaron Ward recalled a personal experience with a hook-me-upper. "One day last year at the mall, I parked my car in a space where there was no other car beside me. When I came out of the mall, there's a cop sitting there with a couple claiming that I hit their car—a white car dented with red paint. Since my car is black, I'm thinking to myself, 'There's not a chance.' Then, while I'm talking to the cop, the other guy says, 'Aren't you Aaron Ward? Didn't you used to play for the Detroit Red Wings? Give me 500 bucks and we can take care of all of this.'"

Multiply incidents like that by a hundred or more, and you have a slice of the athlete's everyday life.

Old joke: A panhandler stops a passing stranger. "Can you let me have ten dollars for a cup of coffee?" "Ten dollars for a cup of coffee!? Why do you need so much?" the stranger asks. "I'm a big tipper," the panhandler replies.

The professional athlete finds himself in the world of panhandlers far too often.

"Who Wants to Be a Millionaire?"

WHAT A SILLY question. Everybody!

Well, let's say at least four-fifths of the world's population. State lotteries generate enormous amounts of money, to say nothing of the millions lost in casinos in Las Vegas, Atlantic City, and every other gambling establishment. Somebody once said, "Money isn't everything, but it's way ahead of whatever is second."

I am opposed to millionaires, but it would be dangerous to offer me the position.
—Mark Twain

Attention, class! It's time for a reality check. The next time you hear or read about an athlete who has just accepted a $40 million contract, or some other such enormous figure, remember that what you have heard does not reflect the whole picture. The athlete does not just ride off into the sunset in his white Mercedes to live happily and outlandishly ever after. Huge salaries evaporate—like puddles of water on a steamy summer day after a thunderstorm. Between the Federal Insurance Contributions Act or FICA (which, in the sports world stands for "Funnel Income Collectively from Athletes"), Supplemental Security Income or SSI, state income tax, federal income tax, agent fees, and fines, an athlete may often wonder what happened to that fantastic salary the media reported he was earning. Fact: Athletes lose up to half or more of their income as a result of these and other unavoidable financial obligations.

Even college graduates salivating over a $60,000–$70,000 anticipated yearly salary need to understand that they won't be taking home anything remotely close to these amounts once Uncle Sam and others get their take. But just like some athletes who spend according to their "gross salary," more than a few college graduates will live it up as though this were really the case too.

I know what you're thinking. "Yeah, but what they have left is more than most ordinary people will ever see in a lifetime." Well, I'd argue with that, if it weren't true.

But my goal here is not to pretend that athletes are poor, underpaid, often penniless, creatures alone in the world at the mercy of federal, state, and city tax wolves. You wouldn't believe that, even if I were crazy enough to say it. My goal is simply to give you a perspective from the other side of those gigantic salary numbers you see spread across the newspapers. Contrary to what most people believe, huge salaries are not just there for enjoyment and endless spending sprees. There are equally huge problems and risks attached, and sometimes those problems and risks can eat up most of the salary. Yes, a six-figure salary is, indeed, a great deal of money, but six or even seven figures don't last forever. Every well has a bottom.

Rookies coming into the professional ranks are in for a rude awakening. If they are fortunate, they might bring home 40 percent of their estimated income, and this does not yet take into account living expenses, tithing or philanthropic commitments, and other notable cash outlays. Worse still, many rookies will not play professionally as long as they had hoped, which makes it doubly important for them to exercise fiscal restraint and to invest wisely, just at the time when they are least likely to want to do so.

Save early, save often, save a lot!

—L. Funderburke

The average career of a professional athlete in basketball, baseball, football, and hockey is anywhere from three to five years, and that is a generous estimate. Unfortunately, no athlete wants to think about what will happen when his playing days are over.

Minimum-salaried and complementary players, in particular, must manage their money carefully, which can be hard when your family and friends are constantly confusing you with Bill Gates.

I spoke with Dennis Hopson about the common misconception that all athletes are millionaires simply by virtue of turning pro.

"What's a millionaire? You might be a millionaire now, but once you stop playing this game and the money stops coming in every two weeks—that is, if you haven't handled it right—you won't be a millionaire for long. So when a person says you are a millionaire, my first question is, 'What's your definition of a millionaire?' Bill Gates is a billionaire and he's still working. That ought to tell us all something."

I asked Steve Sax to comment on the general perception that all pro athletes are millionaires.

"It's not true, although there probably are more millionaires among pro athletes now than ever before. Still, what most people don't know is that a little over 30 percent of all professional baseball players in their first two years are earning salaries that are below the poverty level. The average salary in the minor leagues is about $700 per month. If a guy has a wife and two kids, well…it's pretty crazy. On the other hand, the minimum salary for pro baseball is $300,000, which is darn good. But if you are living in L.A. or New York, where the cost of living is quite high, and you have a car and a wife and kids, that $300,000 may not go as far as you think. Nobody's going to confuse you with Warren Buffett, that's for sure. A few years into the big leagues and you could be making a lot more, but that still doesn't mean you're loaded."

Here's what Anthony Telford had to say:

"People see the professional uniform and they think you're rolling in money. Well, I can't speak for everybody else, but I worked every off-season of my life from 1987 to 1996. I had no choice since I was married and we had a house and I was playing mostly up and down—that is, from the majors down to AAA. Let's say you're making $6,000 a month. That sounds like a lot until you factor in house notes and rent for an apartment, which you use five months out of the year, rental cars, taxes, regular cost of living, etc. Your salary is eaten up pretty fast.

"In baseball we have to play winter ball. So I played in Puerto Rico a couple of years, played in the Dominican Republic once or twice. I used my spring training money to pay my February house note because you don't get paid in the off-season. Don't get me wrong: it was wonderful, but it was not easy.

"The fact is, people tend to believe what they see in the newspaper. So if it says that the average salary for a Major League Baseball player went up, people draw their own conclusions. Unfortunately, the number they see is the mean… Crunch all the numbers, and yes, there are guys making $10 to $20 million a year, but there are also guys making minimum salary. Most of my years in baseball, I made just below the major leage average, even when I was playing in Montreal, where the money was good. At the end of my career I was making very good money, for me, but then I'm pretty low-maintenance. Most people don't understand the reality behind the numbers."

Greg Vaughn agrees: "Most professional athletes are definitely not millionaires, especially in baseball. My wife and I were talking the other day, and we figured I made about $715 a month my first year in baseball. It's still a struggle today, unless you are one of the top two or three picks and you get two, three, or four million dollar signing bonuses. In the off-season, if your parents aren't wealthy, you go back home and get a job or you play winter ball, which helps you improve your game while you're getting paid."

Kris Draper comments further: "Of course, the NHL has its own rules, like the NBA and the NFL. At a certain point in your NHL career, you will be playing under a two-way contract. You get a certain amount of money, and if they send you down to the minors, that amount is cut substantially. And there's always a fine line. When you're in the majors, you're usually making a good living, but if you get sent down, there's a drastic change.

"I played my first two years in the minors. It's a learning process, and you're basically earning your way to a chance to play in the NHL. But you're not going to make the kind of money that will set you up for life in the minors, even though you're still a professional athlete. It's tough in the minors."

It occurred to me after talking to Kris that some hockey players must spend a lot of time wondering what will happen to them and their families if they get sent down to the minors with a drastic salary cut.

Money can't buy happiness, but it can buy the kind of misery you prefer.

—Unknown

Chapter 5

Guilt-tripping

Guilt: the gift that keeps on giving.

—Anonymous

"Keepin' It Real" for Real

"KEEPIN' IT REAL" REFERS TO an athlete's attempts to pay back the debt he is presupposed by many to owe to the community from which he came.

But keepin' it real shouldn't be about assuaging guilt by giving money to the hook-me-uppers. It should be about genuine compassion and philanthropy and giving people, especially young people, the opportunity to strive for a better future. Knowledge-based speaking engagements, scholarships and grant assistance, or simple positive reinforcement that many underprivileged youth need and may only get from pro athletes are the true foundations of keepin' it real. The nonprofit Lawrence Funderburke Youth Organization (LFYO), which I founded, is committed to these services and goals. Many pro athletes and sports franchises are committed to these tasks also.

Athletes, particularly those who come from impoverished backgrounds, never completely distance themselves from the guilt they feel because they made it while others whom they know did not. Thus, athletes become easy targets for the hook-me-uppers from the 'hood who manipulate that guilt to get what they want. And what they want is, of course, money.

Hook-me-uppers often fuel the fire of that guilt with comments such as, "He's so spoiled. He makes millions of dollars for playing a kids' game. He ought to feel guilty!" Or they may say, "Don't you feel like the luckiest person on the planet to make that much money?" or, "How does it feel to wake up every morning and know that all of your bills are taken care of when most folks are out here strugglin' to make ends meet?"

If I sound like I'm more than a little familiar with the dialogue, it's because I was on the hook-me-up end of it for years before I made my way out of the 'hood. Two friends in particular, and with whom I have kept in touch, chide me every now and then about my own hook-me-up days. How tired they must have gotten of reaching into their pockets when I was around, of giving me rides, buying me something to eat, and just plain letting me tag along to mooch off their good fortune. I was the proverbial "strugglin' young brother from the 'hood" with no money in his pockets. How could they say no? No doubt they joked about my constant presence and expectations. "Do you think he's going to ask us?" "Only as soon as he sets foot in the car." And I never failed to ask for something. I was as predictable as a sunrise.

Years later, after I made it to the pros, it was humbling, to say the least, to have some of my own words come back to haunt me. Life does, indeed, come full circle sometimes, as my friends like to point out to me now, albeit in jest and with good humor.

I am blessed in that these two guys have remained my true friends. Never once have they insinuated that I "owe" them for all the things they did for me back in the day. And for that reason, if they needed help, I would give it without hesitation.

I asked Dennis Hopson and Steve Sax about "keepin' it real" and the way some acquaintances play on your emotions to get a hookup.

Dennis Hopson commented, "Yeah, they will, and it doesn't matter how old or young they are. If there is something they want, they will try to use your emotions against you to get it.

"Recently I had someone come in to clean my office. I thought the price he was asking was too high, and I told him so. Then he tried to pull some reverse psychology on me by saying, 'Well, don't worry about it. You don't have to pay me nothing.' He knew I wasn't going to let him clean the office for nothing; he was just trying to get me to agree to his price, which I happen to know was too high for the amount of work he had to do and the size of my office, which is pretty small. Sometimes it's about mind games like that."

Steve Sax added, "Well, there's definitely some psychology at work in situations like the ones we discussed earlier, where you're out to dinner and the bill comes and everybody waits for you to pick it up, or if you're on a trip with a bunch of people and you end up feeling obligated to pay. That happens to me often.

"I also get irritated when people accuse me of being spoiled because I have a nice car and a nice house. They talk as if somebody gave me the things I have. I came from a poor background. Nobody gave me a penny. There were no guarantees I was going to make anything. There still aren't. Every time I stepped up to the plate against the likes of Nolan Ryan, Dwight Gooden, or Roger Clemens, it's all on me. There is no charity involved. I made it because I worked hard. Am I am fortunate? Absolutely! But am I spoiled? The answer is no!"

Here, Sax is right on the money. Many people resent athletes and celebrities. "It's not fair that you get to live like this," they say (or imply), the goal being to make you feel sorry for them and hand over some cash. It should be noted that not all of the hook-me-uppers are poor. Some have just overstretched themselves financially and they want the athlete to bail them out.

I asked my wife, Monya, how she feels when she senses that someone is trying to take advantage of me—of us—financially.

"First of all, a lot of people do try it: those having a close relationship with you, strangers, whoever. You have a kind heart, and people know that. So they feel it's easy to get you to feel sorry for them so they can get whatever it is they want. It happens all the time, and you are a big sucker for it." (Ouch!)

Anthony Telford says he learned very early in his career about the guilt trips hook-me-uppers try to lay on athletes.

"In the beginning, I helped a lot of people. It didn't dawn on me how I was being played until I got older. Then I began to think about how short the career span is for most professional athletes: about four and a half years in baseball and three or four years in the NFL. It dawned on me that I had better start paying attention to my wife, kids, and myself first, and let the hook-me-uppers fend for themselves.

"What most people don't realize is that an athlete has to make all the money he can in a three- to five-year career span to hopefully ensure some financial stability for him and his family to carry them through the transition, and then be prepared to work at something else, which means there better be something else he can do besides throw a baseball. By contrast, the average person in another profession may have twenty to thirty years to work and make a living. Of the sixteen years I played ball, only six were in the big leagues. Only a handful of athletes make enough money so that they never have to work again after their playing days are over. I'm working now, not because I have to, but because I like to keep putting money aside rather than just watching it go out."

And how does Telford handle the guilt if, for example, he refuses to pick up the restaurant tab even if the other person invited him out?

"I actually see that in two ways. I believe God has blessed me so that I can be a blessing, and in that respect I don't mind paying. On the other hand, and as a practical matter, if somebody invites me out, there is a part of me that feels they should take care of the bill. Some people will invite an athlete out and not even bother to bring a wallet! They're so sure he will pay. For many years there was an unspoken rule among baseball players: if a bunch of us went out for a meal, the oldest guy at the table—the veteran—picked up the tab. That's just how it went. Sometimes now if I'm out with a group, I wait awhile just to see if someone else takes the bill. Most of the time everyone folds their hands under the table until I finally say I'll get it. I've even been invited out by one or two people only to have six or eight show up, when word got around that I was going to be there. In situations like that the bill may be five or six hundred dollars. And it just cracks me up how they just assume you'll pay."

I asked Gary Trent if there had been instances when he felt that hook-me-uppers were trying to make him feel guilty if he refused to help them out financially.

"They've tried. When I was younger, early in my career, those feelings were natural when it came to your family. Then, too, if you've got a good heart, you want to help people. But as you get older you begin to change. That may be sad, but it's true. Somebody calls and you can almost hear the violins playing in the background as he pours out the long, sad story. You may very well feel sympathy, but you also know that you don't have enough money—nobody does—to save the world, or solve every problem that comes to your attention. So you compromise. If somebody tells me the roof blew off their house in a hurricane, I make a few phone calls and see if I can talk to some roofers or if I know somebody that works in a roofing company to help the person get the best possible deal on repairs. I may even put a few dollars toward that deal. But I'm not going to rebuild their house. Frankly, they could make the same phone calls to look for the best deal around, maybe get two or three quotes, just as I do. In the end, it depends on the situation. If it does involve some kind of disaster, like hurricane damage to a house, I may front them the down payment, which will leave them with the balance to pay off monthly. But I'm not going to be responsible for the entire cost.

"You were talking before about athletes not wanting to give out their telephone numbers. Well, like I tell people sometimes, we don't need to give out our numbers. Everybody already knows it's 911! We get called every time someone has an emergency. Like I use to tell people, you know what your number really is, your phone number is 911. 'Man, my car got wrecked. The roof on my house fell in, and I ain't got no money. Who do I know got money? I know. I'll call Mr. Millionaire Pro Athlete. He can help me out. He's got plenty of money.' In case of emergency, break glass, and your number is in the glass. You're the first thought they have. Sometimes you are the only thought.

"I don't mind helping out someone who shows some willingness to pitch in and help themselves, even if they do need a little help from me to get started. But I'm not the bank. I can't put up the money to fix everything. Frankly, if I don't give up the money, and the person walks away, even if they walk away angry, it's sort of a relief. It's like I had ten headaches, and when that person leaves, I only have nine left to deal with."

Greg Vaughn remembers some advice he got from former Major League Baseball great Dave Winfield. "The first thing he ever said to me was, 'Save your money. We all have families that have problems, but you owe it to yourself and your immediate family to save your money and take care of them first.'

You can only help those who really want to be helped.
—Greg Vaughn

"Another thing he said to me was that you can only help those who want to be helped. That stuck in my mind, because I do feel guilty when someone comes to me with a money problem and I know I can help, but I say no. For a long time, it was hard for me to say no. I didn't want to be labeled as one of those people who forgot where he came from, who changed once he left the old neighborhood. My wife used to tell me that saying no didn't make me a bad person, and that before I considered giving somebody money I should ask myself whether I would really be helping them or maybe just making a bad situation worse. I tended to feel like I really was helping. Also, I used to think that if something happened to that person, something that I could have prevented if I'd given them the money they'd asked for, I would never be able to forgive myself. Then my wife reminded me that a lot of the people who came to me for money were involved in get-rich-quick scams. Some were alcoholics and/or on drugs.

"Family members or distant, long-lost cousins think because you're a success, you're obligated to support their so-called money-making ideas. I can't do that. I am obligated to a few people, my mom, for example, but I don't have to take care of anybody and everybody.

"Yes, I feel bad when I say no, because I know the people I've turned down will spread the word that I am a terrible, selfish person who wasn't there for them when they needed help. But so be it. I used to worry that people wouldn't like me if I refused to fork over the money they needed. It took a while, but I finally realized that everybody isn't going to like me regardless of what I do. So I live with that and keep a sharp eye on my wallet."

Kris Draper acknowledges that playing on an athlete's emotions, especially guilt, is a frequent tactic. He cites dinner situations where he is always expected to pick up the check, regardless of whose idea it was to go out, as the best examples from his own experiences. "Let's split this" is not something he hears often—if at all. Most athletes can certainly relate to that.

Charley Hannah believes, as do some experts in psychology, that the two easiest targets in terms of manipulating emotions are athletes and doctors.

"Athletes are taught to have absolute faith in their teammates, the people who play right next to them every day. If you do your job, you can count on the next guy to do his. Because an athlete's life revolves to a large extent around implied trust, he is often shocked to learn [usually the hard way] that people off the court or the field will cheat him, lie to him, steal from him, and do whatever it takes to separate him from his money, his possessions, and his peace of mind. That makes athletes easy prey, especially at the beginning of their careers."

Clothing is an excellent example of the point he is trying to make about how easily athletes' emotions can be used against them. All athletes like to dress well. They care about their image and want to present a respectable persona. It gives them a sense of accomplishment, especially if they weren't able to dress so well back in the day.

My freshman year in high school, I had five outfits that I mixed and matched for an entire year. (My mother did the best she could with what she could afford, and I love her to death for it.) Still, poverty is a debilitating mind-set, and being cracked on (made fun of) was common, especially for a lanky kid going through a growth spurt. I'd be a liar if I said the cracks and comments and jokes about what I wore didn't hurt. It hurt, a lot.

Naturally, once I made the pros, it was essential that I always be "cleaner than the board of health," as one of my college teammates, Mark Baker, used to say. Clothes weren't just clothes. They were a statement about how far I had come. And once you hit the pros, it becomes even more important to make the right statement loudly and clearly. Of course, the people who sell clothes know this. So when a visiting team bus comes to town, clothing providers are in the lobby waiting. Many athletes have had prior dealings with some of them; others have not.

For the record, most are quite legitimate and wish only to provide a service to high-profile clientele. I have benefited greatly from the service that several clothing specialists have given me over the years. With that said, here is what Gary Trent had to say about some in the business.

First impressions are lasting impressions, but dressing to impress does not mean wearing the most expensive clothes.
—L. Funderburke

"Athletes are easy targets because they have the means to pay $1,000 to $3,000, if not more, for a custom-made suit, and $100 to $600 for the latest designer dress shoes," Gary Trent notes. "As a practical matter, athletes are usually taller and more muscular than the average person, which makes finding flattering clothing that fits even more essential. It all adds up to an enormous profit for the clothing providers, who very often double and triple the prices because they know athletes will not blanch at the exorbitant costs to maintain that all-important image."

Again, I'm just a small cog in the celebrity wheel, but I cannot count the number of times I've been hounded to buy clothing in hotel lobbies, sometimes before I've had a chance to pick up my key and escape to my room. Even once I'm in there—and keep in mind, a lot of times I may not know anyone at all in this city—I'll find messages either from people trying to sell me clothing (or get free tickets, whatever) or trying to locate one of my teammates who is registered under an alias to hit him up.

Charley Hannah was quick to emphasize that most of the clothing specialists are decent, honorable, respectful, hardworking people. But it may take an athlete a long time (and cost him a ton of money) before he learns to recognize the real deal from the inevitable hustlers and con artists anxious to cash in on his admittedly somewhat manic obsession with clothes and maintaining his image at a certain level.

Gary Trent also noted, "Jewelry specialists, particularly in mega-markets like L.A. and New York, are always there as well, and the same rules apply in terms of how often the prices are doubled and tripled when athletes are the intended customers, or targets. So he who wants a platinum Rolex inlaid with diamonds will find someone who is more than willing to sell it to him.

In fact, that someone will usually find him first. They know that some athletes will buy if they even hear that they can get a good deal from a certain person, without ever bothering to find out if that deal is for real or just another stratospheric

1. Work hard.

2. There is no substitute for hard work.

3. Hard work _always_ pays!
  —**L. Funderburke**

mark-up on a big ticket item that already costs a fortune. And when it comes to rare pieces, how many athletes (or anyone else, for that matter) can tell the difference between the genuine article and a fake?"

On a cautionary note, prices on luxury items are not for the faint of heart. Be prepared to pay tens of thousands, if not hundreds of thousands of dollars. Since few people have these rare jewels, and both competition and consumers are scarce, there is no ceiling.

I asked Dennis Hopson about his experiences with some clothing and jewelry specialists and the unconscionable markups.

"Every single road trip I went on, every single hotel you stayed in, I guarantee when I walked in that room the red light indicating that you have messages would be flashing, and there would be somebody on the line: 'I am new in the game and I'm making clothes. I'm new in this business, so why don't you try me out? Let me make you just one outfit. See how you like it.' They know that athletes, in particular, pride themselves on their appearance and that most athletes don't know what is considered a fair price, if there is such a thing on luxury items, to pay. Then, too, as far as clothing goes, most athletes, because of the way we are built, know we look better in clothes tailor-made for us.

"The younger players, in particular, don't really think about the money when it comes to clothes and jewelry. When I was younger, if I saw something I liked, I bought it and paid whatever they were asking. It's that attitude, along with a deep-seated need to let the world know that [they have] made it, that makes young athletes especially such easy targets.

"Older players, some of whom may be in business, as I am, may know a little more about what things should cost. I mean, I could look over a lot of cars and make a reasonable estimate about what a fair price should be. As for things like jewelry, I check the Internet and other places before making any final decisions. Nine times out of ten, I find out that the price some guy is quoting me may represent a 500 percent markup. So I walk away. Better yet, I run. But it's a never-ending cycle for an athlete. We have to watch ourselves all the time to keep from being taken in one way or another."

As Hopson and I agreed, this is one reason (among many) why athletes are so skeptical of outsiders, even loyal fans.

I asked Steve Sax about his experiences in terms of shopping for clothing and high-end luxury items.

"I was never into jewelry, but I did buy some leather stuff in New York, even though I really didn't know the source, whether the people who sold me the things had licenses or established businesses, etc. They'd usually have rented a room where you could see some pretty nice pieces. I bought a couple of things there and didn't think twice about it.

"As far as the inevitable blinking red light with messages as soon as you enter your hotel room, unless I know people in a certain city, it's almost always a hookup, usually something like, 'Hey, my name is so-and-so, and I'm with so-and-so car dealership. I met you once when you came in to test-drive a car, and we just happened to be here in Atlanta (or whatever the city is), and we're wondering if you had any tickets.' I always listen to the messages, but I only call back if the call really is from somebody I know."

Like other athletes, Anthony Telford recalls being approached in a hotel to buy clothes, jewelry, or other things during road trips.

"A lot of times, there'll be a guy in a city that hooks everybody up, but when you look at his prices you know they're a rip-off. Athletes get hit on clothes, jewelry, you name it, all the time. They come straight to spring training and wait for you in the hotel lobby—no shop or anything. They just sit there waiting for the athletes to come in. There's usually a pretty girl along to be sure they get his attention. And whatever they're selling, it's always expensive."

Gary Trent said that most of the time he doesn't buy anything from people he doesn't know.

"If I don't need anything, I tell those guys in the hotels with the clothes and jewelry, 'No, thanks.' It's too much like harassment to me, and if I feel like I'm being harassed, right away I think the person has got some kind of scheme going on. Real professionals, real businessmen, will not hit you up every time they see you. There's a guy in L.A. who sells sweat suits, and I told him that I get mine free from sponsoring companies: Nike, Adidas. He told me that if I ever wanted to try something different, I should get in touch with him. And he never bothered me again. That impressed me. There was no harassment, just a businessman with a product to sell. A couple of years ago, I was in L.A. and I needed some sweat suits, so I bought two or three from him. I've even bought a couple from him when I was getting them free from some sponsor. But, like I said, he impressed me. There was no pressure.

"High-pressure tactics turn me off. If somebody is pressing you to buy something, it's a scam. Real businesspeople find a way of letting you know about their products and services without getting in your face, so to speak. Players may have known the concierge at a certain hotel for ten years, so if that guy hands them a business card or a flyer or gives him a tip about where to buy something, the player may get in touch. For me, anyway, that's a much better approach than chasing me through the lobby.

"Of course, the other issue is how much he really knows about what constitutes a good price for a certain item. It's like buying a one-carat diamond ring without knowing anything about clarity, cut, color, facets, etc. If you don't know something about diamonds, then you just paid what you were asked or what you were able to pay. You have no way of knowing the true value of the ring, or the amount for which it should be insured. Basically, you don't know what you bought. In the jewelry business especially, most people, including athletes buying jewelry, know very little about it. They buy by the naked eye.

"Whatever the merchandise, if you've been in the league long enough, you already have people whom you deal with regularly for suits, jewelry, and what-have-you. Why would you need to hookup, in a hotel lobby, with some guy you've never seen before? Doesn't make sense. That's why they pick on the rookies and the newcomers most. The young guys are ready to buy new things. Me? My money is old, and I don't have a boatload of fresh money coming in every day. So they don't get any business from me."

I asked Greg Vaughn if he had ever been approached to buy items such as jewelry or clothing on the street or in a hotel room or elsewhere.

"Yes. For awhile, at the beginning of my career, I was buying clothes all the time. It took awhile, but I finally realized that I just didn't need any more. Right now I've got two boxes of clothes I'm trying to ship to my brother, not to mention two cars I'm trying to sell.

"I was never really one of those 'keep up with the Joneses' types. But sometimes buying things is an emotional response. You buy something when you are not feeling good about yourself, when you want to cheer yourself up.

> *It is not the man who has little, but he who desires more, who is poor.*
> — **Roman Seneca**

"As far as getting phone messages in my hotel room even before I've had a chance to get checked in, I started changing my name so people couldn't find me. The people from whom I bought clothes regularly had my cell phone number, so there was no problem there."

Kris Draper believes that people in the bigger markets check all the major sports schedules to see which teams are coming to the area and when so that they can be ready to stake them out. They know exactly how to find out where a team will be staying, and they set up shop to sell as much clothing, jewelry, and other items as they can for as long as the team stays. Your best bet is to walk away from them, though some guys do end up buying suits there. Half the time—in fact, three-quarters of the time—by the time the bill comes, the athletes find out that they got two suits and paid for three, maybe even four.

Kris adds, "As for those blinking red message lights that are on as soon as you walk into your hotel room, it's almost always somebody trying to sell you something. The first thing I do when I check into a hotel is put a 'do not disturb' on my phone, and have the front desk hold all messages until we check out. I always have my cell phone with me, and my wife has that number. So if someone genuinely needs to reach me, they can. Otherwise, I don't even bother to listen to the messages on the hotel phone.

"Why do I do this? Because I don't want people disturbing me in the middle of the night or during my nap before the game or during any other part of my normal pre-game routine. When I'm at home, my wife shields me from interruptions and distractions. But when you are on the road you don't have that luxury, so you have to arrange to shield yourself from distractions."

There's always some new distraction going on somewhere, and it takes tremendous self-restraint not to priortize those above more difficult and time-consuming, but ultimately higher-value projects.
—Charley Hannah

Charley Hannah notes that it wasn't so much the fact that you were being accosted in a hotel lobby as it was the constant pursuit.

"It's non-stop. 'I know a guy that can get you a deal on a Rolex watch,' or, 'I know a guy that can get you a deal on a Mercedes and bring it in from Europe.' And so many of them are dealing in hot merchandise or illegal substances. I knew a guy who opened the glove compartment of his car and found a plastic bag full of rock cocaine. He immediately got in touch with someone on the team, and they called league security, which conducted a thorough investigation. Eventually the situation was cleared up, but it scared the heck out of the guy, as it should have.

"Clothes, jewelry, you name it. Guys come in unfolding black velvet rollers with gold chains and diamonds and stuff for players to buy. And [their] lifestyle is, to a large extent, based on consumption, which many times is their downfall. You see a guy with the best clothes and the best jewelry and driving the best cars, and his wife is decked out and has loads of jewelry, and you wonder if all that spending is leaving them enough to pay rent and put food on the table for themselves and their children or keep the utilities turned on." Regardless of your level of income, this is practical advice that anyone can benefit from.

Be wary of the term "good deal."
—L. Funderburke

Lest I leave the impression that every single businessperson with whom an athlete comes into contact is a scam artist (because most of them are not), here is a different perspective.

I was curious to know why health professionals, among some other businesspeople, often seek athletes as clients. For an explanation, I talked to Rick Oliver, a registered and certified reflexology therapist who has worked with several professional athletes.

"As a health-care provider, I do a lot of charity work, seminars, and community service, much of it pro bono: that is, without pay," he says.

"Still, I can't eat pro bono. So I offset some of the charity work with clients who can pay. Working with an athlete or actor or any high-profile client helps to boost business. The more big names you can mention, the better the chances that others will respect your line of work or your business. Recommendations from athletes can be quite valuable. Their opinions carry a lot of weight because they are looked up to and considered, for the most part, to be believable, especially among other athletes. So if an athlete puts his stamp of approval on your shoes, jersey, product, or service, that can mean an incredible boost in business.

"Of course, the problem for him is the perception, often correct, that he pays more for products and services than the average person because of who he is. I can only speak with regard to physical therapy, of course, but in this instance athletes should keep in mind that they have extraordinary bodies with necessarily different physical characteristics than ordinary people. For one thing, his body is designed to take a considerable amount of punishment. An athlete has more muscle mass; therefore, it is going to take more effort, more manipulation, more strength, and more time to get that professional body ready for more action. Higher prices reflect that extra time, attention, and effort.

"Still, there is no doubt that the hook-me-up syndrome comes into play when unscrupulous characters jack up the prices to rip off a professional athlete. Apart from being unfair to him, such unconscionable behavior tarnishes the good names of legitimate businesses and service providers. We all get tarred with the same brush."

So the public stereotypes the athlete and he, in turn, stereotypes the public, including just about everyone he meets.

You've heard the expression "win-win" situation? Well, in this situation there are very few winners.

Keeping Up with the Jordans

IT IS OFTEN hard, if not downright impossible, for the average working man or woman to understand how an athlete or a celebrity can earn so much money, and yet end up poorer than the proverbial church mice when their athletic career ends. Yet this phenomenon is not at all difficult to explain.

People with lots of money go broke the same way people with very little money go broke: *by spending more than they earn*! It's all on a scale. If you earn $30,000 a year, you're probably not living in a grand house with servants, driving grand cars, or spending $500 per ticket to see your favorite entertainer. Still, if you are earning $30,000 a year and spending $40,000, at some point your odds will run out, and you will find yourself in the middle of a deep financial hole. Now, if you earn $30,000 a week, your home is probably quite grand, and there are servants, and chauffeur-driven cars, and twice-yearly trips to Europe, and weekly massages. *But* if you are earning

$30,000 a week and spending $40,000, at some point you, too, will find yourself staring down the middle of a financial black hole.

Rob Sanford, author of *Infinite Financial Freedom*, advises anyone who is suddenly wealthy to permit themselves one moment of financial decadence and then to return immediately to sound thinking and fiscal responsibility—the true paths to prosperity.

Lending a helping hand on occasion is commendable. However, high-profile athletes, in particular, are often deceived into believing that satisfying every personal whim, and the whims of close associates, can never compromise their financial security. Certainly, donations to good causes are to be encouraged, but cars (a weakness of mine in the past), trips, jewelry, and grand homes do not fall into that category when an athlete first enters the pro ranks.

Save more than you spend. A _lot_ more!
—L. Funderburke

For a young player, the sheer enormity of his first multi-million dollar contract may cause him to believe that it would be impossible to squander away such a fortune.

Here is an interesting exercise, courtesy of the Punahou Coeducational College Preparatory Day School in Honolulu, Hawaii.

Exactly how much is one million dollars? There are one hundred one-dollar bills in $100. Five hundred dollars composed of one-dollar bills would be the size of a thick paperback book. Put forty such 'paperbacks' into an ordinary piece of carry-on luggage, and you would have $20,000. To carry $1 million dollars, you would need fifty suitcases!

Now imagine that you are an eighteen-year-old from an impoverished neighborhood, and one day somebody comes along and offers to *pay* you $25 or $30 million to play ball—something you've been doing just for fun most of your life. Well, after you stop jumping up and down and hugging everyone within a few feet, you would probably take your entire hometown—make that the entire state—to lunch.

In Paris.

And that's just this week. Next week, who knows? You're happy (actually, you're delirious), and you want all your close friends and family to be happy, too. Maybe you've always wanted that, but now you have the money to make it happen. So it's mansions, Mercedes, and Grand Marnier for everybody! Cost? Who cares?! You've got all the money in the world!

Really? Do you really think so? Well, so did dozens of famous athletes, actors, actresses, and big-name entertainers—all names that you would instantly recognize. After years of splurging and spending, most are now leading the lifestyles of the famous and used-to-be-rich.

The truth is that wealth, if not carefully tended, disappears. And the blow, for an athlete, is doubled by the fact that by the time his money is gone, so are his skills, and along with them the limelight he both cursed and savored.

Financial solvency is achievable, but it is by no means guaranteed for anyone, however wealthy. Moreover, no one person, certainly not someone with the short career span of an athlete, can guarantee a lifetime of solvency to those in his "inner circle," however much he might wish to do so.

In their heyday both M.C. Hammer and Mike Tyson accumulated massive fortunes in excess of $100 million. Also, they were each handicapped by what was euphemistically referred to as their entourage, and more than likely, by their own insatiable materialistic appetites.

Nor should an athlete who has allowed himself to slide into financial turmoil expect sympathy from either his Uncle Sam or the general public, who more than likely begrudged him the millions he made anyway.

> *There is nothing wrong when men possess riches but the wrong comes when riches possess men.*
> *—Billy Graham*

I asked Dennis Hopson what he thought readers should know about the phenomenon of high-profile athletes who end up broke.

"That it's not as bizarre as it sounds. Look at Mike Tyson, a professional fighter that filed bankruptcy. He said that he was living on zero. Actually, his exact words were 'subzero.' He literally lost $300 million, which to most people sounds too farfetched to be possible. Of course, for most people, having $300 million to lose *is* too farfetched to be possible. But in the world Tyson lived in, it's the type of thing that could happen to anybody, depending on the person and his dealings with people. You're never really secure. I mean, Donald Trump can't even tell you he's secure. So it really depends on how you run your situation. If you stay on the conservative side, you might be okay. But even then, you could get sick or something, and maybe the medicine you need is so costly that you end up going through your fortune. It could happen. Of course, having the money to take care of emergencies is a lot better than not having it. People just need to understand that athletes, even though they make a lot of money, are human beings, and things happen to them that can wipe out all the money they make, regardless of how much it is. Sometimes it's their fault for not planning wisely. Sometimes they get conned by the people around them. One way or the other, athletes can and often do end up with nothing to show for those early years with the fat contracts.

"Some athletes are just too wide open with their finances. They make so much, they don't see any need to look for bargains or try to get the best possible price for a product or a service. They just pay whatever is asked, figuring the next paycheck will more than cover it. And then one day there is no next paycheck.

"Then, of course, there's that whole thing about trying to fill every hand that's out for whatever reason, trying to take on everyone's problems, instead of handling their own responsibilities first. Sometimes there may be family members who don't understand that, but if not, they have to learn.

You take care of your immediate family—wife, children, and yourself—first. That's where your priority has to be. That's where your money has to go, for them and for your future as a family. An athlete who gets guilt-tripped into believing he is obligated to help everybody who says they need help is looking for a fast trip to the poorhouse.

"In a lot of ways, this is the hardest thing for a professional athlete to learn—not what he has to do on the court or the field or on the ice, but learning how to say no. I haven't played the game in years, and people are still calling me asking for things. It's nerve-wracking, and that's putting it mildly."

Steve Sax said he would like to spend just twenty minutes with some players, especially the rookies, explaining a few of the financial facts of life.

"I could change their lives, just twenty minutes in front of me in my business chair. It's about taking an interest in your financial condition and being prudent, investing for the future, and knowing that those paychecks, regardless of how big they are, won't be coming in forever.

"Albert Einstein said that compounding interest was one of the most amazing things he'd seen in his life. It's not about what you make, it's about what you keep. I've had a job and I've been on a budget since I was ten years old. Yes, I was fortunate to make all the money I made as a professional athlete, but it's the basic principles I learned from childhood that have allowed me to achieve and maintain a measure of financial security.

"And those principles have not changed. I use the same basic financial model now that I used then. I knew that some of the money at the restaurant [where I worked as a teenager] was going to go to taxes. I knew that I had to pay for my car. I knew that I had to save for the insurance. The budget I set up as a ten-year-old paperboy allowed me to buy my own car when I was sixteen. It doesn't matter how much money you make. You still need a plan, and it's the plan that will help you achieve financial freedom. So many athletes, and people in general, have the idea that they need more money to get past the bad spending habits they have created for themselves. But it's not the amount of money, it's the principles and model and the plan that make the whole thing work."

Planning without action is futile. Action without planning is fatal.

—Unknown

Sax may not know it, but his solid financial philosophy has more than withstood the test of time. For the sake of comparison, consider the trajectory of another prudent man.

In 1855, a young man left school to find work in Cleveland. Eventually securing a position as a clerk, he began keeping a detailed written account of what he earned and what he spent. This account was called Ledger A. "I learned to keep my money," he later said, and he saved with a religious fervor.

In 1857, the young man's employer offered to raise his salary. They could not agree on the amount of the raise, however, so the young man accepted an opportunity to go into business with another man ten years his senior.

Although the new business prospered, the young man continued to live as if his earnings had never increased, and to record every penny of income, expenditure, and savings in Ledger A.

Eventually, his eye for business opportunity led him to a new industry: oil refining. By 1870, the boy who kept Ledger A was a rich man, and in 1909 he became the world's first billionaire.

His name, as you must have guessed by now, was John D. Rockefeller.

Today, the fortune that had its beginnings in a young man's frugality and keen business sense continues to have a profound influence on our lives through the support of institutions and organizations that include the Grand Teton National Park, New York's Lincoln Center for the Performing Arts, and Harvard University, to name only a few.

As you can see, Steve Sax is in very good company with his philosophy about savings and investments. What a shame all the rookie athletes (and some of the veterans) can't spend a little time discussing finance with Sax. Talk about a life-altering experience!

"So many athletes when they reach the end of their careers are frightened by the future," Sax continues. "It's 'Oh, no, now what? I can't play anymore, and I don't have the tools I need to take the next step in life.' Spending $40,000 every two weeks is a tough habit to break. I

Good spending habits with less money are better than bad spending habits with a lot of money.

—Steve Sax

know your readers will laugh at that because some of them, probably most of them, can't imagine making $40,000 every two weeks. But, again, the amount of money is not the issue. It's what you do with it. Good habits with less money are better than wasteful habits with a ton of it, because the money will run out. Too many athletes wait until their careers are over to decide that it's time to start paying attention to their finances. That's almost a certain recipe for disaster.

"People, especially athletes themselves, don't realize how easy it is to start out making what seems like a fortune and end up with nothing to show for a lot of hard work. And it's almost always because they didn't exercise prudence or show any forethought about how to take care of the money, and learn how to pay the least amount of tax to maximize their earnings. That and budgeting, those are the keys to financial solvency.

"I believe in dollar cost averaging, where every month you put so much away. When the markets are high you are actually investing less. When the markets are low you are investing a little more, but the same amount of money every month. That's a great tool for players. Then they know they can't go out and spend another $60,000 on another [Cadillac] Escalade or more bling bling. I see people do it all the time, or go to Vegas and gamble most of it away. And God forbid that you are into bad stuff like drugs and all that. That's a whole story on another level, apart from being financially disastrous.

"I can tell you that during my pro career I felt completely secure when I was on the diamond. The times I felt insecure were when I was off the field."

Most people have no idea that the most challenging part of being a professional athlete is not the competition on the court or the field or the ice, but the people you come up against outside the playing arena.

It is difficult to explain to those outside the world of athletics how it is possible to end one's career with nothing of substantial value after having earned millions. Practical explanations for this phenomenon include investing in depreciating assets. (As a magna cum laude finance graduate from Ohio State University I should have known better, but I admit to having invested in some depreciating assets in the past.)

According to the 2003–2004 *Guide to Depreciating Assets*, a depreciating asset is something that has a limited effective life and can reasonably be expected to decline in value over the time it is used. Depreciating assets include items such as computers, electric tools, furniture, and cars.

One person who I interviewed (but who wished to remain anonymous) believes that another major reason that so many athletes are broke at the end of their careers is their tendency to support an array of acquaintances. These people know that many athletes are kind-hearted and feel guilty about succeeding when their contemporaries have not done as well. Thus, athletes can be easily guilt-tripped into becoming the community meal ticket. While taking a weekend trip occasionally is no big deal, no one—athlete or otherwise—should be funding regular vacation trips for eight or nine close acquaintances with accommodations running $500 to $1,000 a night. Do that for ten or fifteen years, and throw in taking care of other members of an athlete's "innermost" circle (immediate and less immediate), and you have a recipe for bankruptcy.

Most of the athletes I know are generous almost to a fault in part because they feel so blessed to be getting paid to play a game they love. Then, too, the amount of money they make is so mind-boggling that they seize on almost any opportunity to share the wealth.

We can only hope that new athletes coming into the business have good managers and advisors to invest their earnings, set up stock portfolios, and stash the money away. (Young people from all walks of life could benefit from these things as well.)

Of course, not all athletes are incapable of handling money. One financial management expert I interviewed said he has seen a lot of well-grounded, educated athletes who are financially astute.

"A football player I know comes to mind. He lives in a modest house and drives a six-year-old car. He doesn't get into that hoopla of, 'I've got to have a new car every camp. I've got to show up with all this stuff.' He's looking out for his future, and he's also investing in real estate. He's creating positive cash flow because he knows that the day will come when he cannot play anymore, and he's securing his future and his family's future, which is smart.

"As you said, many athletes are very generous and regularly make sizeable donations to various charitable organizations. I'm also not suggesting that there is anything wrong with taking care of family members who are genuinely in need. That said, however, there have to be financial limits on how far he can go when it comes to family. It sounds like something out of a bad movie, but it's amazing how many second, third, and fourth cousins an athlete—or anybody who comes into some money—will suddenly run into. Your house can literally become a hook-me-uppers' convention!

"For that reason, he has to be even more financially disciplined. Play every game as though it might be your last, and save every dollar possible. Don't let money slip through your fingers so fast that you have no idea where it went. I've seen it happen with a couple of hockey players that I've worked with. One broken leg can end a career. Now what are they doing? They're working in a sporting goods shop somewhere because that's all they can do. They were only in the league for two or three years, and they didn't put enough money aside to provide for the future. Athletes have got to be well-grounded. They have to set spending limits and stick by them, and they have to find good personal managers and financial advisors to keep them on track."

One of the reasons I wrote this book is to dissuade the public perception of athletes as big, dumb jocks, a perception that is sometimes fueled by the media and sometimes, to be honest, by the athletes themselves. The truth is that a great many professional athletes are bright and intelligent, in addition to being physically gifted.

Perhaps this is a good place to bring up another misconception that is common among many people: that sports require only brawn and no brains. Nothing could be further from the truth. There

Exercise daily—your body and your brain.
—L. Funderburke

is intricate reasoning behind every play, regardless of how erratic the action may appear to the spectator. To beat a competitor, a team cannot just play better; they must play smarter as well. Brains and brawn win championships. Either one, without the other, won't get you into the Hall of Fame.

Some athletes have also become successful businessmen when their playing days were over. Here are just a few.

- Danan Hughes (formerly with the NFL Kansas City Chiefs) is now a mortgage banker who helps other athletes manage their newfound wealth.
- Andrew Kline (formerly with the NFL St. Louis Rams) founded a sports-based speakers' bureau called Athletic Appearance, which arranges appearances by top athletes for corporate and community events.
- Former USC star and All Pro defensive back Ronnie Lott founded HRJ Capital with former teammate Harris Barton.
- Former NHL greats Wayne Gretzky and Mario Lemieux now own NHL franchises.
- NBA legend Earvin "Magic" Johnson has commercial real estate and movie theater interests.

There are hundreds of post-pro career success stories like these. Still, the fact remains that many athletes do not have the necessary skills to survive in the real world. In one respect this is understandable. To make it to the pros in any sport requires the kind of intense mental and physical focus of which few people are capable. The athlete must be willing to eat, sleep, and breathe his chosen sport—to give 110 percent to every effort. This is the stuff of which champions are made.

Unfortunately, this level of concentration often doesn't leave room for the athlete to develop the skills to harness his enterprising or entrepreneurial spirit, without which he will have nothing to fall back on when his pro career comes to an end.

Anthony Telford recounts the story of a friend.

"After playing in the NFL for eight years, he has nothing. He didn't work for two years after he retired. Because he . . . was uncomfortable and never felt like he found a place for himself. He'd been in that NFL spotlight for eight years spending every Sunday playing a game he loved in front of 65,000 fans. Then it ended. Eventually, his wife left and took the children."

Life is about making adjustments.

—L. Funderburke

Part of the problem with being an athlete is that when you are really good at something, maybe even considered the best at what you do, it's a transcendent feeling that you don't want to give up. Then the day comes (and it always does) when your body and mind can no longer handle the demands of that life. So there you are in your mid- to late thirties or early forties, and suddenly it feels as though the bottom has fallen out of your world. If you are not "the athlete" anymore, then who are you? It's a tough transition for most athletes psychologically as well as financially.

Telford adds: "When you go from making $500,000 to $1 million a year (after taxes) for eight or nine years all you need is one bad investment or just a little too much bling. Some guys make the mistake of not changing their lifestyles after their pro careers end. It's easy to get used to living from paycheck to paycheck, the first and the fifteenth of every month like clockwork. Let's say you made $5 million a year for three years, half of which goes for taxes, but you bought a $5 million house, a $1 million boat, a couple of high-end expensive cars. When those checks stop coming in, you will not be able to afford to maintain that lifestyle.

"I remember one year when I made $1,150,000 and ended up with $200,000. I bought this house (the one I live in now) and I paid cash for it. Of course, I will have to pay taxes on this house for the rest of my life, unless I decide to move. But then, that same year, I bought a couple of cars at $70,000 apiece. And I had a $2 million umbrella policy, just in case I got sued for some reason. And so on and so on. It's easy to meet those obligations while the checks are coming in. But when they stop, you're over your skis in a hurry."

What a great analogy! Going downhill on skis with the momentum building, and suddenly you look for some brakes to slow your descent before you crash, and you realize there are no brakes!

"Where did all the money go?" It's a common refrain among retired athletes.

I wanted *Hook Me Up, Playa!* to be a wakeup call for young athletes, and young people in general, to help them begin the process of planning ahead and avoiding some of the pitfalls. Unfortunately, the information and advice provided here by experts and athletes who have been there, personally, will be too late to help a lot of athletes who have already reached the end of their careers, and the end of the money as well.

I cannot stress enough, however, that this book is not a plea for sympathy. While it is true that many athletes are the victims of fraud and deceit, many have also been their own worst enemy. They allowed themselves to become so absorbed in the fun they were having on the field or the court or the ice that they forgot about the real world—the adult world, where there are bills, taxes, and consequences of ill-considered actions. Nobody knows this better than they do. So they neither want nor expect sympathy.

Hook Me Up, Playa! is meant to educate athletes—and young people in general—about taking control of their lives. It is also my hope to educate you, the public, about what it means to be a professional athlete, the good, the not-so-good, and the terrible. Every life, no matter how good it appears to the people in the audience or the stands, has its downside. We put the people who entertain us, who make us marvel at their skills and ability, on pedestals. Then we are surprised when they fall off because, as it turns out, they are every bit as human as the next person, and human beings do stupid things. We can only thank God that there is no law against stupidity, otherwise we couldn't build enough jails to hold us all.

A person earning $40,000 or $50,000 a year, with a family, and struggling to make ends meet cannot be expected to understand how an athlete making twenty or thirty times that much can complain about losing half his income to taxes, and squander away the rest by the time his career ends. Yet this phenomenon occurs more often than one cares to imagine.

The post-career lifestyle change is a major shock to athletes who didn't invest in sound instruments, such as tax-free municipal bonds, real estate or rental properties, etc. that would produce residual income. A great deal of careful planning is necessary.

I asked Gary Trent for his thoughts on athletes and the lack of financial planning.

Material possessions do not define you. What you make of your life defines who you are.

—L. Funderburke

"Much of the problem stems from not knowing where your money is and from ill-advised investments. If you have a million dollars, you should never invest $700,000 of it in any one thing. Invest no more than $50,000 to $100,000—in other words, no more than you could comfortably afford to lose if the investment doesn't pan out.

"There is a point in every athlete's career where he spends his money before he gets it. In the beginning, an athlete will spend money like water if, let's say, he has a three-year deal worth several million dollars and he knows there's more money on the way. He gets reckless. Maybe he puts six or seven TV's in his car. Is it unnecessary? Of course it is. But he's not thinking about that. He's responding to that peer pressure that says 'Wow! He's drivin' a Benz! He must be makin' serious money!' He's in the league now, so that means appearances on BET to show the world his big new crib, and the bling bling, and the girls, and this and that. And you take it all for granted. 'Sure. I went over my budget this month, but I'll get back on track next month.' But next month something else happens.

"The advantage of maturity is, or should be, that you become more detached from the material side of things. You're not pressed about what people think about you. You're more in touch with your own reality, versus someone else's reality for you."

Motivational speaker Les Brown said a teacher once told him, "Never let someone's opinion of you become your reality." That's another way of defining maturity.

"Bottom line?" says Trent. "It's not how much you make, it's how much you save. Do the math. If you make a million dollars a year and you save $50,000 of it a year, and I make $200,000 a year and I save $100,000 a year, in ten years I will have more money than you. In fact, you could run out of money, depending on investments, taxes, lifestyle, cost of living, etc. Your house may be paid for, but property taxes go on. Your health may be fine today, but not so fine tomorrow. Health insurance goes on. Your car may be paid for, but car insurance goes on. (Sometimes car insurance can cost more than the car!) If somebody asked me to buy them a brand new Cadillac Escalade, I'd ask them a few questions first. Such as, 'Can you afford the insurance? Can you afford the maintenance? Can you even afford to put gas in it?' If the answer is yes, if you can afford all that, then you can afford to buy your own Escalade!

"A lot of people, especially young people, don't know what it means to be able to afford something. It's an interesting word: 'afford.' If you buy a car and then you have to get a second job to pay for it, you couldn't really afford that car. If buying something adds stress and anxiety and headaches to your life, you can't afford it. It's just that simple."

You may be surprised to find out how much you can learn from professional athletes. Many professional athletes often have a lot to teach about money management and financial planning primarily because they've done it wrong before. I admit that I have made my share of financial mistakes.

You may never receive a $10 million signing bonus, but you could come into a large sum of money from an inheritance, a lump-sum pension plan payout, or a successful business venture. The steps you need to take to secure this income are the same regardless of the source. For example, many people wonder why a professional athlete who earns millions even needs a **budget.** The truth is that a surprisingly high number of professional athletes have ended up broke by the time their (short) career ended because they mismanaged their money during the early years. Thus, smart athletes put themselves on a core budget (or hire a financial planner to do it) that covers basic expenses—including off-season living expenses.

Financial planners often work with professional athletes to compile an **emergency fund** in the event of worst-case scenarios such as injuries and work stoppages, which can jeopardize an athlete's financial security as well as that of his family. Thus, professional athletes must put aside enough money to cover three to six months of basic living expenses. (You should, too!)

Personal long-term disability insurance is another crucial element of financial planning for the professional athlete. An athlete can blow out a knee or suffer other serious injuries in a matter of minutes. This type of insurance will make up for the lost earnings in case he can never play again.

For the professional athlete (and for you as well), **life insurance and estate planning** are also crucial. There is no substitute for having one's affairs in order in case the worst happens.

Finally, the professional athlete learns often from bitter experience to be aware of **investment scams.** Professional athletes are ripe targets for scam artists because of the busy schedules that often leave little time for keeping up with personal finances. Regardless of your profession, however, it just makes good sense to be closely involved with your finances and to educate yourself about money management, even if you have a trusted financial advisor.

My hope is that the information provided here will be useful for everyone, not just professional athletes.

Danny Levitt, Assistant Vice President and financial advisor at Merrill Lynch, recalls a couple of investment situations that serve well as cautionary tales.

"Athletes will sometimes rely on their agents to help them in the placement of their assets with trusted advisors. This example will show that this is not always the best course of action.

"In the past couple of years there was a high-end boutique investment firm here in Houston that was giving clients a guarantee of a 12 percent return. These assets were invested primarily in mortgage-backed instruments. This particular firm happened to have a number of local professional athletes as clients, and most of them were investing through the advice of their agents. One thing that needs to be said is that the word 'guarantee' should not be used in the investment industry; if it is, it should be researched thoroughly.

"Eventually, as the economy started to turn, the investment did as well. Not only were the clients/athletes losing their guaranteed income, but they were losing their principal as well—all of it. To make matters worse, the people involved in the investment firm were able to pull their personal and family assets out of the venture before it went up in flames. This is not only a severe breach of trust, but it is also a classic example of taking advantage of highly-compensated athletes who obviously never really understood the risk. If income was their objective, they would have been better served by investing in AAA insured tax-free bonds.

"Another prominent example of a highly-compensated athlete being defrauded by someone close to them was the tragic situation involving professional golfer, Davis Love III. This was a very public case of a professional athlete relying on people whom he thought he could trust. Davis allowed his brother-in-law to be his manager, and his responsibilities clearly included certain financial matters. It was soon discovered that substantial funds were unaccounted for and that the brother-in-law had taken advantage of his position of trust. Sometime thereafter, he committed suicide. Davis found the body along with a note."

These tragic situations further illustrate the difficulty athletes have in identifying people whom they can trust, and the cynicism toward everyone after that trust has been betrayed, particularly by people close to them. Even honest fans bare the brunt of this cynicism.

"Athletes, particularly young athletes, need guidance when it comes to financial planning," notes Greg Vaughn. "I see it in football a lot more than I've seen it in baseball, but it's true for every sport. These guys just buy, buy, and buy. They sign a $40 million contract without realizing that it's actually $20 million after taxes, and that's before they've spent so much as one dime. I knew someone who signed a $25 million contract and then promptly went out and bought a $23 million house. That was years ago. Now he can't even pay the taxes on it. That's one of the differences, I guess, between what they call 'old money' and 'new money.' The 'old money' crowd pay their own bills, and they don't give power of attorney to just anybody, if anybody at all.

"If I could give athletes any advice at all there would be three main things. First, if you sign a contract, your objective shouldn't be to double or triple that amount. Your objective should be to keep that amount and live off the interest, without ever touching the principal. Second, make it your business to be involved in your own financial affairs. Personally involved. Know where your money is going and why at all times. Don't give anybody power of attorney, and pay all your own bills. Third, don't fall for any get-rich-quick-schemes. Your home run is your interest."

Kris Draper believes the primary reason so many athletes are financially insolvent by the end of their careers is lifestyle.

"It's all about 'which boys end up with the most toys.' I mean, these things add up. You go out and start buying Mercedes, and then you move up to Ferraris, and then it's houses and then summer houses. Bills don't magically disappear. For us, we get paid from October to April. When your career is over, you have a list of who knows how many millions of dollars in bills that you have run up, and now, with no money coming in, there is no way to pay them. Suppose you have two or three houses, and each one has a twenty-five-year mortgage? What then? Banks and credit card companies don't care whether you're playing or not. They just expect to be paid.

"Then there are the homies with their hands out, and you're shelling out a little here and a little there. Over the years it adds up. Throw in one or two bad investments, and you're basically sunk. That's the situation every athlete wants to make sure that they guard against.

"Athletes have to remember that they have only a certain amount of time to build financial security, to set up things for their kids and for themselves. That's the goal—not trying to see which boy ends up with the most toys."

Charley Hannah thinks a "scared-straight" approach might be helpful in dissuading young athletes, and young people in general, from throwing their financial future away.

"You know how they sometimes take troubled teens into prison and let them listen to some of the guys inside talk about what big shots they were in their teens? How they thought they were bulletproof, even when their friends were dead and dying all around them? Well, maybe it wouldn't hurt to take a few rookie athletes out to meet a first-round draft pick from thirty years ago who is picking fruit for a living now. 'Yeah, I had nice cars and nice clothes and great houses. It's all gone now. I spent too much.' Then take them to see former athletes who are doing well, and who can say, 'All I'm doing is applying the same hard-work ethic that I did with sports to my work ethic now in business.'

"Most people cannot comprehend the hard work that goes into becoming a professional athlete. You have to be special, physically and mentally. Every athlete who makes it to the pros has the necessary fortitude and drive, or they wouldn't have made it. The trick is helping them learn to apply that same fortitude and drive in business or elsewhere so that they can support themselves and their families, make a contribution, and be as happy in what they're doing behind a desk as they were on the field. It pains me to hear an athlete at the end of his career say, 'Well, now I can't do anything,' when that is absolutely not true.

"A guy once asked me the most important thing I learned from being in the NFL. I told him it was that I will do whatever it takes to succeed. And he said, 'Well, what does it take?' And I said, 'Whatever it takes.' And he said, 'What do you mean?' I said, 'Whatever it takes. Whatever the effort, whatever kind of work, I'll do it. I know I'll do it. I won't steal, and I won't be dishonest, but I will put forward whatever effort is necessary. It may not guarantee success, but even if I fail, I'll go back and do it again. Eventually, it will pay off for me.'"

It is interesting to note that Charley Hannah played for legendary coach Paul "Bear" Bryant, who once said, "Show class, have pride, and display character. If you do, winning takes care of itself."

If you learn from your setbacks, you get better every time.

—Charley Hannah

"Sports are the greatest teacher of life," Hannah went on to say. "It teaches you about winning and losing. If you lose a game, you don't quit. You go back, you learn from your mistakes, so that you can be better the next time out. Same is true for life. I laugh when people say to me 'It's nice to see you do well in real life after football is over.' I tell them, 'You know what? Life doesn't get any more real than when you're playing football because the competition is much more intense, and you are on public display.' In sports, you have to do your best in front of the world, and sometimes your best isn't good enough. And the world sees that, too. Over time you come to an understanding that it's not just about who won or who lost, but about who put forth the best effort that will pay off in the long run. I had twelve seasons, but we only won the Super Bowl once. If you learn from your setbacks, you get better every time."

If life knocks you down, try to land on your back, because if you can look up you can get up.

—Les Brown

I asked Charley Hannah about professional athletes who end up broke when their careers are over.

"It's real easy to do," Hannah said. "If a guy lives off his money—paycheck to paycheck, they call it—then at the end of the year has nothing left, he's already traveling down the path to bankruptcy, and it's going to hit him real fast and real hard. Or if he's spending more than what his savings and investments can conservatively generate, again, he's heading down that path to financial ruin. Our careers are short—three to four years, on average. So, to my way of thinking, your first year should be your most frugal. As each year passes, and there is more money, [an athlete] needs to ensure future financial security becomes more firmly established. Of course, everyone is going to reward himself a little, but primarily a first-year pro athlete should live so that if his career ended the following year, he would have a nest egg for himself and his family to start over and reestablish themselves somewhere else.

"There's always time to enhance a lifestyle. You don't have to live rich at twenty-five. You can do that later on in your life, and it will be much nicer to do it then than to live rich while you're young and be destitute when you're older. I've seen that happen with first-round draft picks. They had an opportunity to help themselves. Instead, they were done for as soon as the door closed on their athletic career.

"The other problem, too, is that spending money is addictive. If the player is spending, and his wife is spending, and maybe the kids are spending, then consumption becomes a family dynamic. Then when the money stops coming in, the entire family is thrown for a loop, and [the athlete] is left feeling like a failure because he can no longer provide the lifestyle to which the family has become accustomed.

"I hear stories of guys that are getting ready to sign a pro contract or [are] in college, and agents are already feeding a lifestyle. There are insurance policies on players when they are in college so that if they get a career-ending injury they will have something. This started out as a good idea, but then players started taking out loans and borrowing against the policies. In effect, an athlete can come out of college already in financial trouble with debt-based insurance policies, and most of the time, if he doesn't sign a pro contract, he can't pay. That means he's in trouble in terms of contract negotiations right off the bat.

"On the other hand, I remember a friend of mine that I played with here in Tampa (for the Buccaneers). He was from Norman, Oklahoma. One day he was talking about some things he was doing and I said, 'Next thing you know you'll be living in one of these houses.' I think I was referring to some big house that I saw while we were driving through town. 'You know,' he said, 'I don't think I'll ever do that because I don't want to put that type of pressure on my children.' In addition to a degree in ancient philosophy, this guy had some real insights into life.

"I think an athlete should really think about what he's going to do after his career is over before he goes to the pros. There are numerous educational opportunities and contacts afforded to the professional athlete. If he is a good person and well-respected, the networking opportunities are practically endless. I'm not against the idea of an athlete leaving college to make the jump to the pros. But I do believe he should spend some of the money he earns in the pros on education, so that when his career is over, he will have some working knowledge (particularly a working knowledge of investments) that he can use to go on.

"There are really two extremes: the players who live off their paychecks and have nothing to show at the end of the year and those at the opposite end of the spectrum, who are ruled by a fear of the future. Their motto is, 'I don't ever want to work again.' I think the people who are most content exist somewhere between the two extremes. I wouldn't be happy if I weren't working, but I made sure I would have some security so that I don't have to sweat it. But that's just me. There are athletes who really don't want to do anything when their careers are over so they arrange their finances so that they won't have to. Then there are others who reached a point of financial security and when their careers ended dedicated themselves to something else: education, coaching, a favorite cause, whatever. They don't need the income. They are doing something because they want to do it."

Never quit. It is the easiest cop-out in the world. Set a goal and don't quit until you attain it. When you do attain it, set another goal, and don't quit until you reach it. Never quit.
—Bear Bryant

Chapter 6

Avoiding the Traps

The safest way to double your money
is to fold it over once and put it in your pocket.
—Frank Hubbard

Separating the Wolves from the Sheep

Hands off the man, the flim flam man.
His mind is up his sleeve and his talk is make believe.
Oh, Lord. The man's a fraud, he's a flim flam man.
He's so cagey, he's a flim flam man.

TRUER WORDS WERE NEVER WRITTEN (by Laura Nyro) or recorded (by Barbara Streisand) back in the day. Somebody once said, "Truth is whatever a con artist can lead you to believe at any given moment in time."

Mr. Webster (of dictionary fame) defines the words "con" as "swindle or manipulate" and "scam" as "a fraudulent or deceptive act or operation."

The confidence trickster (a.k.a., con man, scam artist, or con artist) usually works in conjunction with an accomplice, called the shill ("one who acts as a decoy, as for a pitchman or gambler, or one who makes a sales pitch or serves a promoter"). In other words, the shill diligently pursues and encourages the mark (that's you) by pretending to believe the pitch (whatever they're selling).

The mark in a traditional swindle assumes that he is well aware of the con being played (at the expense of a gullible third party). Later, and to his eventual dismay, he shockingly finds out that the gullible third party is none other than himself. Generally speaking, the term con or swindle refers to any scam where the victim loses money under the illusion of guaranteed profits.

Although confidence tricks primarily target the implicit greed and dishonesty of their marks, con artists also prey heavily on the naiveté of key players who regrettably place their undivided trust in high-risk schemes and improbable investment strategies. It is safe to say that society as a whole may not fully comprehend that these schemes are fraudulent in nature for many years to come, and by then I'm afraid, it will be too late. As a result, many people will lose their life or retirement savings in the process. How tragic.

It must also be noted that the boundary between the legal promotion and sale of a product or service, and scamming is fluid: that is, what some people clearly believe to be a scam may not be so identified by legal authorities.

In a warning issued online, the police department of Napa, California, acknowledged that spotting con artists is not always easy. They are among the smartest, most persuasive, and most aggressive criminals. They may invade your home by telephone and/or mail, or by advertising in respected newspapers and magazines. They may even come directly to your door. And nothing intrigues a con artist more than people who smugly insist that they are too smart to fall for a scam. Fact: Given the right set of circumstances, *anybody*, regardless of intelligence or level of skepticism, can be fooled. Every year con artists swindle all kinds of people—from investment bankers and engineers to teenagers and senior citizens—out of billions of dollars.

> *It's all about sincerity. If you can fake that, you've got it made.*
>
> *—Jean Giraudoux, French Writer*

Professional athletes are very near the top of the list of people who get conned out of millions annually. Rookies especially are prime targets for scams because they are usually too excited by the newfound wealth to think clearly, have little or no education on financial matters, and have not yet engaged the services of a reliable financial advisor.

Scammers, like all predators, have an uncanny instinct for recognizing vulnerability. They can sense what the prospective mark is looking for and which buttons to push to gain his trust.

A pastor (and ex-con) named John Gillette used a phony investment program to bilk millions from professional athletes. With religion as the hook, he presented himself as a believer in Christian values and used their money to support his own lavish lifestyle.

Barry Minkow, another ex-con, built a phony, publicly-held business, which at one time had a market value of $240 million. Unfortunately for investors, the company was a fraud. His victims included not only professional athletes, but also bankers, and other highly paid professionals.

As Gillette and Minkow prove, a successful con man could teach a course in how to fake a sincere, even passionate, interest in anything about which the mark is sincere and passionate. Scam artists are smooth talkers and smooth dressers who usually travel first class, drive the finest cars, and stay in the best places. The window dressing is part of the package that helps to gain your trust, which is essential to separating you from your money.

Another essential element, when conning an athlete, is the implied trust of other athletes, preferably the victim's teammates and colleagues.

An autographed photo of the con artist with one of your teammates, or perhaps a football or basketball signed by some mega-star athlete, all but guarantees that the scam will succeed. The scammer may also throw in comments such as, "Well, I've done such-and-such for so-and-so, and their portfolios have nearly doubled," or, "You can ask your teammates, X and Y. They've been my clients for years." If you do ask and your friends and colleagues verify the relationship, it is only natural to think yourself, "Well, if so-and-so trusts this guy, he must be all right."

Sometimes the scammer will go so far as to make sure that the first few monthly residual checks or statements from the so-called investment are on time and accurate. Sooner or later, though, the truth will come out, and the victim will learn that his faith was tragically misplaced.

Another popular way of swindling professional athletes (and many other people as well) is called the Ponzi scheme, named after the infamous American swindler, Charles Ponzi, the quintessential scam artist.

One day in 1919, Carlo "Charles" Ponzi (then a clerk in Boston), received an international postal reply coupon from Spain. Ponzi immediately realized that the coupon could be redeemed in Boston at a rate of six times its value in Spain. This discovery gave him the idea that he could make money buying up stamps from foreign countries and then reselling them. By promising a 50 percent return in forty-five days, he soon enticed others to join him in this so-called business.

At first, Ponzi was able to pay huge profits, which of course attracted hordes of new investors. Still, as there was *no real product* and the number of foreign stamps was limited, it soon became clear that the only way for investors to be paid was from the money put in by those who came into the scheme later. The scheme eventually collapsed. Ponzi declared bankruptcy, was subsequently tried and sent to prison.

Not only are investors in today's (numerous!) variations on the Ponzi scheme likely to lose their money or life savings when the pyramid collapses, but even those who profit can be sued and end up having to pay out more than their original investment.

It is the Charles Ponzis of the world who make life difficult for sincere people with legitimate business propositions. Professional athletes, in particular, are loathe to trust strangers, especially if they have been burned before. It's hard to differentiate between a fan and a hook-me-upper, or between an honest businessperson and a scam artist. Rather than spending time trying to discern each person's motives and finding out, in many cases and to their dismay, that their initial worst instincts were right, it's easier—and safer—for the athlete to just to turn them all away.

Even if an athlete wanted to make the effort to separate the sheep from the wolves, he wouldn't have the time. He is accosted too often, in too many places, by too many people. San Francisco 49ers tight end Eric Johnson has seen it with a former, mega-star teammate. "People are always all over him," Johnson said. "They all want something from him. He has to be hardened on the outside. He shuts people out whom he doesn't believe to be honest."

Every professional athlete receives tons of mail from would-be financial advisors, non-profit organizations, and other business entities. The mailing itself allows them to use his name to market their services without paying for the unauthorized endorsement. Still, most athletes treat that mail the same way every one treats "junk mail"—they toss it in the trash. Again, there is no doubt that this lack of trust closes the door to many legitimate—even lucrative—business opportunities. Yet, athletes live by the motto "better safe than sorry."

For the potential scam artist, the hardest part is getting into the locker room. That's where those in an athlete's inner circle have an advantage, which many have been known to abuse. Once an athlete has been impressed by a service or product, the word spreads to his teammates and beyond, and the ground grows more fertile for the scam artists.

As noted earlier, players tend to trust homeboys and teammates, sometimes to their eventual dismay. One in particular, a star football player from my alma mater, met and developed a relationship with his eventual agent, also a former Ohio State athlete. The athlete was to have lost over a million dollars at the hands of his agent, who had cultivated relationships with other OSU star athletes, allegedly misappropriating nearly two million dollars from fourteen of his clients. The SEC later charged the sports agent with fraud. He had used the stolen funds to pay his expenses, pad his equity accounts, and pay residual income to ranking constituents of his Ponzi scheme. He later filed for bankruptcy protection to avoid claims against his assets.

I was once approached about a potential partnership venture, but when I asked to see the company's financial statements (so that I might have an opportunity to determine the feasibility of the proposed partnership), their representative balked at the request and grew defensive. (Flag on the play! Time out!) In a move to deflect my request, the rep asked to see my financial documents. In the end, I turned down the partnership, and as it turned out, our first potential deal would have netted me roughly a 3 percent return on my investment after expenditures. I could get a better return on an interest-bearing money market account.

Although I was not surprised by the scam, I was angry about the insult to my intelligence and about their assumption that I was a "typical dumb jock."

On another occasion I met with a group of businessmen at a restaurant to discuss a possible joint partnership. They wanted me to invest several hundreds of thousands of dollars; however, I noted that at the end of the meal they did not offer to pick up the tab. The bill was not consequential, but as a matter of business etiquette and normal practice the meal should have been a business expense for them, particularly since they called me—not the other way around. The incident was enough to make me suspicious of their proposal, and I declined to participate in the partnership.

One of the more popular scams today is the Nigerian Advance Fee (or 419) Fraud.

The mark (i.e., the intended victim of the scam) receives an unsolicited letter, fax, or e-mail from someone who claims to be an official of the Nigerian government or an agency thereof. The letter offers to transfer several million dollars into the mark's bank account. As to the source of this sudden windfall, if queried, the scammer may claim that the money is part of a currency conversion scam, or part of the purchase of some unspecified real estate. There are a dozen explanations—each distinctly implausible and all lies.

The mark is told that his assistance is needed to thwart corruption in the Nigerian government. To sweeten the deal, the letter also promises a return of 10 to 30 percent of the total sum to be funneled to the bank account. There's nothing like the promise of fast money to reel in a mark.

Inevitably, of course, certain problems surface to hinder the smooth transfer of funds. Advance fees are required from the mark to combat these problems, which generally are also attributed to corruption in the bureaucracy.

Sometimes the mark is even asked to go to Nigeria to complete the transaction, and told that a visa is unnecessary. If the mark makes the trip, the scammers have enormously increased their power over him since it is, in fact, a serious breach of law to enter Nigeria without a visa.

Of the many people who are taken in by the 419 Fraud each year, most are too embarrassed to come forward, thus making investigation and apprehension of the scammers far more difficult.

Spotting Scams

WHILE IT IS clear that avoiding scams like the 419 Fraud is as simple as ignoring any suspicious unsolicited letter, fax or email, not all advance fee frauds are as overt. You may find yourself involved with an individual or company that initially seems legitimate, but continually charges for "services" not rendered. Given that the stringent privacy laws in offshore centers can be used to mask unsavory activities, particular consideration is necessary when dealing with unknown professionals and companies. Even if you realize you have been scammed after the fact, foreign judgments may not be recognized in the offshore jurisdiction, and you could be in for a lengthy and expensive legal battle.

In writing this book, I have been reminded of how blessed and fortunate I have been to have invested soundly (as have many other athletes), and thus to be able to live comfortably if I never play professional sports again. Even so, I feel the pain, sadness, and anger of athletes who lose their hard-earned fortunes, either through trickery and deceit or by their own unbridled spending. I therefore applaud any and all efforts by the Securities and Exchange Commission (SEC) and the National Association of Securities Dealers (NASD) to catch and punish con artists. As a taxpayer, I feel that this is an instance in which my money is well spent.

There is some comfort in knowing that no matter how smart the scammer, he cannot forever escape the truth of Proverbs 27:19 (NIV): "As water reflects a face, so a man's heart reflects the man."

Con artists find potential marks in all sorts of places—country clubs, small cruises, high-end restaurants and stores—in short, anywhere people with money and an appreciation of the good life can be found.

Con artists will attempt to mirror your interests, beliefs, and passions. They will become a kindred spirit. If you fall for it, the bait comes next: "You are just the kind of person I've been looking for," or "I need your help," or "I've been looking for an honest person to work with me."

More complicated scams usually feature a middleman who will attempt to gain your confidence. One particularly neat trick is to make you feel as though you need to prove yourself worthy of being part of this so-called investment opportunity. To this end, the middleman may ask you to sign a letter of intent or even a power of attorney before steering you to the inside man. He's the one who is running the show, although he is likely to tell you that there is someone else "higher up." This increases the pressure on you once they have your money. It also provides a built-in alibi. When the checks stop coming (as they will), the con can always say that he is at the mercy of this "higher up" and, therefore, caught in the middle just like you are—still the kindred spirit.

Depending on how badly they need your money and your level of naiveté, the inside man may tell you that the scheme is, in fact, dishonest or he may continue to pretend that the scheme is a legitimate investment. From their perspective, it doesn't matter. They will get their money either way.

By returning some of your money to you at decent intervals, the con can fool you into believing that you really are making the profits promised. By this point, your level of trust in the con artist is secure enough so that you will invest more. To pressure you into bringing in other investors, you will be led to believe that this window of business opportunity is closing rapidly. So your friends need to act now!

Here the con will either end the scheme or hit you for additional (phony) expenses. Whatever the lie, scammers will do their best to make it convincing. After all, that's what they do best.

Should you happen to uncover the scam, it may be possible to recover a portion of your money, if you can act quickly, though in these days of electronic transfers that has become problematic.

Another way to spot and avoid a scam is to know what kinds of questions to ask which a con artist will not answer. Remember: A con artist will tell you anything they think you want to hear, right up to the point where you start asking real questions. If the person refuses to answer these sorts of questions, or hesitates, or makes excuses, or appears to be giving you false information, *run, do not walk, through the nearest exit.* And don't come back.

The basic strategy for detecting a scam before you are hooked is to ask for the credentials of the con artist and his business, e.g., a contractor's license number, whether he is registered with governmental or international agencies (and which ones), the name of his banker, references that you can check. If the person either can't or refuses to answer even one of these questions again, run—don't walk—through the nearest exit.

Certainly, before you reach any kind of agreement, consult with your own attorney.

To further protect athletes from scams and fraudulent investment schemes, the NFL Players' Association has instituted a program that calls for all players' financial advisors to register with the union.

When it comes to scams, con games, and the like, there is, quite understandably, a high degree of paranoia among professional athletes, a sort of "who's after me next?" feeling that makes them wary of friends, acquaintances, and fans, as well as perfect strangers.

Regardless of what position an athlete plays on the team of his particular sport, he must play defense when it comes to watching out for shady deals and scams. A good friend of mine has a voice prompt on his cell phone that asks callers to identify unblocked phone numbers if they are restricted. Those who do not comply with this request will not have their call answered. The assumption behind this defensive posture, popular with many athletes, is clear: people who will not identify themselves want something, usually money, in one form or another.

Here is a true story. After losing a hotly-contested playoff game, an NBA team returned home and was greeted at the airport by a throng of fans. Naturally, the players were thrilled by the show of continued support. As they made their way to their cars to go home, they waved and otherwise signaled to show their appreciation to the fans lined up in the streets and anywhere they could find a space just to get a glimpse of the team members. Then things took a strange turn. Some of the fans jumped in front of the cars as the players were trying to leave the area. To the players, this was frightening.

Later some fans who claimed to have been hit while the players were attempting to get onto the nearby freeway sued two players. Although it is likely that the injured fans were pushed into the path of the cars by other fans, it is just as likely that they jumped in front of the cars.

Lawsuits are every professional athlete's worst nightmare. Because it is nearly impossible to avoid them, athletes must have additional insurance coverage to protect themselves. Being in the limelight can sometimes be warm. Other times it burns.

During one of our interviews, Charley Hannah said, "There's more ways to take advantage of an athlete or anyone with money than we can think of and put into a book. A friend of mine says, 'If you try to come up with a foolproof system, all you're going to do is find a more cunning fool.' But if a guy is careful with his relationships, careful about choosing his friends, careful with his money and about choosing the people to help him invest it, then the con men will soon realize that they better look for an easier target."

Here is another true story involving a former Major League Baseball player and his barber. One day the barber mentioned that he needed a new car. The player offered to take him to someone who could help him get a reasonable deal on the purchase. The two went to a dealership, where the barber was shown several cars that were well beyond his financial means. The player and the barber had been friends for some time, and the player offered to buy the car and let the barber pay him back. Ready for the shocking part? The barber turned down the offer! The player probably wouldn't have been more surprised if he'd been hit in the head by a fastball! Athletes are so used to friends who drop hints the size of bricks whenever they hit a financial roadblock.

Too many people spend money they haven't earned, to buy things they don't want, to impress people they don't like.

—Will Rogers

Yet the barber explained that, while he appreciated the kindness and generosity behind the gesture, he simply would not feel right about the arrangement the player proposed.

That baseball player had something that no amount of money can buy: a real friend.

I hesitated to introduce this next topic here because I wasn't sure if, strictly speaking, it could be called fraud. After I thought about it, though, I decided that it is a kind of fraud committed by athletes (and millions of other people) against themselves. I'm talking about frivolous spending prompted by peer pressure.

Mindless, impulse spending is a kind of fraud because you are cheating yourself out of your own future. One afternoon, some years ago, Oprah Winfrey shocked her audience when she said that during a recent cruise vacation she refused to buy a souvenir T-shirt because it was $45 and she thought the price was too high. A barely audible rumble of derisive giggling swept through the room, and you can guess what they were all thinking. "This is one of the richest women on earth, and she wouldn't spend $45 on a T-shirt?!!" One of the ways in which Oprah remains one of the richest women on earth is by not squandering her money foolishly!

If this sounds like the beginning of an anti-shopping crusade, nothing could be further from the truth. You've earned your money, and it would be foolish not to enjoy it. Just be sure that you do so on your own terms, and not because you feel pressured to prove something to other people—or even to yourself. Don't buy a new car because a friend or a fan or some perfect stranger says, "Hey, man. When you going to upgrade that ride? I know you can afford it. You got plenty of money. Don't be so tight with it!" Don't buy a new wardrobe because a teammate or friend chides you, "I've seen you in that outfit three times already this year. When you going to buy some new clothes?"

This is the quintessential definition of a slippery slope. Soon you will find yourself buying things you had never even considered just to stop people from making comments, when there is a much easier (and cheaper!) way to do that. Next time somebody suggests that you need to buy something, ask them if they are going to pay the bill when it comes in. It's a variation on an old saying, put up or shut up!

Aaron Ward had this to say on the subject of pressure-based spending.

"When you're an athlete, people pad your ego all the time. So when you start hearing, 'That looks absolutely great on you, and now I want to show you something better,' it's easy to get caught up in the hype and the pressure to buy something, even if you didn't really want anything right at that moment. My advice? When you get ready to go shopping, go alone. That way you make your own decisions about what to do with your money, which is the way it should be all the time."

Financial Education

PROFESSIONAL ATHLETES LEAD hectic lives, to say the least. The near-breakneck pace demanded by their profession can easily keep them so busy that by the time they are ready to take the time for a thorough and detailed review of their financial situation, it is already too late. Either their money has been stolen or they have frittered it away themselves through frivolous spending habits or, more likely, a combination of both.

Contrary to what many people believe, the majority of athletes are not intellectually incapable of understanding the world of finance.

D'Marco Farr, formerly with the St. Louis Rams, who was defrauded by a trusted financial advisor, tells other players, "When it comes to your money, what you're earning, what your body is producing, do your homework. That's what guys need to learn." That's sound advice.

One way for an athlete to examine his total financial picture is to use the same approach he uses when preparing for an opponent on the court, field, or ice. Assess the strengths and weaknesses of your financial situation

If you can't count, they can cheat you. If you can't read, they can beat you.
—Toni Morrison

and try as much as possible to prepare for the unexpected. It—whatever "it" is—may never happen, but you will feel good knowing that you have a plan of action in place just in case.

I think it is safe to say that most professional athletes begin their careers basically as trusting people. They cannot bring themselves to believe that anyone whom they have invited into their inner circle would have anything but the best and most honorable intentions and that their actions would always reflect those intentions. Quite often they are wrong, and just as often they don't find out how wrong they are until financial tragedy has struck.

The key to avoiding being conned and/or defrauded, or at least decreasing the likelihood of it, is education. You may not have time to go back to school for formal instruction, but you can ask questions (remember: it is your money!).

It is absolutely imperative for professional athletes (and people in general) to devote some part of their free time, even if it's only a few minutes a day, to studying the sensitive subject of personal finance. An excellent way to do this is to read books and other publications on financial planning. There are certain basic elements of which athletes (and everyone else) should have a working knowledge.

An **annuity** is a stream of equal payments to an individual, such as to a retiree that occurs at predetermined intervals (that is, monthly or annually). The payments may continue for a fixed period or for a contingent period, such as for the recipient's lifetime. Although annuities are most often associated with insurance companies and retirement programs, the payment of interest to a bondholder is also an example of an annuity.

Assets are the entries on a balance sheet showing all properties, both tangible and intangible, and claims against others that may be applied to cover the liabilities of a person or business. Assets can include cash, stock, inventories, property rights, and goodwill.

A **tax shelter** is a financial arrangement, such as the use of special depletion allowances, which reduces taxes on current earnings.

A **commodity** is a class of economic goods; especially, an item of merchandise (as soybeans) whose price is the basis of futures trading.

Present value refers to the value today of a future payment, or stream of payments, discounted at some appropriate interest rate.

Inflation is a general increase in the price level of goods and services. Unexpected inflation tends to be detrimental to security prices, primarily because it forces interest rates higher. A point to keep in mind is that a certain amount of inflation is already embodied in security prices.

Interest is the charge for a loan, usually a percentage of the amount loaned; also an excess or bonus beyond what is expected or due.

An **investment** is property acquired for the purpose of producing income for its owner. Just as plants and equipment are investments for manufacturers, stocks and bonds are investments for individuals; expenditures made for income-producing assets.

Liabilities are anything that is owed to someone else.

Stocks are *ownership in* companies.

Bonds are *loans made to* companies.

Another good approach for athletes to educate themselves in this area is to use some of the time they spend traveling to read and learn about financial matters. Check the Internet or your local library for recommended reading.

"Share the wealth," says one old adage, or as Commander Riker once said during a crap game on "Star Trek: The Next Generation," "When the train comes in, everybody rides!" When one achieves a certain level of financial security, whether through hard work, inheritance, or a fortuitous bounce of good fortune, the impulse to try to be all things to all people (i.e., to at least to play Last National Bank to those whose finances are less well-endowed than your own) is very nearly universal. Rob Sanford, in his book *Infinite Financial Freedom*, advises people who suddenly find themselves with access to a lot of money to do nothing for ninety days. If possible, plan to get out of town for a few days, preferably to a quiet place, where you can begin to think clearly about what you wish to do.

This is sound advice, particularly for young athletes newly signed to the pros. A brief hiatus interrupts that impulse to start a tab for everyone in town!

An athlete must play well, but the game cannot be the sum total of who the athlete is.
—*L. Funderburke*

It took me several years to realize that I could not be all things to all people, and to take control of my finances before I fell into the trap of taking my continued life as a professional athlete for granted.

I remember only too well the problems that I had in high school and college, particularly in identifying the attributes that I could bring to the table if my career didn't go as planned. An athlete must play his game well, but the game cannot be the sum total of who he is, and there will come a point in his life when he must transcend the game to achieve the sum total of who he can be. Otherwise he risks becoming a sad figure with nothing more than old video tapes and newspaper clippings to show for his life.

Brent Williams, who played professional football with the New England Patriots from 1986 to 1997, is now a money manager and financial advisor. He uses his experience as a professional athlete and his financial expertise to provide informed advice to athletes, business owners, and non-profit organizations.

Williams grew up in a single-parent home in Flint, Michigan, and the NFL was his ticket out of a tough environment.

Don't help people so much As a young athlete, new to what
that you hinder them from was then considered to be a large salary,
helping themselves. Williams admits to having made every
 —**L. Funderburke** possible financial mistake. "I didn't have
a budget. Anyone who asked me for
money got it. I bought whatever I wanted, and used every credit card I
had." Fortunately, Williams was able to play for eleven years, and he used
that time to build a strong financial foundation.

Williams believes that one of the first mistakes rookies confront is
the feeling that they are going to make this incredible amount of money
forever. He recalls a young, single athlete who, at 21, was spending close
to six figures—a month! Williams eventually convinced him that he could
live quite well off a whole lot less.

Although that's an extreme case, I don't think most of us—whatever
our profession—have a real handle on how much we spend every month.
One afternoon my wife and I sat down to review expenditures for the
previous month—not including car payments, insurance, and other bills,
but just the money we spent on day-to-day activities. Receipts in hand,
we tallied up the numbers. I can only say that I am glad we were sitting
down when we looked at the total. And we are not, by any stretch of the
imagination, spendthrifts! I am also glad that my friends, teammates, and
family members who have accused me of being, shall we say, excessively
frugal didn't see the total. They might have thought we'd been adding up
figures for another family.

Convinced that these figures just didn't add up (so to speak), my wife
and I reviewed the numbers again. The results were not heartening, though
in a sense we were right. They didn't add up. I now encourage everyone
to tabulate expenses for at least three months, including regular monthly
bills. You, too, may be surprised at what the figures show about the need to
establish and maintain a budgeting plan and to curtail excessive spending.

Williams advises his clients to set aside a certain amount of money each
year and to live on that amount for X number of years until 401(k) annuities
kick in. As for the family and friends who expect athletes to provide for them,
Williams suggests that his clients ask family and friends to write down what
they want and submit it in the form of a proposal to the player's financial
advisor. Williams believes that this action will eliminate most requests for
money while at the same time taking the pressure off the young athlete (in
particular) who may still be uncomfortable with the idea that he may be
disappointing some people by refusing to give them money.

Because of the inability to predict exactly when their careers will end,
athletes have to invest their money accordingly. Most people look forward
to retiring at sixty-five or older, but an athlete's career can be ended by
an injury when he is twenty-six. So they cannot invest in the same way
that a corporate executive with a twenty- to thirty-year window invests.

In addition, athletes need to plan ahead for the kind of career they will choose when their sports careers end.

Today, agents are negotiating contracts, instead of players. More than ever before, athletes need advisors who can prepare them for what will happen after the contract is signed, and for how their lives and relationships will change.

The Greek philosopher Aristotle said, "Education is the best provision for old age."

The Ancient Greeks invented sports, too!

May I Have Your Autograph, Please?

IN HIS INTERVIEW WITH Pamela Gerloff, Brent Williams pointed out that most young players do not realize the extent to which their lives will change once they sign a pro contract. Even if they are prepared to be treated differently by fans and strangers, they are almost never prepared for the reactions of close friends and people whom they have known all their lives.

Handling fame and notoriety is a tough balancing act. Well-known players like Michael Jordan can't go to a mall without being mobbed. It's difficult for someone like that to have a normal existence. Mainly, as a professional athlete, you want to have some time when you can just be normal, and that's not always easy to find.

At the height of his career, veteran NBA star Bill Russell was the driving force behind the nearly unstoppable defense of the Boston Celtics, who won eleven championships in thirteen years. In his book *Second Wind: The Memoirs of an Opinionated Man*, Russell relates a telling incident.

Russell was standing by himself in an airport, reading a newspaper while waiting for a flight, when he became aware of a little round man staring up at him.

"Hi, Wilt," the man said.

Although Russell sensed an aggressive attitude in the man, he did not answer. Not surprisingly, the man kept on until Russell finally said, "My name's not Wilt." For a moment, the man actually insisted that Russell was, in fact, Wilt (as in Wilt Chamberlain).

Russell remembers being glad when the man walked away, but not surprised when he came back a few minutes later, irate because Russell had refused to correct the man's mistaken identity of him.

The man then asked for an autograph. (Hard to believe, isn't it?) When Russell informed him that he didn't sign autographs, the man responded, "You have to sign autographs. I'm part of the public. We made you, you know."

For Russell, not signing autographs is about freedom and his personal beliefs.

For other athletes, however, the decision whether or not to give autographs is often grounded in their wariness of people and their motives.

Hustlers will often use children to approach athletes and request autographs, which the hustler will then sell to the highest bidder on eBay or elsewhere. The assumption, in general a correct one, is that an athlete is unlikely to turn down a child requesting an autograph. While selling memorabilia is by no means illegal, using a child to further such a pursuit is at the very least unconscionable.

During the annual rite of passage called spring training, Florida is a magnet for both fans and hustlers. Drew Park, a depressed and disadvantaged neighborhood not far from the heart of Tampa, is just around the corner from Legends Field, where the New York Yankees hold spring training camp every year. Children by the dozens come to the park hoping to meet or get an autograph from Derek Jeter, Gary Sheffield, Alex Rodriguez, or some of the other famed Yankee team members.

Hustlers of memorabilia use the children's attraction to the field as a money-making gambit. One hustler began by selecting five children, each around ten years old. From the trunk of his shiny new car (an attention-getter by itself), he selected, from among dozens, five collectors' items and gave one to each child with the instruction to find a particular athlete and have the item signed. "Make sure you get the players to sign on the 'sweet spot,'" he said, as the kids scurried off with their items to find the players, and unaware that they were being used in a con.

Players are immediately put in an awkward position. If they refuse to sign the item, as requested, the public labels them as arrogant, insensitive, unfeeling, and overpaid. If the child inadvertently gives away the scam, perhaps by repeating the hustler's instructions to him, "Make sure you sign on the sweet spot," the player who refuses to sign still runs the risk of coming off like a jerk.

This practice is legalized child abuse. Yet most players would rather give their signature than question the intentions of an autograph seeker, particularly a child, even though most are aware that the newly-autographed item will be sold. Some athletes are now personalizing autographs to diminish their value on the open market.

This is an example of why professional athletes feel exploited, and may also explain why so many athletes are unwilling to let their guards down, even for an instant. You may be an honest fan just wishing to express your admiration for an athlete's talent and skill. But he has no way of knowing that, and taking your word for it may be, in his mind and based on his experiences, too risky. Professional athletes meet so many people with ulterior motives. Sadly, many athletes become jaded and decide it is safer for them to assume that is the case with nearly everyone they meet.

Autograph and memorabilia scams are not the only ways in which a professional athlete's name can be misused and/or abused. Research scientist Dr. Ariel Roth noted, "The cause of truth would also be generously served if we would drop the practice of name-dropping."

Name-dropping is commonplace with professional athletes. The problem arises when an athlete discovers that his name has been used as a reference without his permission.

Suppose an athlete hires a contractor for some landscaping work. Several thousand dollars later, he is very pleased with the results. A couple of weeks after the job is finished, a representative from the landscape company returns and, without his consent, takes pictures of the newly-beautified surroundings of the home. Only later does the athlete learn that pictures of his home and the landscaping for which he paid are now being used in an advertising brochure for the landscape company, which identifies him by name as a "satisfied customer."

Similarly, athletes often find their names being used to promote or endorse questionable companies or individuals with whom they may have done business, but never agreed to have their names become part of a marketing campaign. An athlete's reputation is very much on the line in these situations, as it is likely to be difficult for him to publicly retract any association with a company or individual. Some suspicion of involvement or a business arrangement is likely to remain.

The biggest issue for athletes, indeed, for all celebrities, with regard to the misuse of their names, is identity theft.

In 2002, Anthony Lemar Taylor, a twice-convicted felon with a record of petty thefts and robberies that spanned seventeen years, was arrested and tried for stealing Tiger Woods' identity. "It's a violation of your persona," said Woods. "You feel like you have been violated."

Thanks to modern technology, a thief can empty a person's bank account and max out credit cards all from the comfort of home.

Charley Hannah had his identity stolen, although the incident took on a bizarre twist. With the unwitting assistance of a stranger who whispered, "There goes Charley Hannah," the impersonator met and subsequently began a relationship with a woman who believed him to be the real football player with the Tampa Bay Buccaneers. The fact that the impersonator bore no resemblance at all to the real Charley Hannah apparently went unnoticed.

Hannah had difficulty convincing people that the impersonator was, in fact, just that—an impersonator. "People would approach me out in public and tell me, 'I am so-and-so, and we met several times at a bar. I am a big fan of Alabama, remember me?' I tried to tell them that I'd never been to that bar, but they insisted that I had."

Aaron Ward, who won two Stanley Cups with the Detroit Red Wings, was victimized by someone who ran up a hotel bill of several thousand dollars in his name. When the hotel management called the team office to state that one of the players was running up an enormous bill, including room service and other amenities, Ward was, to say the least, shocked. "What are you talking about?" he said. "I've never stayed at that hotel before."

On another occasion, sensitive information was stolen from Ward's mailbox owing to the lag time between mail transfer from the city where he played during the season to the city where he and his family lived during the off season. The thief emptied their bank account, although the situation was later rectified. Forwarding mail is always a concern for professional athletes because when they leave town, some mail is usually left behind in spite of address changes with local mail providers.

Safeguards notwithstanding, celebrities and star athletes remain the most vulnerable to this increasingly common crime.

Sadly, identity theft is often easier to commit than an ordinary robbery. Moreover, once a person becomes an identity theft victim, he or she has a fairly high chance of being victimized again.

Players on all Major League Baseball (MLB) teams are briefed about the rise of identity theft during spring training. Perhaps in part as a result of these and other prevention efforts, incidents of identity theft that targeted baseball players, coaches, and personnel have been significantly reduced.

Because of two previous convictions, the man who stole Tiger Woods' identity was punishable under California's "three strikes" rule, and was convicted on eight felony counts and sentenced to twenty years to life.

> *"Who steals my purse, steals trash; 'tis something, nothing;*
> *'Twas mine, 'tis his, and has been slave to thousands;*
> *But he that filches from me my good name...*
> *robs me of that which not enriches him...*
> *and makes me poor indeed."*
>
> **—William Shakespeare**
> **Othello, *Act III, Scene 3***

Financial Emergency—Dial Athlete 911!

Plan ahead. It wasn't raining when Noah built the ark!

I DON'T KNOW who first said that, but there is as much truth in it as there is humor. Everyone hits a financial roadblock now and then. It's a major strain, psychologically as well as financially.

Unfortunately for the professional athlete, he is often viewed as the solution to other people's money problems. Young athletes, especially, feel obligated to fill that role and, as a result, are open to those who would exploit that feeling. One can only hope that the money doesn't run out before they realize that they were never thus obligated.

Some people seem to have the opinion, often unstated, "I don't need to play the lottery or read a book on how to become a millionaire, since my client or my homeboy or my cousin or my whatever is one."

Most people know, intellectually at least, that athletes work hard. Yet there is still the subliminal feeling that the money an athlete makes is free of the constraints attached to the salaries of ordinary working people. It's as though people equate an athlete's salary with winning the lottery—a happy financial accident or a bit of good fortune. And if that is the case (which it isn't), then people tend not to feel bad about asking him for money. Indeed, many feel that they have a right to be angry if their request is turned down.

When I was a child I used to have a recurring dream in which I would be behind a Brinks truck when the doors flew open and I suddenly found myself adrift in a sea of coins, through which I would vigorously dig, finding coin after coin and eventually amassing a great deal of money. It's funny to me now, especially when I realize how many adults out there feel about professional athletes the same way I felt about that Brinks truck in my dream. All you have to do is stand there and wait for the door to fly open, and the money—the athlete's money—will come pouring out.

True story: some time ago a professional athlete found himself stranded on the freeway due to a flat tire. A guy passing by noticed the disabled luxury sports car on the side of the road and stopped—to ask for $60,000. Fooled you, didn't I? You thought the guy was going to offer to change the tire or call a tow truck. Well, it fooled the athlete, too. The guy didn't offer to do anything except relieve him of $60,000 if he happened to have that much handy.

Are there still good Samaritans in the world? Sure. But the next time you're thinking about how great it would be to be rich, just remember: rich people don't meet many good Samaritans.

Nor is it just on the streets and highways that athletes are harassed by the money-challenged. An athlete may find numerous messages from the desperately in need, many of whom are angry when their calls are not returned right away. "What took you so long to call me back?" Rarely is it a matter of life and death: more something on the order of, "Hey, man. Can I get $400 to make my car payment?" or, "Can I get two tickets to the big game tomorrow night?" or, "My car broke down, and I need your help."

Similar to their assumptions about an abundance of cash lying around with no purpose, hook-me-uppers also assume that the nature of an athlete's job leaves him with enormous amounts of free time. After all, the average game

> *No good deed goes unpunished.*
> —*Clare Boothe Luce*

lasts—what?—three or four hours, max? It's not like he is working nine to five like any regular working person.

Well, no, he isn't, primarily because he doesn't have the same type of job. In fact, the average nine-to-five worker would find it nearly impossible to keep the daily schedule of a professional athlete. It's not just the game:

it's the game plus the heavy-duty workouts, plus the practice sessions, plus the team meetings, plus the interviews and league PR obligations—plus and plus and plus. Throw in little things like a wife, children, sleeping, and meals, and what you often get is a guy who wishes there were twenty-five hours in a day. Yes, he is paid handsomely for his efforts, but he doesn't get paid to do nothing, any more than the guy working nine to five gets paid to be unproductive.

I am not by nature a cynical person, as the quotation from Clare Boothe Luce, on page 119, would seem to imply. However, my experience as a professional athlete has taught me a few valuable lessons that do not always show people in their best light. For example, befriending someone who is in the middle of a crisis is an act of kindness that, for the professional athlete, may end up costing him more than he had bargained for.

Public perception of the professional athlete is that of a spoiled, overpaid, arrogant, self-involved person who, were it not for his athletic skills, would hardly be worth knowing. It is an image that the majority of athletes go out of their way to challenge. Think about it. No one, regardless of what they do, wants to be perceived in such a wholly unflattering light. Combine the desire to change our image with general public knowledge of our annual salaries, and you have ripe territory for hook-me-uppers.

Thus, the athlete who offers financial help to someone in distress can pretty much count on being put on that person's long-term sucker list—or the list of someone they know, or the sister-in-law of the second cousin of someone they used to know in school. One act of kindness then burgeons into seemingly endless requests from the person you originally helped and from people they know whom you've never met in your life, all based on the assumption, "Oh, he won't mind helping you out. He's a cool guy." Reach out to help someone once, and it becomes open season on you and your wallet.

As always, it's the athlete who is left in the awkward position. Once he extricates himself from the entanglements precipitated by his generous gesture, he can never so much as call to see if the person is all right without fear of reopening Pandora's box. The end result is that he may not reach out to some people at times when he genuinely should. For better or worse, he will never feel comfortable in the future beginning an offer of help with, "Look. I'm only going to do this once, and please don't put my name on a mailing list of people with financial problems."

Sort of takes the charity out of an otherwise charitable gesture, don't you think?

In a different vein, I have another friend for whom I would do just about anything and who, ironically, has never asked me for anything. As strange as it sounds, that is why I have given him tickets to my games, and why I help him whenever I can, and why he is always welcome in my home.

Athletes are used to an implied, if not stated, expectation of reciprocity if someone does something for them. But this man has supported me and been there for me when I needed him most with no strings attached. My wife and I both feel that our lives are richer for his presence. Nothing that I can give him or do for him could equal the gift of our friendship. Most athletes have at least one or two people like this in their lives, and they feel, as I do, blessed.

Contrary to what seems to be accepted opinion, athletes do work for a living. The fact that what we do is called "playing a game" unfortunately lends credibility to the public perception that it isn't a real job. Yet if we use the definition of a job as provided in *Webster's Collegiate Dictionary,* "a piece of work undertaken on order at a stated rate," then what we as athletes do meets that criterion and is, therefore, a job. Granted, to some spectators who observe from afar, we may look like a bunch of overgrown two-year-olds chasing each other up and down the court (or field or ice) playing a strange form of tag-you're-it, but that's just appearance. When we are on the court (or field or ice), we are working.

Within this context, then, perhaps you can understand why we may seem a trifle annoyed when approached by those who feel that we are obligated to share our earnings with them because of some affiliation. "Hey, man. I'm [black, white, brown, Native American, your sister-in-law, your cousin twice-removed, a vegetarian, a member of the Club, your homie], so you know you have to do business with me! You got to hook me up!"

Young athletes are probably more inclined to fall for this than the veterans, but we are all vulnerable to it at times. Yet, as long as helping someone, doing someone a favor, whatever you wish to call it, remains a voluntary act, an athlete must be on guard against those who would use psychological and emotional manipulation to coerce from him that which is his to give or keep. As for the hook-me-uppers, there should be a level to which even they will not stoop.

There should be.

Among the many types of hook-me-uppers about whom I spoke, possibly the most offensive is that group for whom nothing is ever enough— for whom merely good is never good enough. Wouldn't you think a person would be satisfied just being a moocher? Wouldn't you think it would occur to them that if they complained too much about the stuff they mooch, the moochee (the athlete) might cut off the supply?

As Gary Trent said, "They ask for $1,000. You give them $500, and they still have the nerve to complain." Aren't you glad you don't have that kind of nerve in a tooth? The sheer audacity is mind-boggling.

Similarly, one of the most prominent and influential members of the African American entertainment community reported giving a car to a person who then complained because she wanted a higher-end car. Apparently, the fact that the car was free was not a consideration for the recipient.

I've had my own experiences along this line, of course. Recently, when I told a friend about my plans for a financial gift to another mutual acquaintance, the reply came, "I don't think he is going to be happy with that because he knows you can give him more."

It is important to remember that man was created at the end of the week.

—***Mark Twain***

The Pain and the Gain

ONE THING AN athlete learns quickly about his place on the wrong end of a hookup: He must never:

- Expect to be repaid
- Say the hook-me-upper is asking for too much
- Question the reliability (let alone the legality) of any business venture
- Cut them off for good if they've already conned him once.

Do you suppose the hook-me-uppers would even mention those "rules" if the person being hit on for money was—oh, I don't know—say, a loan shark? Well, let's put it this way. If they did, they would only do it once.

I usually have a good feel for whether an inquiry is legit. An ex-NFL player who himself got burned more than a few times, but who is now a successful businessman, had some sound advice. He said that professional athletes, like everyone else, need to understand the risk-ratio analysis when contemplating whether to invest in a project.

According to the website Financial Pipeline (www.finpipe.com), risk (or financial) ratio analysis is "the calculation and comparison of ratios which are derived from the information in a company's financial statements. The level and historical trends of these ratios can be used to make inferences about a company's financial condition, its operations and attractiveness as an investment."

If the odds for a particular investment are somewhat high or significantly higher than competing investments or alternatives, an investor must be acutely aware that his principal will be exposed and possibly jeopardized. For instance, if the likelihood is that five percent of a hundred investors will lose their principal, then that must mean that five of these investors will lose a hundred percent of their money. To some people, an investment with such a high risk of significant financial loss is not sound.

The bottom line is really taking a common-sense approach to risk management. Sadly, some athletes have not yet learned how to do this, and they should because it is a useful tool not only in analyzing investment decisions, but also in things like buying a new car or deciding whether to loan someone a large amount of money.

No doubt we've all been told as children about the importance of saving for a rainy day. We may not have understood the significance of that then, but as adults we do, even if we have yet to accomplish it.

The fact is that curtailing and amending one's spending habits is hard. Even so, it is still arguably the best approach for athletes and non-athletes alike. Save and invest a considerable portion of your wealth—however large or small—in conservative, sustainable investment instruments, even though a portion of your investments are apt to incur a little more risk depending on your age and income level. This advice is universally applicable unless an athlete or entertainer has made hundreds of millions of dollars, and even then, he or she may not be able to retain his or her fortune in the absence of some level of diligent investing and saving.

No Work, No Pay

"WITH THE CANCELLATION of the 2004–05 season—a first for a North American sports league—the NHL has started down a path into the unknown," reported Scott Burnside in an online article for ESPN in February.

Burnside added that, given that the average NHL career is about four years, many in the rank and file face losing one-half of their NHL earning potential.

Although this is the first season cancellation in memory, lockouts and work stoppages have become more common in recent years, particularly during the era of big contracts and heightened publicity (the NBA had a lockout in 1998).

Before getting into the financial and emotional toll of these actions, and in line with our overall theme about the importance of education in the athlete's process of establishing financial security, I wanted to provide some basic information on work stoppages, lockouts, the meaning of collective bargaining, and revenue sharing in professional sports.

(*Warning*: The following comments in the next several paragraphs may precipitate a sudden desire to take a nap. It is recommended that you have coffee, tea, or a spray bottle filled with very cold water on hand. If these substances fail to keep you awake, have a loved one beat you over the head—lightly, of course—with a small pillow or a lightweight rubber hammer. We have found that children are usually very willing participants in this activity, though they can, on occasion, get a little carried away.)

One of the most difficult issues that must be addressed during player/owner negotiations is the *salary cap*—a league-mandated limit on the size of players' salaries.

Ideally, after deliberations are concluded, both sides sign a *collective bargaining agreement.* These agreements are designed to assure both players and owners that they are getting a fair deal regarding profit sharing as a percentage of total revenues and *free agency* (a system that allows athletes without a contract to sign with the team that offers them the best salary). Collective bargaining agreements are used in all four major professional U.S. sports leagues: the National Basketball Association (NBA), the National Football League (NFL), Major League Baseball (MLB), and the National Hockey League (NHL).

Collective bargaining agreements expire after a certain amount of time and must be renegotiated and renewed. If during that process the two sides cannot reach an agreement, player-organized strikes or owner-imposed lockouts or suspensions usually result. Both strikes and lockouts have occurred in every major pro team sport at some time during the past twenty years.

There now. That wasn't so bad, was it? Okay, so maybe it was, but hopefully you learned at least a few things that you didn't know before.

The financial and emotional toll of work stoppages and lockouts are staggering. Paychecks stop coming in. The bills do not. It's important to remember that this affects not only athletes, but also workers at the arenas and venues, as well as businesses in the immediate vicinities.

When players are going through a lockout, the tension—and fear—can be gut-wrenching. Wives, children, and other loved ones begin to wonder when Daddy is going back to work. To make matters worse, Daddy is wondering, too.

As players and owners jockey over their share of revenue dollars, lockouts and work stoppages are likely to be part of the future of sports for many years to come. These impasses can blindside an athlete who is unprepared, especially the minimum-salary and lower-tiered players.

Preparation is the key, as Aaron Ward noted in our conversation.

"Obviously your salaries are public knowledge. The key, as always, is investments and putting aside money for the bedrock things like your kids' education. If a lookout is looming, even before then, you need to begin prioritizing your finances and your daily lifestyle, which will change with a lockout or work stoppage. Obviously, living day to day is the most important, and you need a long-term plan in place so that you are prepared for that."

I asked Aaron to comment on the strain for NHL players who experienced a lockout in late 2004.

"The union knew this was coming," he explained. "Since '95 they were preaching to us that the owners had put away the expansion money they got from teams that came into the league. They pretty much started the conference with the $300 million in expansion money. I think they [the NHL] asked the owners to place like $10 million each in terms of [equity] at the beginning of the lockout. We were made aware of this much earlier, so our committee asked us to put aside a paycheck every year to be placed in an investment fund. They kept back the payment of union dues, and monies from merchandising and licensing arrangements went into this fund also. Basically, if the total allocated amount of what each player put in grew to $5 million, we would at least be able to survive on it."

I then asked Aaron about how players cope with a lockout psychologically.

"That was the part I didn't prepare for. As an athlete you look forward to the time you spend playing your sport. It's part of our competitive nature. Then, too, my family has never been used to me being at home so much. I think the toughest part is sitting around feeling as though you have no purpose. I feel like I have been put in a situation where I have to start making decisions. I'm looking at possibly going back to school or getting a job. If you sit around doing nothing too long, you begin to feel mentally and physically lethargic. You work out every day for a couple of hours, but after that there really isn't much to do."

Of course, an athlete's career can be interrupted (or ended) by circumstances other than work stoppages and lockouts. I was reminded of this one morning during ESPN's "Outside the Lines," a weekly program hosted by Bob Ley.

Ley was talking with quarterbacks Heath Shuler, Akili Smith, Cade McNown, Tim Couch, and Ryan Leaf, each of whom, despite brilliant college careers and being high draft picks, had not found tremendous success after turning pro.

I particularly remember the conversation with Akili Smith, former Oregon Ducks standout and quarterback for the Cincinnati Bengals. Smith is not currently playing in the NFL, but he is trying to make a comeback. But he did something early in his career that more athletes should do for their own protection. He saved and invested a sizeable portion of his salary and signing bonus. He may not have been psychologically prepared for an early end to (interruption in?) his career, but he was financially prepared.

The point is that sometimes careers don't go as planned, and a professional athlete must prepare himself and his family for this possibility. That same tenacity and resolve that propelled them to the top of their sport should be used to build a strong financial foundation that will support their next career moves, regardless of the direction. Since pension and 401(k) plans can't be touched for several years, an athlete needs to decide what he will do when the checks stop coming in. In most cases, he must be able to depend on residual income-generating investments or be prepared to venture out into the business world.

This is not easy if sports have been the center of your life. But just as every team makes the necessary adjustments from game to game, so, too, must the athlete in the game of life outside the arena once his career concludes after college or the pros.

An athlete can prepare for work stoppages and lockouts. He cannot, realistically, anticipate injuries, which can derail a career before it starts.

An athlete's body is, after all, his meal ticket. A back or disk problem, a torn anterior cruciate ligament (ACL), a torn Achilles tendon, or a head or neck injury can leave an athlete wondering if he will ever play professionally again.

Understandably, most athletes prefer not to think of these outcomes. But the fact remains that injured players are expendable. Thus, it is prudent for athletes to at least consider the possibility that they may not be able to play out their careers to their natural conclusion, leaving the game at a certain age, depending on the established standards of the sport.

An injury, temporary or career-ending, can be a financial and emotional setback for an athlete and his family. Coping with an injury presents a tremendous challenge.

Only after being injured for the last two years did I become acutely aware of the importance of having a plan in place to deal with the financial and emotional ramifications of an injury and its impact on my career. While it is always possible that an athlete will never be injured, the very nature of sports makes that an unlikely outcome. In short, injuries are a distinct possibility in any athletic career, collegiate or professional.

Over the past two years Rickey Dudley, a former teammate from Ohio State University who is currently a tight end with the Tampa Bay Buccaneers, has suffered a number of injuries, each of which he says has hampered his future income even though he is still likely to be playing for some time.

Injuries, particularly those that happen during the last year of a contract or near the end of a career, hurt athletes in more ways than the obvious. Injuries also create questions, and questions create doubt in the minds of general managers. (In his novel *Bleachers*, author John Grisham tells the story of a high school All American named Neely Crenshaw, who returns home when he learns of the impending death of his old coach, Eddie Rake. As the best quarterback ever to play for Rake's famed Messina Spartans, Crenshaw went on to the NFL, but his career was cut short by a knee injury. In the novel, Crenshaw and his old high school teammates reflect on their feelings—good and bad—for Coach Rake as they wait for word of his death.)

To the extent possible, an athlete must have a financial plan for himself and his family in case he is injured. This is relevant to non-athletes as well; everyone must have a backup plan for unforeseen financial circumstances, such as being laid off or suffering a debilitating injury which prevents one from working.

The strength of an athlete's financial plan will dictate how well he and his family hold together emotionally. It is a good idea to have both a best- and worst-case plan. The worst-case would, of course, be a career-ending injury. That means that the plan should be set up to help ease the athlete's transition from the world of sports to the working world of everyday Americans.

According to the NCAA, prospective college pros can obtain disability insurance up to a certain amount. This is called the Exceptional Student-Athlete Disability Insurance (ESDI) program. Under the ESDI program, maximum coverage is as follows (these figures were accurate at the time of my research):

- Men's basketball: $4.4 million
- Football: $3.0 million
- Baseball: $1.5 million
- Men's ice hockey: $1.2 million
- Women's basketball: $250,000

It is possible to live comfortably on these sums, but certainly not lavishly, as many athletes quickly become accustomed to living. And remember: these figures represent income *before* Uncle Sam, premium repayments, close acquaintances, and business associates get their take. In many cases, there may not be that much left. Trust me on this.

And now a word about one of the athlete's least favorite subjects: fines.

In late November 2004, there was a much-publicized (and videotaped) brawl during a game between the Indiana Pacers and the Detroit Pistons. A fan or fans apparently precipitated the melee, but soon fists and fur were flying in every direction from the court and the stands. By the time the smoke cleared, it was the NBA's equivalent of the shot heard 'round the world, not to mention one *gi-normous* black eye in the already none-too-pleasant image of the professional athlete.

It was a troublesome spectacle for all involved. Children, in the stands to see and enjoy their favorite athletes in action, instead were witness to a display (from both fans and athletes) of shocking actions and the resulting repercussions.

Someone once said, "Don't worry about the fact that children may not listen to what you say. Worry that they watch everything you do." With that said, it is a disservice to paint all athletes with the same brush (especially when those involved have asked for and sought forgiveness).

Here are a few personal observations.

1. I am confident that those players who received the stiffest penalties, suspensions, and loss of pay for a good portion of the season had financial plans in place for their salaries, which were derailed when this unexpected incident occurred.
2. These players have people who depend on them financially, including close acquaintances, and business associates. Thus, the impact of the penalties and suspensions will not be limited to the players.
3. The best options to cover living expenses in a situation like this are a line of credit from a bank against future earnings and interest from

investments and/or endorsements. Borrowing dramatically increases overall debt in cases like this.

4. The court of public opinion has rendered a verdict. Players involved in this debacle can expect boos and verbal attacks from the stands in opposing arenas for some time to come. Envisioning themselves in the place of those fans who were involved in the brawl, opposing fans will ask themselves, "What if that had been me?"

It may seem inappropriate at this point to discuss collegiate athletes and scholarship hunting, but I believe there is a connection with the overall theme of this section on paying and playing.

> *There's no free lunch. Don't feel entitled to anything you don't sweat and struggle for.*
> —**Marian Wright Edelman**

Professional athletes who went to college before turning pro remember their college days, especially if they were fortunate enough (or talented or smart enough) to land a scholarship. The advantages for a college athlete on scholarship were undeniable and often lucrative.

I'm not here to debate superstar college athletes and whether they should receive additional stipends above and beyond a scholarship. But on top of free tuition and room and board, as well as tutors and other "legal" fringe benefits, scholarship athletes clearly receive a great many perks not available to non-scholarship students. Moreover, it is a well-known fact that college coaches will practically line up for miles to offer prize recruits scholarships to their schools of higher learning. Competition for the best talent is nothing, if not keen. And if he is smart, an athlete can take advantage of the opportunity to obtain a meaningful degree secure in the knowledge that no outstanding student loans will await him (or his parents) the day after graduation, as will await "regular" students and their parents.

As Gary Trent observed, "People are looking for scholarships and a free ride."

It's a view shared by many athletes who have been confronted by people seeking connections to free money, free vacations, free tickets, free passes, free perks, and on and on *ad nauseum*. It is as though being on scholarship has become a mode of living that some people wish to extend well beyond the campus into the real world.

Beyond the ethical considerations, professional athletes are just too busy—being professional athletes and trying to hang on to what they earn long enough to retire and enjoy it.

Chapter 7

"You Ain't All That!"—
Ignore the Fans at Your Own Risk

So you want to be a star, huh? Well, it's not a bad way to make a living. But, like everything else in life, it does have a price tag. Consider the following true story involving Tom Kenny, the voice behind the highly successful animated character SpongeBob SquarePants.

As the show became popular, people started to recognize Kenny. As he discovered, fame can bring out the worst in some fans.

One summer, Kenny's father died unexpectedly. He recalled being overwhelmed by the larger than expected gathering to pay tribute to his late father. In fact, he said it reminded him of a scene from Frank Capra's classic film, *It's a Wonderful Life*.

It was reported that one woman who approached him offered condolences, and then abruptly reached into her handbag and pulled out a "SpongeBob" CD.

"I hope this isn't inappropriate, but could you sign this?" she asked.

Although he signed without comment, he later remarked, "The only thing that would have been more inappropriate is if I had leaned over and used my father's forehead to steady myself."

Every sports league owes its very existence to fans.
—NHL Commissioner Gary Bettman

I want to make it clear that, as a professional athlete, I would be the last person to understate or underestimate the importance of fans.

On February 16, when NHL Commissioner Gary Bettman announced the cancellation of the 2005 NHL season due to unresolved salary issues between the players and the owners, he apologized to the fans—more than once. He said the fans deserved better. The question remains, however: Did the fans take him at his word?

The owners and the players face what sportswriter Scott Burnside called "the ominous task" of repairing relationships with fans. But Commissioner Bettman knows, just as everyone connected with the business of sports knows, that without fans who are eager to spend money to watch us do what we do, there would be no celebrities. And while there might be professional athletes, we wouldn't get paid as much were it not for the fans we attract.

But just as all professional athletes and celebrities are tarred with the same brush when one of our number behaves badly, so too are fans. All it takes is one—like the woman who didn't see anything wrong with asking Tom Kenny for an autograph at his father's funeral (!)—to give all fans a bad name (and, perhaps, to remind us that the word "fan" is derived from "fanatic").

Yet if Mr. Kenny had pointed out, however politely, the inappropriateness of the timing of her request, guess who would have borne the brunt of the bad publicity that would have ensued. I'll give you a hint. It's not the lady with the SpongeBob CD.

In an article called "The Culture of Celebrity," journalist Jill Neimark argues that fans and celebrities are diminished by the ways in which the nature of fame has changed in modern times. Thanks in no small measure to technology, celebrities (or, more accurately, concocted images) are rapidly disseminated, marketed, and sold. Fame is thus immediate and instantaneous, and public fascination with it is more fickle than ever.

"As our culture generates endless images, we are fed more and more information about people who are less and less real," Neimark states. She believes that the scope of world events is thus reduced to personalities, and that our vision becomes limited to the foibles and failings of those particular individuals.

Neimark goes on to note that because information comes at us with incredible speed and in innumerable changing faces and stories (such as through the networks Court TV or CNN), we know far too much (or think we do, at any rate) about celebrities—their love affairs, their private conversations, the color of their underwear, how many nose jobs they've had, and on and on *ad nauseum.*

Someone once observed that the "hero was distinguished by his achievement, the celebrity by his image." Put another way, a celebrity is well known for being—well known. We could become the first society in history to make our illusions so vivid, persuasive, and realistic that we can live in them.

If my fans think I can do everything I say I can do, then they're crazier than I am.
—Muhammad Ali

I don't know about you, but to me that's a frightening thought. The public, some portion of it anyway, looks at athletes (and other celebrities) and sees a person—or a world—that does not really exist. Yet they want to be near that person or in that world, which is not possible. Nor can most people understand what it is like to be the center of this kind of "fishbowl" attention.

In his article "What Do Superstar Athletes Really Owe the Mere Mortals?" Christopher Young wrote about the unexpected responses of some superstar athletes when confronted by awestruck and adoring fans. Quite often the fans walk away disappointed because the *star* failed to shine—at least, he didn't seem to want to shine on them. It's an encounter the fan will not forget. It's also an encounter that the professional athlete is unlikely to remember.

Young added, "When we root for players on our favorite team, we feel like we know them." Unfortunately, that is a misconception and fans often come away from even brief personal contact with some pro athletes disappointed and feeling that their idols have turned out to be first-class jerks instead.

Young went on to highlight a series of questions that every athlete must seriously consider: "So what is reasonable to expect of our sports heroes, during and after their professional lives? What do these athletes owe the people with whom they interact on and off the field? What is the minimum standard of conduct and obligation?"

Evidence suggests that because of their off-court, seemingly unfriendly personas, some professional athletes may be losing their appeal to fans. Sportswriter Mike White has noted, "Television ratings, as well as attendance figures in [some] professional sports, are down . . ."

In a *Washington Post* article, writer Sally Jenkins noted that sports fame is a different kind of fame than any other. The public seems to react more intensely to it and to imbue sports figures with a kind of Greco-Roman greatness, which we, the public, are then prepared to worship. Based on that impossible ideal, we classify athletes as good or bad, winner or loser. Small wonder that we are surprised when an athlete turns out to have many of the same complexities common to ordinary folk.

When we watch an athlete perform, we believe he's real and that the game is a real event in which people demonstrate genuine human behavior. So we feel justified in drawing tidy conclusions about him based on demeanor and appearance. Even commercial enhancements further present athletes as characters vs. flesh and blood and often flawed human beings like the rest of us.

For better or worse (usually worse), some people want desperately to believe that athletes are not strangers.

Jenkins has a point, especially about fans' expectations of athletes. While I don't think fans are becoming disenchanted with sports as a form of entertainment, it is possible that they are becoming more and more turned off by what they perceive as the arrogant air of self-importance that some athletes display, albeit sometimes unintentionally.

Still, it is or should be a two-way street. Certainly athletes should, to the extent possible, show themselves in the best light when confronted by an ordinary working fan who may have shelled out fifty bucks (or more) for a ticket to the game. By the same token, fans should, to the extent possible, remember that an athlete is not an android or a robot. He is a human being, and like everyone else at the end of a tough day, he may be tired, cranky, annoyed, and frustrated. Or maybe he had an argument with a family member, or his son is flunking geometry, or his mother is sick.

Or he thinks you're going to ask for money (or something else) instead of an autograph, and he doesn't feel like taking the time to figure out how to say no politely.

Whatever. The fact that the professional athlete makes more money than the average person does not mean that he is exempt from the same bad hands that life deals to all of us sooner or later. So if he isn't all smiles and handshakes and gratitude when you ask for that autograph, just cut the man a little slack!

This holds especially true for those occasions when fans and athletes "collide" (so to speak) away from the athletic event.

No doubt you have heard stories about celebrities and athletes who literally cannot go out in public without being mobbed. Since this is something that will never happen to most ordinary people, it is difficult to explain how disturbing—even frightening—it can be.

The story is told that one day back in the day, while Marilyn Monroe and an actress friend were walking down the street in New York City, the friend expressed her surprise that they had not been mobbed by adoring fans. Monroe, it seems, had developed an effective disguise for occasional forays into the public. Surprisingly, there were no wigs or dark glasses involved, only a raincoat with a small hood. She simply used her skills as an actress to project an entirely different persona. In effect, she dissociated herself from "Marilyn Monroe," and became, for that moment, Norma Jeanne Mortenson (her real name.) "Do you want to see me do 'her?,'" Marilyn is said to have asked her friend. With that, she took off the raincoat, shook her blonde mane into place, and flashed the smile that broke a thousand male hearts in the '50s. Within seconds, a mob formed, and the two women had to make a run for it to escape being trampled. The crowd wanted Marilyn Monroe. They neither knew nor cared about Norma Jeanne Mortenson. The fact that these two seemingly separate and distinct women existed in the same package is something only a psychiatrist could explain.

Oprah Winfrey has remarked on similar experiences of times when she was not recognized simply because she was not wearing make up.

Ninety percent of the information (on websites) isn't true, (and) the pictures aren't really me.

—Denise Richards

In the same vein, albeit to a lesser extreme, fans often perceive athletes as having two distinct and conflicting personalities. This explains why Michael Jordan can't walk down to the corner grocery store to pick up a few things. Inside, he may feel just like any other guy who needs to pick up a few things from the grocery store, but to the public, the minute he steps outside he's "Michael Jordan Superstar," and for better or worse, he becomes fair game.

Small wonder that athletes and celebrities go to such great lengths to maintain their privacy. Apart from any other considerations, it is first and foremost an effort to introduce at least some semblance of normalcy into their otherwise completely abnormal lives.

One afternoon as I was leaving a golf course near my home, I ran into the owner. "Where have you been?" she asked, pleasantly. When I told her I'd been working on *Hook Me Up, Playa!* and what it was about, she told me about an incident with a mega-star athlete in the Tampa Bay area who also frequented the club. Approached by an autograph-seeker, the player had been (to her way of thinking) unnecessarily rude, and her opinion of him was thus less than exemplary.

Similarly, my neighbor, Mr. Evans, told me of an encounter with a famous Major League Baseball player. Let's just say that the meeting did not leave Mr. Evans with a positive impression. Here is his account of what happened.

"I first met this particular athlete in Milwaukee many years ago, when his team was playing in the World Series. He was meeting with some upper-echelon executives from my company about a possible endorsement opportunity. Executives from the company brought him over to my table, where a group of employees and I were sitting at a local restaurant, just to say hello. It was a brief encounter and certainly a bigger moment for me than it was for him.

"Many years later, in a sporting goods store here in Tampa, I ran into the same player. I was talking to another gentleman about a pair of shoes I was thinking of buying, and the player overheard our conversation. I recognized him and started to say hello and engage him in a little small talk, but before I could get the words out he cut me off and walked out of the shoe department and presumably out of the store. I've thought about that encounter a lot, and it still seemed odd for him to react that way."

It should also be noted that Mr. Evans didn't ask the (then ex-) athlete for an autograph or anything else, nor was he trying to be imposing. Yet somehow the former sport's icon apparently felt threatened.

Let me say, first of all, that like it or not, athletes have an obligation to be courteous and to conduct themselves in a manner that does not perpetuate the already tarnished image of athletes to which the general public subscribes.

> *No one is too big to be courteous, but some are too small.*
> *—Unknown*

That said, however, the public should know that a lot of professional athletes who may be comfortable interacting with fans at sporting events or during interviews with media reps may actually be quite reserved in other circumstances. It is easy and even understandable for a fan to misinterpret this as deliberate rudeness personally directed toward him or her for no apparent reason.

Then, too, it is difficult for fans to understand how much an athlete values his "downtime," the time when he is away from the court and the press—the time when he comes closest to being himself. Athletes jealously guard that time and are loathe to give it up—even the few minutes it takes to sign an autograph or exchange a few words of greeting.

Mutual understanding, as difficult as that may be for two groups of people who live in different worlds, is the only true bridge across the chasm that separates professional athletes from the fans on whom their livelihood depends.

Chapter 8

Plan B

Expect the best, plan for the worst, and prepare to be surprised.
—Dennis Waitley

You've Got What It Takes

"Tough ain't enough."
—Clint Eastwood
Million Dollar Baby

PRODUCER, ACTOR, AND AWARD-WINNING director Clint Eastwood, who has coined a number of phrases that became part of American (indeed, world) jargon, has done it again. In the multi-Oscar Award-winning film *Million Dollar Baby*, speaking to would-be boxer Hillary Swank, Eastwood gruffs out the soon-to-be-immortal phrase, "Tough ain't enough." (Get your bumper stickers and T-shirts now! Avoid the rush.)

In professional sports (some might even go so far as to say in life in general), "tough" really isn't enough. The competition in professional sports is fierce and intense. Through the various media (primarily television), the public gets to know about players' skills, the strategies of various coaches, and which athletes stand out from the others as particularly gifted and talented.

But the smart athletes (and doctors and lawyers, for example) know that to assure personal, professional, and especially financial survival, you have to bring more than just talent and skill to the table. Determination is the other essential element. Talent and skill can be learned and enhanced. That's what coaches do. They teach aspiring athletes how to be stronger and faster. But there are those who believe that determination cannot be taught. Those who have more of it will go further in sports—and in life—than others who may be more talented and possess greater skills.

It is my belief that parents, especially the parents of athletically-gifted children, must be the source of the intellectual and psychological stamina from which determination springs. To a large extent, that is what *Hook Me Up, Playa!* is about: teaching young athletes (and other young people as well) about intellectual and psychological survival in a competitive environment where "tough" isn't enough.

Parents must also be the source of a realistic world-view for their children. Some young people will make it to the pros. Many will not. Either way, every young person needs to know the value of planning. In the world of professional sports, Plan A is what you will do if you get to the pros. Plan B is what you will do if you don't, or if you get there, but unforeseen circumstances bring your career to an early end.

Please note: this is not about failure. Here (from an unknown author) is a partial list of famous failures.

- **Michael Jordan** was cut from his high school basketball team.
- Boston Celtics Hall of Famer **Bob Cousy** suffered the same fate.
- **Babe Ruth** struck out 1,300 times—a major league record.
- A newspaper editor fired **Walt Disney** because he *"lacked imagination and had no good ideas."*
- **Einstein** was four years old before he could speak.
- **Isaac Newton** did poorly in grade school and was considered "unpromising."
- **Beethoven's** music teacher once said of him, "As a composer, he is hopeless."
- When **Thomas Edison** was a youngster, his teacher told him he was too stupid to learn anything. He was counseled to go into a field where he might succeed by virtue of his pleasant personality.
- **The Beatles** were refused a contract and dismissed by Decca Records executives in 1962. "We don't like their sound. Groups of guitars are on the way out."

Heavy hitters, the ones who hit the most home runs, also strike out a lot.

—Unknown

You will make mistakes, but you are not a failure until you start to blame someone else. Parents must teach their children to believe in themselves. Parents must see greatness in their children. Let them know it. Expect it of them. This is the key to success, regardless of the chosen career path.

Parents: make it clear that goofing off and playing around in the back of the room in high school—because, after all, you've got the moves and you're goin' to the pros—is unacceptable. Make sure your young athlete knows that even if he makes it to the pros, if he can't read a financial statement, the chances are very high that somebody smarter than he is will steal most, if not all, of the money that comes from that zillion-dollar pro contract. Uneducated, but physically skilled and talented amateur and

You can get robbed with a piece of paper, the same as you can by someone with a gun.

—Gary Trent

pro athletes are just so much raw meat for scam artists, so-called financial advisors, crooked accountants, and other such scavengers.

So, even if you make it to the pros, it's important to continue to educate yourself. Learn as much as you can as often as you can about everything—but especially about finances. Use the same tenacity and skill that comes into play when avoiding tacklers to avoid being ripped off by people you thought you could trust. Then, if you make it to the pros, you may get to keep whatever Uncle Sam and his state relatives don't take.

As for Plan B? Surprise! Get your education. Learn as much as you can as often as you can about everything—but especially about finances.

As has been stated more than once in these pages, an athlete's career, assuming he stays healthy and remains a valuable asset to the franchise, is short: three to five years. That means an eighteen- to twenty-one-year-old first-round draft pick will likely find himself out of work (out of this line of work, anyway) well before his thirtieth birthday.

Out—of—work. As in, no check every two weeks. If he hasn't planned ahead, if he hasn't saved and invested a sizeable portion of the money he earned during his career, an athlete will find himself in big trouble. And if he has a wife and children, he will not be alone in that floundering boat.

Failing to plan is the same as planning to fail!
—Martin Lemieux

One businessman commented, "We've got a huge population of young people who can't adequately read or write and therefore are unemployable, except for manual labor or low-paying service industry jobs. They end up being frustrated and unhappy because they can't support themselves, much less a family." Certainly, he wasn't the first one to make this observation. Nor is he likely to be the last. But it is serious food for thought.

Financial planning is crucial regardless of what your career goals may be, but especially for professional athletes since their career span is very short and equally unpredictable.

Get into the habit of planning ahead regularly and be sure to consider business and family together when setting up a financial plan. (It is surprising how many athletes—and people in other professions—forget to do this.) Keep a list of your goals, and develop plans for your long-term future—as well as for the coming day, month, and year. These goals will help you budget your time and money and move toward fulfillment of your dreams, which includes financial security for your family.

Sports history is rife with sad tales of great athletes who ended their careers with nothing except a few newspaper clippings to show for years of hard work. A young athlete with a "that'll never happen to me" attitude might as well set fire to his paychecks because he won't have them long enough to enjoy them—that is, beyond the temporary pleasures of high-end cars and expensive clothes and jewelry that are all a part of what is called livin' large.

And while we're on the subject, this is a good place to bring up the subject of debt—more specifically, young people and debt.

Two sobering statistics from the MSN Money website (source: www.moneycentral.msn.com):

- Americans between *twenty-five and thirty-four* have the second highest rate of bankruptcy, after those in the thirty-five to forty-four-year-old age group.
- If you have a $2,000 credit card balance and you only make the minimum payment each month, with no new charges, it will take sixteen and a half years to pay off! That adds up to more than $2,500 in interest fees.

In her article "A Generation Weighed Down by Debt," Marilyn Gardner offers some equally sobering thoughts.

Gardner interviewed a young publicist and recent graduate of Boston University who lamented having already maxed out her credit cards and being unable to keep up with the credit cards and other bills even though she was making a decent salary. "I'm just trying to get by," the young woman said.

Hoping and trying to get by. Those six little words echo around the country as young adults struggle to stay financially afloat. Gardner believes that this may be the most indebted generation of young Americans ever.

In trying to determine what is behind this trend, Gardner identifies two possible causative factors: exponential increases in college costs and the aggressive marketing of credit cards to college students.

College costs soared in the 1990s and by the end of that decade a large percentage of students had borrowed money. According to Ms. Gardner's article, in 2002, the average graduate owed nearly $19,000 in student loans.

And then there are the credit cards. Gardner points out, "Many indebted young adults trace the beginning of their slippery economic slope to the first day of college." At the registration desks, credit card companies often hand out free T-shirts to anyone who completes an application. To sweeten the deal, there are usually offers of 0 percent interest! (an offer, which, if one reads the fine print, is often only good through the first month.)

While young people incur considerable debt just to pay for basics, they also get into financial trouble because of impulse spending.

As of December 2004 three credit reporting agencies—TransUnion, Experian, and Equifax—offer consumers a free credit report annually. Everyone, but especially young adults, should get copies of all three. It's a much needed eye-opener as well as a reality check.

Perhaps Charley Hannah summarized it best. "The simple truth is that there is no place for [financial] innocence among young athletes—or young people in general. They are going to have to grow up real fast."

I am indeed rich, since my income is superior to my expense, and my expense is equal to my wishes.
                                                              —*Kahlil Gibran*

There Really Is No Free Lunch

WHAT IS A perk? First, there is no such noun, as a form of speech. A perk, in the manner that is used by most people, in fact refers to "a perquisite—a privilege, gain, or profit incident to regular salary or wages; especially one that is expected or promised."

I don't know how the word "free" came to be associated with perks. As you can see, there is nothing in the definition to suggest that perks are free. Yet for some reason, we have come to believe that they are.

Well, the truth is, perks are not free. They almost always come with strings attached—monetary strings. For example, as noted earlier, NBA players are given four complimentary tickets to every home game. Close associates and even complete strangers covet these tickets, particularly if the team is on a winning streak. Thus, it is often difficult for an athlete to decide who gets them, especially since there are likely to be hard feelings on the part of those who are left out. But here's the interesting part. Because of government-imposed legislation, some NBA franchises are now requiring players to pay income tax on the value of those "free" tickets. Just as company employees in the corporate world must pay tax on so-called perks, professional athletes now must do likewise. Whether this new requirement will spread beyond the NBA, I cannot say, although if I were a gambling man, I would put money on it. But one thing is crystal clear: those "free" tickets are not free.

Let's do a little math here. With forty-five games (four preseason and forty-one regular season) at approximately $90 a ticket, let's say, each player will have to pay income tax on $4,050. This does *not* include playoff game tickets, which of course cost more. Okay. So that's not a huge tax bill, but it is a bill. Moreover, teams advancing well into the playoffs can expect an incrementally higher tax liability.

These sorts of issues go a long way toward explaining the frustration many athletes experience (and young athletes will experience if they are in the business long enough) confronting the incessant array of hook-me-uppers looking for handouts and favors. Gary Trent summarized it well.

"I want to tell them, 'Get out there and get your own.' It's harsh, but it's just that simple. I have a salary because I am earning a salary—every play. When I go up to get a rebound, I earn it over another player's back.

That player may be a friend of mine, but doesn't mean he will give me that rebound. If he does, he won't be playing very long. We each earn every steal. My doctor tells me that the vertebrae in my back are out of line from all the pounding my spine took throughout my career. I have scars on my knees from being scoped. I literally put my life at risk, even if it's just getting on a plane to fly to the East Coast to make sure a game gets on TNT tomorrow.

"I'm not whining, and I'm not complaining. What I am saying is, 'Don't ask me for anything.' And don't believe all the glamour and glitz from the NBA highlights. That's not even half the story. To an outsider it may not look like I'm earning my salary. But I know that I am. And that means I'm not going to part with it lightly or easily, and certainly not just because somebody asks for part of it. Not going to happen."

Gary added, quite rightly, that most of the stress, especially the financial stress, in the life of an athlete comes from other people—people whom motivational speaker Les Brown has called "toxic." You have to get the toxic people out of your life.

"People will drain you, financially and emotionally," Gary said. "So whether it is a family member, a friend, a homeboy, a woman, whoever it is, you have to bring that relationship to an end. It's that simple."

Call it a subset of Plans A and B.

Chapter 9

Maturity: Believe the Hype!

During my career, people would come up to me and say, "Great Game, Bill. I want my son to grow up just like you." But then I begin to wonder. Those people didn't know a thing about me personally; for all they knew, I might be a child molester. Yet here were parents saying they wanted to model their children after me, instead of after themselves. I began to cringe at those moments; instead of flattering me, they made me sad.

—Bill Russell

IN A NATIONALLY TELEVISED INTERVIEW, former NFL star and Heisman Trophy Winner Ricky Williams admitted to struggling with cravings for marijuana. He had, he said, used marijuana in an effort to find that state of bliss which he had not found playing pro football. He had also sought and failed to find that bliss in various religions. For me, his most troubling confession was that he had thought money would bring him freedom. Instead, it became a form of bondage.

I've never met Williams, but I tried to read between the lines to see if I could understand the pain he was clearly suffering. As a star running back at the University of Texas, no doubt he couldn't wait to get his first taste of the good life. Indeed, he amassed great fortunes as a pro athlete. Yet, somehow, that wasn't enough.

For better or worse, Williams is not an aberration. Nor does his story represent some phenomenon peculiar to the late twentieth and early twenty-first centuries. Only technology and the times change. Human behavior—human desire—is the same now as it has always been. People have always believed that money is the solution to life's problems. What most people don't know, until and unless they achieve a degree of wealth, is that money creates almost as many problems as it solves.

I would as soon leave my son a curse as the almighty dollar.

—Andrew Carnegie

Still, as noted earlier, everybody wants to be a millionaire. State lotteries are based on the fundamental desire of all people to be rich. Hundreds of books are written on it, and dozens of so-called reality shows are designed around people's fundamental willingness to do frequently bizarre and outright insane things in pursuit of a promised fortune.

I believe another lesson that young people need to learn, from their parents, if possible, involves not just the value of saving and investing money, but also a sober and realistic appreciation of the things that money can and cannot do.

Suffice it to say, there is a great deal of humor, but little if any truth, in the old saying, "Anyone who says money can't buy happiness doesn't know where to shop."

Much of this book has been devoted to the problems and feelings of athletes in a world full of people whose sole desire appears to be finding ways—whether illegal or simply unethical—to separate them from their money. In spite of those difficulties, I believe that the overwhelming majority of athletes care about the welfare of others. Beyond generous monetary donations, most give much of their time to community outreach and youth programs. A great deal of these activities do not receive media attention, in part because an athlete who is behaving badly, and thus living up (or down, as the case may be) to public perceptions, makes better copy than an athlete who spends Saturday afternoons working with kids at a community center. Then, too, an athlete often prefers that these types of activities get no media attention. Absent cameras, lights, and reporters, he is more free to be himself and thus to "be real" with and for the kids, who get to see him as a person and a mentor, and not just as a superstar.

Part of the maturity process that an athlete (or any young person) must exude is giving back to others in meaningful ways. Here are a few examples of community and youth-centered efforts sponsored in whole or in part by professional athletes or their organizations.

1. **The Washington Redskins Charitable Foundation**, established in the year 2000, is committed to raising awareness of issues influencing youth in the region and using the unique assets of the Washington Redskins organization and its corporate and community partners to achieve measurable results that improve communities. (See www.washingtonredskins.com.)

2. **The Baltimore Ravens Annual Honor Rolls Program** salutes youth groups or organizations that provide outstanding volunteer service to communities. During each Ravens home game throughout the regular season, the winning groups receive up to 100 tickets to a game, Honor Roll T-shirts for all participants, official recognition during the game on the SMARTVISION screens, and further recognition in a public service announcement on WBFF Fox 45 in Baltimore the following week. (See www.baltimoreravens.com.)

3. **The New Jersey Nets and Devils Foundation** scholarship program recognizes students who have demonstrated leadership qualities and the desire to make a difference in the community. Students are selected based on their history of community service, financial need, and academic standing. Established in 1998, the program provides recipients with a $4,000 scholarship over a four-year period. Each scholarship is matched by a participating educational institution, raising the total financial package to $8,000.
(See www.newjerseydevils.com.)

4. **New York Yankee Derek Jeter's Turn 2 Foundation** has a threefold mission: to create signature programs that will acknowledge and reward youths who avoid drugs and alcohol and those who choose a healthy lifestyle; to fund organizations that help prevent and treat teenage substance abuse; and to leverage the integrity and popularity of Derek Jeter by hosting special events for today's youth that serve as a platform for his message. (See www.turn2foundation.org.)

5. **The Jalen Rose Foundation**, named after its founder, former Chicago Bulls guard Jalen Rose, provides funding for programs that support single-parent families, works with community kitchens to provide meals to individuals and families in need, and supports non-profit organizations that assist deserving children in achieving their educational goals. Rose also established the **Jalen Rose Chicago Children's Foundation** to aid local children who have lost a parent. (See www.jalenrose.com.)

6. Five-time NBA All Star Chris Webber founded the **Chris Webber Foundation for Troubled Youth** in his hometown of Detroit. The foundation provides scholarships to students who strive to do their best in the classroom and in the community.
(See www.nba.com/community/webber.)

It is important for you to understand that I did not include this information just to give "bragging rights" to my fellow athletes. My goal here, as in the rest of this book, is to ameliorate, to the extent possible, the public perception of athletes as perpetually arrogant, hopelessly self-involved, mindlessly self-indulgent, and essentially overgrown jocks. This is no more true of athletes 100 percent of the time than it is of doctors or lawyers or people in any other profession. We just get the light shined on us more often.

My hope is that the next time (or the first time) you run into a pro athlete, be it after a game or in a shoe store, you will think twice before judging him too harshly should he fail to treat you with the courtesy you unquestionably deserve. Keep in mind that if his guard seems to be up, it could be because he thinks you're about to ask him for a hookup, even though your only goal may be to express your appreciation for his skills and talent.

Or it could be that he's just having a bad day. All the money in the world doesn't stop those from cropping up in everyone's life from time to time. So if he's grumpy, tell him you read *Hook Me Up, Playa!*, then leave him be.

On a personal note, writing this book was a kind of catharsis for me. Psychologists (and theologians) tell us that forgiveness is about letting go of the past. It doesn't mean that whatever wrong was done to you is suddenly okay. It means you are prepared to move on without bitterness, which is excess baggage you refuse to carry down the new roads of the future.

With *Hook Me Up, Playa!* I have already released the vestiges of frustration and hostility toward those who have treated me unfairly whether by accident or by design. Without extending forgiveness, how can we ever be forgiven when we offend others?

The word "closure" gets tossed around a great deal these days, sometimes to the point where I'm not sure it has any real meaning. I do know that it is a personal goal that can only be achieved by each of us in our own and individual ways. As the old hymn goes:

You got to walk that lonesome valley.
You got to walk it by yourself.
Ain't nobody here can walk it for you.
You got to walk it by yourself.

Pain is mandatory. Suffering is optional.

—An elderly black woman

Often we do not recognize the magnitude of our pain until we realize that we are not alone in having survived certain experiences. It's easy—far too easy—to feel that you are the only one who has been plunged into financial, psychological, and/or emotional turmoil.

Then, too, although I could (of course) be wrong, I believe that most people who have taken unfair advantage of an athlete's resources (time, money, whatever) are unaware of it, perhaps even blissfully so. Or perhaps they are aware of it, but prefer to assume that he will "get over it," thus equating strong muscles and athletic skills with a superhuman ability to ignore emotional pain. General Norman Schwarzkopf once said, "I don't want a man around me who can't be moved to tears. He's not human."

In the end, I know that if I allow those who have treated me unfairly to determine my mood and state of mind, then I will have allowed them to take from me something far more valuable than money and time. I will have allowed

Laughter is inner jogging.
—Norman Cousins

them to take a piece of my soul. Can't do that. I'm going to need my soul—all of it—in the future, even if I don't have a dime.

With this book, I have also learned more about the value of laughter, particularly the ability to laugh at oneself. I don't know how people who can't laugh at themselves get through a day, let alone an entire lifetime. Laughter is indeed therapeutic.

Hopefully, the lessons learned in dealing with financial issues and entanglements from a pro athlete's perspective will be beneficial to every reader, including trust, honesty, integrity, and due diligence among many others. My ultimate lesson learned: Being a blessing to others (who haven't breached the code of friendship) in spite of prior financial grievances with close acquaintances is necessary, but it doesn't always have to be monetarily. This book is my gift to you, with no strings attached.

Finally, it has been said that in times of crisis you find out who your true friends are. In the world of the professional athlete, where enemies too often masquerade as friends, people who have proven their friendship are more valuable than all the money in every contract that has ever been signed by any athlete in any sport on the planet.

> *Friendships born on the field of athletic strife are the real gold of competition. Awards become corroded, friends gather no dust.*
>
> *—Jesse Owens*
> *Four-time Gold Medalist in Track and Field*
> *at the 1936 Olympic Games*

My wish for you is friendship, in whatever the arena of your life.

Appendix A

Turning Pro: The Pros and Cons

You have teenagers thinking they're going to make millions as
NBA stars when that's not realistic for even 1 percent of them.
Becoming a scientist or engineer is.

—Dean Kamen

IN THE RECENTLY RELEASED MOVIE *Coach Carter*, actor Samuel L. Jackson portrays real-life former inner city high school basketball coach Ken Carter.

In an Associated Press (AP) interview with Colleen Young, Jackson acknowledged that the film isn't likely to elicit any big change in public school education, but said he will be happy if only a few kids see the film and rethink their priorities. Asked what he thought about Carter when he first heard about him, Jackson said he thought the coach's ideas were a refreshing change from the constant emphasis on winning at any cost. "I liked that about what he was doing, putting the idea out there that education is worth something," Jackson said.

As for Carter's methods and approach, Jackson sees value in those as well. He believes that somewhere along the line we have mistakenly replaced the student-athlete with the athlete-student and, in the process may have abandoned the truth that, while winning on the floor is fleeting, albeit a good feeling, an education is something that can't be taken away.

They don't need a handout.
They need a hand.
—Ken Carter

Although the real Coach Carter is no longer a coach, he is still teaching life lessons, as Joey Johnston, a reporter for the *Tampa Tribune* wrote in an article earlier this year.

A few months earlier, Carter spoke at a high school celebration of Martin Luther King's legacy.

"How many of you guys would like to make a lot of money?" asked Carter.

Hundreds of hands shot skyward.

Carter then asked how many of those in the young audience knew whose picture was on a fifty-dollar bill.

Silence and uncomfortable shuffling ensued.

One student finally called out the correct answer (it's Grant, by the way) and Carter summoned the young man to the stage and handed him a fifty-dollar bill.

He then asked the young people how they could expect to earn a lot of money (the already acknowledged universal goal of the assembled group) when they didn't know who was on the money? "You earn money with knowledge," Carter said, and went on to point out that this is the way the young man who knew who was on the fifty-dollar bill had gotten the money.

The foundation for Carter's wealth, notoriety, and celebrity status can be traced to his inner city alma mater. In 1999, as coach of the basketball team, he required players to sign a contract in which they agreed to maintain a 2.3 grade point average (GPA), to sit in the first row of all their classes, to perform community service, to address all teachers as sir or ma'am, and to wear sports coats and ties on game days.

By the time Carter received the first academic progress reports that year, the team was 13–0 after having won just four games in the previous season. Unfortunately, the academic reports showed that one-third of the players in his program were either failing or skipping classes. Carter's response was swift and, some would later say, harsh. The next day he wrapped padlocks around the gymnasium doors and hung a sign, "Practice Canceled. Report to the Library."

Holding up the signed contracts, Carter told the team members that because of their failure to carry out the agreement they signed, there would be no practices—or games—until the team raised its GPA to the agreed-upon level. It should be noted that the team included Carter's son, Damien, who had a 3.7 GPA, and two players who had been making straight A's. Still, Carter believed that a team is only as strong as its weakest link. So he held fast to his decision to cancel practices and games. Two games were forfeited. Practice time was devoted to studying with tutors.

If you think the community rallied around Carter for this decision, think again. Obsessed with the number one–ranked team, people called for Carter to be fired. It wasn't long before angry words became even angrier actions. Bricks were tossed through the window of Carter's sporting goods store. People drove alongside his car, trying to spit into the window. Asked how he could take away the game when that was the one thing the kids were going to cherish for the rest of their lives, Carter stated that there was a serious problem at hand if, in fact, winning at sports was the biggest thing in their lives. Taking the ball from his team and forcing them to go to class turned out to be a far more unusual step than he had anticipated.

Still, the decision earned Carter strong admiration from his fellow coaches across the country, who praised him for, among other things, choosing to be respected over being liked.

Carter told his audience that while it was okay to have dreams of professional athletics, they needed a backup plan, and that while sports is great, it is education that gives one a chance at life—education and holding oneself accountable, treating people with respect, and integrity. These are qualities that will never go out of style and for which one will be remembered long after the highest score of the last game is forgotten.

When USC's dynamic quarterback Matt Leinart announced his decision to remain in school and finish his degree rather than accepting a multi-million-dollar contract to make an immediate jump to the NFL, there was a degree of astonishment in the sports community. This is, after all, the age of instant gratification. And it doesn't get much more instant than a fat contract with the NFL.

During the coin-toss ceremony at Super Bowl XXXIX, in the middle of the field, along with the team captains, there were also four young children in peewee uniforms present. By way of noting their presence, one of the commentators quipped that we were looking at four future NFL prospects. It was a casual remark, and certainly no harm was intended by it. Still, I couldn't help wondering how many of the children's classmates, friends, neighbors, and family members saw them there and took the commentator's words to heart. More important, I wondered whether their parents would read too much into the innocent comment, not realizing how very few—very few—hopefuls make it to the NFL (or to pro sports in general).

Like the rest of *Hook Me Up, Playa!*, this section is meant to educate, especially young people and their parents. I am not about to condemn professional sports, the field of endeavor from which I have richly benefited. But as both a parent and a pro athlete, I believe I can offer a unique perspective and, maybe, throw a little reality check into the mix.

I must admit to being surprised by the depth of the controversy surrounding the issue of professional sports as a career choice. An (to my mind) alarming number of middle- and upper middle-class parents are pushing their children to excel in sports, with a view toward a scholarship and a lucrative professional contract. There was a time when this was almost entirely an inner city, poor neighborhood phenomenon.

Last September, *Sports Illustrated* profiled a successful businessman who is spending several thousand dollars a year on concentrated sports training for his young children to pave their way toward sport's stardom. As added insurance for his dreams for his children, he has also assembled an adult staff of trainers and nutrition experts to work with them.

"I love my kids," he declared. "I want to be a real father." He went on to say that, for him, one of the components of being a real father is providing a support system that will take his kids to number one in their field—or rather in the field he has chosen for them. Although he acknowledges the importance of their becoming good people, too, he also makes no apologies for his intention to make as much money as possible off their success.

It will be interesting to see how his children feel about his dreams when they are old enough to have a voice of their own.

Perhaps cause for more worry is the fact that doctors are seeing an exponential rise in the number of injuries in young athletes who, more often than not at the insistence of their parents, overtrain.

Many pediatric sports medicine specialists feel as if they have stumbled upon a new childhood disease, and they believe the culprit is the overaggressive culture of organized youth sports—and the overaggressive parents behind it.

"These are overuse injuries, pure and simple," a nationally prominent sports orthopedist noted in a recent *New York Times* article.

Many of the injuries, e.g., stress fractures, cracked kneecaps, frayed heel tendons, growth plate disorders, which were once found primarily in adults, are now becoming commonplace among children and adolescents.

Back in the day, which is to say as recently as the 1980s, sports for children was still little more than pickup games in parks and schoolyards—just good healthy outdoor exercise where the kids could enjoy themselves. At that time, only a fraction of the sports-related injuries doctors saw in children were the result of overtraining.

Now specialization in one sport at an early age and the year-round, almost manic, training that often follows, is the cause in more than half the sports-related injuries doctors are seeing in young people. It's no longer enough for kids to just play on a school team. They have to travel with two teams, go to four special camps in the summer, meet with nutritionists, and work with private instructors twice a week. Talk about no rest for the weary!

More troubling, these extreme regimens mean no rest and recovery time for overused young muscles, tendons, ligaments, and joints. Ironically, by pushing their children in this extreme manner, parents are more likely to be hurting their child's chances of making it to the top of the professional ranks, rather than helping.

It is not uncommon for the damage done by an overuse injury to be irrevocable. Should the doctor advise that the child give up the sport, it is often the parents who seem hardest hit by the news. Kids are usually happy to get back to just being kids, though they may never admit as much for fear of disappointing the parents.

In extreme cases, parents have even asked whether there is some type of surgery their children can undergo in order to maintain their ability to train and get ahead in the sport of choice. In other words, they want to know what medical science can do so that their children can keep doing the things that caused the injuries!

This is not to suggest that overtraining hurts all young athletes. Parents should be aware, however, that children (like many adults) may dismiss pain as the price one pays for getting to the top. Children may also force themselves to play in pain so as not to disappoint their parents.

To address these issues and to help parents with athletically-gifted children to maintain a proper and healthy perspective, the American

Academy of Orthopedic Surgeons and the National Athletic Trainers' Association has launched an educational campaign. They have summarized the theme of the campaign with the headline: "What will they have longer, their trophies or their injuries?"

It is generally agreed that a healthy and successful sports experience for a child depends on the parents' ability to build confidence and self-esteem and to make the sports experience rewarding, but more important, to make it fun. Parents need to teach their children to focus on the big picture, i.e., a healthy, successful, fulfilling life. For sports, as any professional athlete will attest, the best, perhaps the only way to succeed, is to focus on the process of the game—not the game itself and the outcome, whatever it may be. In the end, execution and doing one's best is more important than trophies and prizes.

After a game or other competition, parents should refrain from asking, first, whether the child or the child's team won. This sends the wrong message, i.e., that winning is the most important part of the game and that losing is the end of the world, as they know it. Instead, parents should simply ask if the child had fun. This gives the child the right impression and helps him or her focus on having a good time, which is (or should be) the true objective of the activity. Parents need to show their children that they support them as people—not just as potential superstar millionaire athletes and pint-sized bread winners.

Parents also need to help children learn not to equate performance outcomes with self-worth. A child (or an adult) is a person first and an athlete second. Success should never determine a person's self-esteem.

Sadly, the unsportsmanlike, often violent behavior of parents on the sidelines at children's games is becoming more and more prevalent. Parents are, first and foremost, role models, and as such, it is up to them to show composure and poise at all times. As every parent knows (or should know), children mimic parental behavior. Thus, parents need to provide a positive image—being particularly mindful of their reactions during a close game and/or in the face of questionable behavior by a competitor. If a child is to stay calm, composed, and in control, he or she must see that behavior in parents who show, by their good grace, that the most important value of the game is being a good sport.

Also, parents should never coach during competition. Too much coaching can lead to mistakes and cautious performance. The best thing a parent can do at a game is to be encouraging. If parents must coach, they should do it during practice sessions, and even then it should never be over done.

Society places too much emphasis on winning. Parents have to be the buffer zone for their children between what society deems to be important and what is really important for the health and well-being of the child—regardless of his or her athletic potential. Winning comes from working the process and enjoying the ride. Our children need to focus on and enjoy the challenge of each element of the sport.

Sports for a child should be a game—not a business. Let your child just have fun and enjoy the healthy competition.

Finally, parents should never attempt to substitute their agenda for the child's. Athletes (young and old) compete for many reasons. Some just enjoy the competition. Some like the social interaction. Others enjoy being part of a team, or enjoy the challenge of setting goals. Whatever the reasons, parents should never confuse their goals with their children's goals.

All of this is sound advice for all parents, of course, regardless of their economic status or whether their children are athletically-gifted.

Still, if you are a parent bringing up a child in an impoverished or disadvantaged neighborhood, you may be less inclined to heed it. At last estimate, more than 60 percent of the young black males in inner city neighborhoods believe that excelling in the sports arena is their only way out. That is not true, but try telling that to a young man living in an environment where the trash cans are always full; dilapidated (often hazardous) buildings are commonplace; drugs are prevalent; single-parent households are common; living conditions are deplorable; refrigerators and cupboards are often bare; crime, especially gang violence, is a constant presence; anxiety, chaos, and tension are relentless; and the only role models are on television. Under such conditions, the fact that the odds against a career in the pros are astronomical seems almost irrelevant. Just as the person who buys a lottery ticket every week in full knowledge of the outrageous odds thinks, "but somebody will win," so the young black male in impoverished circumstances thinks, "I'll be the one who makes it, in spite of the odds." That mind-set fuels their hunger to escape from the nightmare of their lives, as well as the belief that excelling in sports is the fastest way to achieve that goal.

There are, of course, many thousands of young people pursuing law, medicine, financial services, and other traditional careers. As a pro athlete, I would argue that none of these professions are less psychologically (or financially!) rewarding than professional sports. (Depending on the circumstances, they may be less glamorous, but I don't believe that is necessarily a bad thing.)

The larger point is that there are more jobs available, over the long haul, in traditional fields than in sports: jobs that, all other things being equal, will last exponentially longer than the average three- to five-year career of a professional athlete.

Perhaps the harshest reality for parents and their athletically-gifted children is this: most aspiring athletes will never play on the professional level.

As difficult as it may be for many people—especially parents—to accept and believe, *fewer than 2.9 percent* of high school males will play at the big-time NCAA level. *Fewer than 1 percent* will make it to the NBA. Percentages for the NFL, MLB, and NHL are slightly higher, but no less grim. (Source: www.ncaa.org.)

Does this mean young athletes shouldn't try? Absolutely not! It just means that they—and their parents—need to be realistic about the odds.

It is interesting to note that careers in professional sports were not a major objective in the '40s, '50s, and '60s. There were millions of fans, yet a large percentage of parents were not pushing their children in the direction of professional sports as a career. One reason for the change is, of course, the multi-million dollar salaries many professional athletes now earn. Throw in television's twenty-four hour sports stations and prime time games, and it is easy to understand what is attracting so many young people—and the enthusiastic support of their parents. A career in professional sports has achieved the same status as winning the lottery. But just as with the lottery, nobody talks much about the downside.

Please understand. I am not saying that professional sports are a bad way to earn a living. I am saying that they are not, as many would have you believe, the "perfect" way to earn a living. Far from it.

Parents, and their children, are attracted by the possibility of media attention, status, endorsement opportunities, and the pre-packaged appearance of lavish lifestyles. Some parents have gone so far as to take on second and third jobs in the hope of ensuring that their child makes it to the pros. Others are quitting their jobs entirely to manage their child's athletic career.

Coaches, teachers, psychologists, even some school administrators are sounding the alarm about this phenomenon. So far it appears that their warnings are falling on deaf ears. A tee-ball coach with whom I spoke said many parents become obsessed with the possibility of a career in professional sports for their children. Just in the past ten years, the increase in specialized sports coaching, enrollment in gymnastic academies, multiple camp and AAU tournament participation, and even special nutritional protocols is nothing short of astounding.

Sadly, there has also been a dramatic increase in violence among parents, for whom the drive to secure a place in the pros for their child can quickly turn ugly. One out-of-control parent savagely beat to death another parent at a hockey game while their children played. Unbelievable? Yes. Senseless? Incredibly! But a fact, nevertheless. And keep in mind this is just the behavior the public sees. What happens to some of the children behind closed doors is no doubt even more unthinkable.

When I was a small child, organized sports certainly had its share of, shall we say, overly committed parents who occasionally barked at officials because of an unfavorable or missed call. Yet, to my knowledge, there were few if any incidents of parents losing control to the point of violence, nor did they interpret any action, no matter how slight, against their child-athlete as a roadblock to a future career in professional sports.

It is true that gifted athletes enjoy a special place in society. And, as a practical matter, given the ever-increasing cost of college tuition, an athletic scholarship is nearly every parent's dream, particularly those parents who may not be able to afford to send their children to college on their own salary. Sure, there is a lot of talk about stock portfolios and investments, but to paraphrase the once-famous (and infamous) television character Archie Bunker, the average person's money is tied up in makin' a living. From that perspective, it's easy to understand why so many parents are pushing their children toward sports, a possible college scholarship, and ultimately, a career in the pros.

Even so, the extent to which the parental mind-set is skewed in the direction of sports is (or should be) disturbing. Alas, there appears to be no limit as to how far some parents will go in pursuit of a career in professional sports for their children.

A pint cannot hold a quart— if it holds a pint, it is doing all that can be expected of it.
—Margaret Deland

In an ESPN.com article, "Growing Up Next," Tom Farrey reported that a company in Melbourne, Australia, has devised and is marketing a DNA test for sports performance.

The test is based on the principle that certain people may have an inborn gift or talent for one activity while other people may have an inborn gift or talent for a different activity. The company's chief pathologist/geneticist is quick to add, however, "Sports performance is a jigsaw puzzle, and this is just piece No. 1."

This type of genetic research is still in its infancy. For now, the fact remains that a savvy coach with a stopwatch and yardstick can still gauge athletic ability with greater accuracy than any currently available tests.

As Farrey humorously but shockingly points out while discussing this test on his infant son, "How bizarre will it be if (when?) he's cut out for sprinting while he still can only crawl?"

Sports specialization is considered by many to be crucial if a young athlete is to achieve and maintain a competitive edge. Absent focus on a particular sport, a child's chances for a career in the pros dwindle substantially. Professional athletes who excel at more than one sport, while not unheard of, are rare today.

Not surprisingly, and for better or worse, media attention on superstar elite athletes and their lavish salaries has done more to reinforce the trend toward early specialization than anything else.

If tennis star Jennifer Capriati and former high school and USC football standout Todd Marinovich had not worked with specialized mentors and coaches starting in grade school and continuing in high school, it is arguable that they might never have been as successful as they became. Many parents are finding that they don't know how to maximize their child's sports potential. Absent this knowledge, it is all but impossible for a parent to grasp the magnitude of work necessary for a young athlete to reach the pinnacle of success in sports.

Of course, there are exceptions to every rule. According to some basketball fans' viewpoint, legendary NBA star Larry Bird used guts and determination to compete on the professional level against more physically-gifted opponents (although I don't agree that he was limited physically). Exceptionally driven to be the best, Larry outworked and outsmarted his opponents, they said. Psychological strength and mental agility as well as a deft shooting touch, which Bird displayed in abundance, can on occasion, overcome physical deficiencies.

> **Learn to lead without coercion.**
> **—Lao Tzu**

Yet it must be said that there are tremendous potential drawbacks to specialization. Not the least of these are the detrimental effects of specialization when it becomes a form of coercion, when parents coerce their children into a field (be it sports or something else) to which the child is not naturally drawn.

My personal view is that, given the very high odds against a young athlete making it to the pros, children should be encouraged to participate in a variety of sports, although specialization does serve its purpose in rare cases. Beyond career considerations, participation in sports helps children develop good fitness habits, build self-esteem, and learn the importance of having the right attitude. In addition, children learn:

- Teamwork
- Determination
- Critical thinking
- Strategy enhancement
- Focus
- Cooperation
- Goal planning

All of these traits are invaluable regardless of what career one chooses.

More particularly, a child who is under constant parental pressure to sacrifice his or her childhood for the sake of a future career in the pros usually reaches a boiling point, which can manifest itself in dangerous behaviors, such as drug and/or alcohol abuse, and in stress-related health problems. One or all of these can be part of something called the "specialization bug."

Todd Marinovich's NFL pro career went into a well-documented tailspin with the Oakland Raiders in the early '90s. Billed as the next prototypical quarterback, Todd never met his own expectations or those of others.

Jennifer Capriati's recently resuscitated tennis career has been one of the most remarkable sports stories in recent years. She, too, struggled in her early years as a professional, and many people saw her as the victim of overcontrolling parents.

Gymnast Dominique Moceanu and, from the entertainment field, McCauley Caulkin and Gary Coleman, are other examples of children seemingly lost to dreams of fame and fortune, whether parental or their own.

As difficult as it may be, parents need to remember that, ultimately, the decision to pursue a career in sports should belong to the young person.

For some parents, a career in pro sports for their children is a way to vicariously live out the dreams of their own youth. This does the young person a tremendous disservice.

My parents put skates on me at age two, the way it should be if you're serious, and I've always liked it.
—Bonnie Blair

But whatever the reasoning, in the end, it is the young person who will have to put in the time and the effort and face the tremendous mental and physical challenges involved. There is far too much at stake—far too much involved on many levels—for parents to push a young person into sports if that young person is not fully and personally dedicated to the pursuit.

Pros and Cons of Pursuing a Career in Professional Sports

Pros	Cons
College scholarships	Overburdening of children
Potentially lucrative signing contracts	Parental misunderstanding of full ramifications
Recognition	Extremely high odds against making it to the pros

Although some parents of gifted child-athletes are driven by the desire to vicariously live out dreams of their youth through the experiences of the children, many parents believe that the road to wealth lies in a professional career for their children. Thus, the "child as an investment commodity" is another increasingly commonplace phenomenon. This goes far beyond normal parental ambitions for their children. Moreover, children sense the reduction in their status from being loved for who and what they are to being viewed as the financial basis of future retirement plans.

Yes, pro contracts can be amazingly lucrative. The fact remains, however, that most professional athletes are not multi-millionaires. Moreover, the focus on wealth can rob children of their right to be children, since they cannot (nor should they have to) fast-forward their physical and cognitive growth to accommodate parental dreams. The resulting tension, stress, and anxiety can have undesirable—even tragic—results.

One day a couple who were in my home to provide me with an estimate for some closets told me about their son and his desperate desire for a career in professional sports. Apparently, he is an extremely bright child with potentially unlimited career opportunities, and they are, by all accounts, a middle-class family. They knew another couple who were pushing their child toward an athletic career, and still another couple whose son was an outstanding high school quarterback and had received a college athletic scholarship. They wanted to know what they could do to help their son move in that direction.

Although I was certainly aware that many parents were interested in possible career opportunities in professional sports for their children, I don't think the pervasiveness of the idea hit me until that day. Seemingly unfazed by the sheer odds against their son making it to the professional ranks, many parents assume that if he can get into college on an athletic scholarship, the move to the pros is more or less guaranteed. If there is something that could be further from the truth, I don't know what it is.

The fact remains that children crave love and attention, and most children want to please their parents, whether the career dreams involve pro sports or entertainment or beauty pageants for toddlers. Given media attention and ever-increasing salaries, it is doubtful that driven parents can be convinced to let their children choose the direction of their own lives.

With this in mind, based on my experience as a college graduate (now pursuing my MBA), a college athlete, and a professional athlete, I have provided some tips for parents and young athletes.

22 Tips for Current Athletes, Young Athletes, and Parents of Athletically-Promising Children

Some of these tips have been stated elsewhere in the book. But they all are important enough to be listed separately for you to clip and save for future reference.

1   Make education "Plan A." Plan B can be a career in professional sports—or not.
2   Realistically assess your chances (or, if you are a parent, your child's chances) of a career in pro sports.
3   **Parents:** Your child must be self-motivated. If you have to push him or her to practice and compete, then your child is not interested in a career in professional sports. **This is not a bad thing!** Find out what your child's interests are, and help him or her to move in that direction.
4   **Parents:** Icons are rare. Do not push your child to become "another" Tiger Woods or Michael Jordan or Wayne Gretzky or Venus (or Serena) Williams—or Rudolph Nureyev! However gifted your child

may be, the odds against him or her becoming a superstar are too high to calculate.

5 **Parents:** If, because of limited finances, you have to choose between investing in your child's education and investing in the possibility of a career for him or her in professional sports, **choose education.** This is especially true if potential income is the driving force behind the decision. There are many career choices for which the potential earning power is both very high and long-term.

6 **Parents:** Never deprive your child of the joys of being a child. Controlling their every move will only lead to resentment.

7 The key to happiness is having a purpose in life. If that includes a career in professional sports, fine. If it does not, that is also fine.

8 If you are committed to a pro sports career (or if your child is committed to it), find out what it takes—specifically—to have the best chance of reaching that goal. For example, a high school athlete must first be one of the best in the city, then in the state, then on a national level. Also, be aware that today's competition includes young people from other countries.

9 Work harder than you thought was possible, but at the same time, accept the fact that no matter how hard you work or how gifted you are, you may not make it to the pros. This is no cause for shame. **Parents:** Help your child understand this.

10 Treat your body well. That means nutritional eating and exercise, including training for strength, agility, speed, and flexibility. **Get the proper amount of sleep every night.** Without enough sleep, neither your body nor your mind will function at peak efficiency.

11 Never underestimate the importance of R.E.D.D.: Resilience, Effort, Discipline, and Determination. (Milwaukee Bucks All-Star Guard Michael Redd created this acronym to help him overcome his doubters. It worked.)

12 Take advantage of the opportunities afforded to you through competitive sports (such as seminars and tutors).

13 Never be selfish or stingy with your time in helping others improve. Always cheer and support them, even if they do not return the sentiment.

14 Be prepared to sacrifice leisure activities and unproductive acquaintances to improve your chances for success.

15 Regardless of what career you choose, **develop math skills, the capacity for critical thinking, *and* the ability to speak well.** If necessary, get help from a tutor.

16 Be personally involved in your financial affairs. Make it your business to know where your money is going and why.

17 If you sign a pro contract, your objective should be to invest and save the money you earn so that you can live off the interest without ever touching the principal.
18 It is the quality, not the quantity, of your practice that makes the difference between winning and losing.
19 In the beginning, at least, imitate successful athletes. This is a humbling process, but it works.
20 If you are one of the fortunate few who makes it to the pros, enjoy it while it lasts.
21 Do not allow your image to be tarnished. This has kept many deserving athletes from a career in pro sports.
22 Be cordial to the media. They bridge the gap between fans and players, and fans form their opinions of athletes based on what is reported in the media.

In truth, a high school athlete who believes he will make it to the pros stands a significant chance of corralling a college scholarship. So the goal for his parents, and for society in general, is to convince him to take advantage of the academic opportunities.

You have to expect things of yourself before you can do them.

—Michael Jordan

In a bold move to encourage college athletes to work as hard academically as they do athletically, the NCAA recently announced a novel program that will go into effect in 2006. The new program ties academic achievement to athletic competition. The idea, which first surfaced in 1991 as the brainchild of the Knight Commission on Intercollegiate Athletics, was initially dismissed as coming from reformers and "ivory-tower academics who weren't operating in the real world." No one thought it had a prayer of ever being enacted.

In the ensuing years, however, continuing academic scandals, along with the controversies surrounding the increased commercialization of college sports, prompted renewed and more vigorous calls for action.

So, beginning in 2006, teams on which fewer than 50 percent of team members graduate will lose scholarships. This action could be followed by ineligibility for bowl games and NCAA championships.

Although the full impact will not be known until after the NCAA releases data collected after these sanctions are in place, it is known that the effects will be felt most strongly in football, men's basketball, and baseball.

Under the new rules, a grant-in-aid cannot be re-awarded to an athlete who left the university having made no significant progress toward earning a degree. This rule will apply to all NCAA teams on an individual basis.

Penalties will be based on a newly devised measurement, the Academic Progress Rate (APR). With a maximum rate of 1,000, teams scoring below

925 will be penalized. Thus, an academically ineligible athlete who is not returning as a full-time student will lose his or her scholarship. Further, the number of scholarships a team can lose will be capped at 10 percent. This means an NCAA football team with an APR below 925 could lose nine scholarships.

The team would receive the full allotment of scholarships if the problems are corrected prior to the start of the following season.

Some question a strategy that clearly uses money to enforce academic progress. Others wonder whether schools will look for ways to create more courses or entire majors designed to keep athletes within the confines of the newly instituted and stringent academic standards, i.e., the creation of meaningless, but at the same time, "acceptable" degrees. It is also felt that coaches may be less likely to recruit athletes, who for whatever reasons, are less academically gifted and may have trouble adjusting to a rigorous college curriculum.

Whatever the potential downsides, the NCAA is generally being applauded for these academic policies and standards. Hopefully, student-athletes will graciously accept the challenge with vigor and determination, and truly take advantage of their "free" scholarship opportunities.

(For more details on the new NCAA academic policies, go to www.ncaa.org.)

But most young athletes who make the jump to the pros before graduation are black, and balancing the lures of a well-paying professional sports career with the less immediate benefits of an education is not easy. Asking a young man from an impoverished neighborhood to turn down a pro contract worth millions to stay in school long enough to graduate is, from the young man's standpoint, a lot to ask. A whole lot. And it goes well beyond the concept of instant gratification, with which we all grapple from time to time, be it about money or who gets the last piece of chocolate cake. For the young man, on one side are two or three more years of study toward a degree. On the other is being only two or three inches away from moving your family out of an undesirable neighborhood, and a dramatic (albeit possibly temporary) financial shift that takes them from nothing (or sometimes less than nothing) to lavish in a heartbeat. In short, it's asking a nineteen- or twenty-year-old to think well beyond his years of maturity, something that most young people are not emotionally, psychologically, or technically equipped to do.

Know also that sudden wealth will skew personal relationships, creating paranoia, greed, mistrust, anger, fear, shame, guilt, anxiety, and any number of other psychologically detrimental responses. Most people find it hard to believe that newly acquired wealth could bring about such problems, but financial experts say that experience is very common.

In an online article, "You're Suddenly Rich? Bummer," M.P. Dunleavy provides some helpful strategies for people who come into sudden wealth whether by having signed a lucrative pro sports contract, received a sudden and unexpected inheritance, or profited greatly from a business venture. (Oddly enough, these same strategies can also be helpful if you have just lost a great deal of money.)

First, park the money (however much there is) in a bank. Then don't do anything. Don't quit your job. Don't make any major financial decisions for at least three months. Give yourself time to think.

Next, get organized. Look at your assets and liabilities. Pay any taxes and high-interest debt (e.g., credit cards!). Review your insurance coverage.

Consider your situation in light of your income, net worth, fixed expenses, tax obligations, and perhaps most important, how much is left after all those things are accounted for.

Think about what you want to do. This will be particularly difficult if you have just come into what may be considered a fortune. The first thing many people—heck, most people—want to do is celebrate! In a *Columbus Dispatch* article, sportswriter Ken Gordon called it "the Austin Powers voice in your head that hollers, 'Yeah, baby!'"

But that's not about long-term goals. That's just a momentary emotional (albeit very pleasant) high. What you must do now is think seriously about what you want to do in the long term—about how you want to live, and what is important to you. Take all the time you need to establish priorities and decide how the money can be used to move in those directions.

Finally, consider the benefits of retaining a financial advisor—or team of advisors, to include an accountant, an investment person, and an estate attorney. After the initial emotional reaction, you may decide that your new financial situation is too large for you to handle personally. NOTE: Even if you hire financial advisors, always be aware of what your financial situation is and how your money is being handled. Having financial advisors does not absolve you of that responsibility.

Although money can create a lifestyle that is second to none, left unharnessed, that lifestyle can easily leave an athlete and his family no better off than when the ride began.

Thanks in no small measure to the media, most people idealize what life would be like with "Big Money." They cannot envision the dark side of the equation. Large amounts of money, like large quantities of drugs, can distort one's life. As Dunleavy rightly concludes, huge sums of money can change your parameters—change what you can do, what you no longer have to do, where you can live, how much you can travel, and so forth. It is no exaggeration to say that a sudden windfall induces a kind of shock to the system, making the necessity to move carefully and cautiously even more critical.

This last item brings us to another financial point already discussed earlier in this book, but which is worth repeating, about the importance of selecting the right financial advisor. Under no circumstances should you, as a young athlete (or a young anything else) abdicate responsibility for your own finances once you've found an advisor you can trust.

Always know where your money is going and why, regardless of whom you have hired or how much you feel you can trust that person.

Even keeping that in mind, however, you will need help in the proper handling, saving, and investing of your money (including things like planning for retirement, finding the best way to finance a new home, saving for your children's education, or simply putting your finances in order). This is particularly true for young athletes because their earning careers in the pros will be short. Thus, it becomes all the more important that they invest their money wisely.

The Certified Financial Planners (CFP) Standards Council offers some valuable suggestions to help you interview and evaluate financial planners to find a competent, qualified professional with whom you feel comfortable and whose business style suits your financial needs (see www.cfp-ca.org). The take-home news? Start by interviewing more than one financial planner so that you can get a good idea what services are available. Don't be afraid to ask as many questions as you need to for a full and open answer. Any professional will welcome them. Find out about the planners' qualifications and experience. Get a full explanation of their services and their approach to financial planning. Find out who will be working with you and how much they charge for their services. And as with any kind of contractual relationship, get the agreement in writing, and read the contract carefully before you sign it.

Of course, the planner will need to ask you many questions as well about your priorities, future plans, and family situation. Remember, however, that it is entirely up to you how much information you wish to provide. Also, this information will be recorded, and in many cases you will be asked to sign a document verifying that the information you provided is correct.

Financial planning is important not only as you look toward the future, but also if you are planning to get married. The USAA Education Foundation website provides a list of suggested questions to ask your significant other *before* you get married (see www.usaaedfoundation.org). Given the salaries of some professional athletes, this is particularly important.

I know. I know. It takes some of the romance out of an otherwise blissful event. But the more you know about each other, the better your chances of weathering the inevitable storms—particularly the financial storms—to come. Money is one of the major sources of stress in relationships. Ideally, your marriage will be a financial partnership as well as a partnership in other ways. You and your spouse must be prepared to make financial decisions and develop financial solutions as a team.

> **Question: Do you want to be right, or do you want to be happy?**
> **—Unknown**

To make that a reality, you must talk about your respective financial attitudes and expectations before you marry. Discuss spending habits, financial values, and priorities. Develop a dialogue that will allow you to understand each other's points of view—perhaps even the psychological basis for your individual views about money and money management.

If you decide to use the questions available on the USAA Education Foundation website, answer them individually first. Then compare your answers to those of your future spouse, paying special attention to areas of difference. Ideally, the results of your conversations, along with the answers to the questions, will provide the basis for some jointly agreed-upon decisions about how you want to handle money after you marry. Remember, of course, that there will have to be room for compromise. This type of financial preparation for marriage, particularly if you plan to have children, is an important and worthwhile investment in your relationship.

There is one other area for discussion, already touched on in Chapter 8, but which, in my opinion, cannot be overemphasized: credit cards. The seductive appeal of credit cards is the illusion of "free money." But the money you borrow comes at the cost of high interest, and if you don't pay off your balance each month, the interest charges can easily wind up costing you more—a whole lot more—than what you originally borrowed. That's right. Borrowed. Do yourself a favor and learn to think of credit cards as nothing more than high interest loans that can skyrocket if you miss just one payment. Some cards also charge annual membership fees just for you to have the *privilege* of holding the card. Know also that the way you handle your payments is compiled into a credit report. Missed payments mean a poor credit rating—and that can come back to haunt you, for example, if you want to buy a house or encounter an emergency that requires a loan.

The Collegeboard website (www.collegeboard.com) provides detailed suggestions on using credit cards wisely. In addition, the Federal Trade Commission provides free information to consumers on dozens of topics related to credit and credit cards, ranging from "Choosing and Using Credit Cards" to "Avoiding Credit and Charge Card Fraud." Take the time to learn their strategies and develop sound credit habits.

Apart from financial issues, being a professional athlete comes with a great deal of baggage—some good, some bad. Professional athletes have access to tremendous networking opportunities. Doors that are closed to the average person miraculously swing open when a professional athlete knocks. (Taking advantage of the business contacts can, if done wisely, be more lucrative than playing the game!)

Many professional athletes resist the idea of being a role model. This is understandable, albeit somewhat unrealistic. As a professional athlete, you'll find that your moves will be imitated both on the court (or ice or field) and off. So it's up to you to make sure you make the right moves.

Are professional athletes the only viable role models? Absolutely not!

As a child from a single-parent home, Ben Carson was called "dummy" and responded by almost killing a friend with a knife. Today (and I think

I can say this without fear of dispute) even Michael Jordan would agree that no young person, whatever his or her background, could find a better role model than Dr. Ben Carson, Director of The Johns Hopkins University Division of Pediatric Neurosurgery and Professor of Neurology, Plastic Surgery, Oncology, and Pediatrics.

> *If we recognize our talents and use them appropriately, and choose a field that uses those talents, we will rise to the top of our field.*
> —*Dr. Ben Carson*

A discussion of why millions of young people who know (or think they know) every detail about Michael and Shaq and "Sir Charles" have never heard of Dr. Carson or others in his "league" would fill another book. Certainly media attention is a primary factor. Young people, particularly those living in poor neighborhoods, are attracted to money and status. Professional athletes have (or seem to have) enormous quantities of both. Enormous responsibilities are part of the package.

> *To whom much is given, much is required.*
> —*Biblical Proverb*

Making a difference in people's lives—particularly young people's lives—is something that professional athletes can (and should) do. Most prefer to do so anonymously, or, at the very least, away from the media spotlight, lest they be accused of grandstanding and flagrant self-promotion. In my opinion, this is one of the greatest joys of a career as a professional athlete. To the extent that there is a selfish motive, it is the good feeling that comes from being able to help people who genuinely need help.

It's a feeling that no amount of money can buy.

> *You are only as wealthy as you are happy, so invest in yourself. Invest in your education, health, family, culture, and relationships.*
> —*Vince Fudzie and Andre N. Hayes*

Appendix B

Professional Advice: The Attorney

You Got My Back?

A COMMON MISCONCEPTION AMONG MANY professional athletes and some celebrities is that they have enough money to cover all of their personal obligations and enough left over to consider many, if not most, of the myriad investment opportunities that come their way. Certainly, not all of these opportunities are bad or fraudulent, but almost all of them involve a degree of risk. Alas, the higher the degree of risk in a particular opportunity, the more likely it is to be brought to a professional athlete or entertainer for consideration.

In contemplating investment opportunities, many athletes overlook the important role that advisors and attorneys can play in these decisions. Before taking the plunge into any investment, athletes must be sure that they are fully and honestly apprised of all the potential risks. Regardless of how well-versed or savvy the athlete may be, input from competent advisors is an essential part of every investment decision.

Another area in which professional expertise is paramount is contractual agreements. Attorneys have always been the targets of a great deal of humor. Indeed, without attorneys, some comedians might not have any material at all! Still, when all the jokes have been made, there is no substitute for an experienced attorney when it comes to drafting effective contracts. For professional athletes, high-profile entertainers, or, in fact, anyone who is about to enter into an agreement, a contract that outlines all of the terms and remedies for breach is, *without exception*, the most important part of the transaction. Many people are inclined to ignore the need for such a contract, especially if they are dealing with a trusted friend, family member, or long-time acquaintance. This is unwise and can leave one open to all manner of difficulties and issues that could have been avoided had there been a signed contract in place.

Certainly, not everyone is out to cheat you. People will often make promises without thinking and with no thought of malice or attempt to defraud. Yet verbal promises, however well-intentioned, are unenforceable in the absence of a signed contract in which the expectations of both parties are clearly stated and understood. A well-drafted contract protects both parties. In particular, it protects the investor by setting out specific remedies in the event that an investment or business venture fails to materialize as hoped and/or predicted.

The ease of Internet access now makes it possible to download sample contracts of nearly every kind, either at the local library or in your own home. Thus, the temptation to bypass the expense of an attorney is often great. Remember, however, that contracts need to be specific and should cover all the minute details that are unique to your agreement. A boilerplate contract, while legally acceptable, is unlikely to fully protect the interests of the investor.

So before making any investment decision, and certainly before signing any contracts, ask yourself, "Who has my back?" True, your family, friends, colleagues, and teammates may look out for you, but ask yourself:

- Do they have the professional skill and expertise to protect your financial interests?
- Can they draft a contract that allows you to quickly and inexpensively collect the return on your investment?
- Can they draw up a document that insulates you from liability and bad publicity for involvement in a deal that goes south or, worse, turns out to be illegal?

Finally, it is important to remember that all deals are not created equal, nor are all advisors and attorneys. It is almost never advisable to put all of your trust into one person or firm. Checks and balances keep people honest. Just as one player cannot cover all positions, one attorney is unlikely to have sufficient expertise in all areas of the law. So before considering an investment or even signing with a publicist, take the time and, if necessary, spend the money to find the right advisors and attorneys to help you.

Putting in the time and money on the front end will save you exponentially more time and money in the long run.

Who's got your back? You do!

—Jephtha J. Paul, Esq.

≈≈≈

Jephtha J. Paul has served on numerous nonprofit boards in various capacities and has worked in the private sector and in education using her fundraising/development, event management, and legal skills. Ms. Paul holds a B.A. from Miami University and a J.D. from Georgetown University Law Center, and currently resides in Columbus, Ohio.

Appendix C

Reflections on "The General"

All of us learn to write in the second grade.
Most of us go on to greater things.
—Bobby Knight

HE'S BEEN CALLED COLORFUL, COMBUSTIBLE, combative, and a number of other things, most of which are unprintable. Some say he is among the most intriguing sports figures the amateur ranks have ever produced. One thing no one disputes: Bobby Knight is one of the most successful coaches in college basketball history. He is opinionated, controversial and, in my opinion, an absolute genius.

Born October 25, 1940, in Massillon, Ohio, Robert Montgomery Knight discovered basketball in high school, where he played four years. His early skill and feel for the game led to participation in two All Conference Championships, one All State Championship, and recognition as the Team MVP in 1957. At Ohio State University, Knight joined the basketball team under the late Hall of Fame coach Fred Taylor, and was part of the team that won the 1960 NCAA Championship.

After graduating with a bachelor's degree, Knight moved on to become assistant basketball coach for the U.S. Military Academy at West Point in 1963. By 1965 he was head coach and, at twenty-four, was the youngest varsity coach in college basketball history. This was the first in what would become a long list of record-setting achievements. (It is believed that Knight acquired the nickname "The General" during his coaching years at West Point.)

Knight stayed with West Point until 1971, when he accepted the position as head coach at Indiana University, where he remained for more than thirty years building a record that is practically unmatched in college basketball history. At Indiana, his teams

- Won eleven Big Ten Conference titles
- Participated in five Final Four berths
- Were undefeated in 1976
- Won NCAA Championships in 1976, 1981, and 1987

- Won the National Invitational Tournament (NIT) Championship in 1979

(Statistics compiled from www.hoophall.com/Hall of Famers)

Knight himself was named National Coach of the Year in 1975, 1976, 1987, and 1989, and Big Ten Coach of the Year in 1973, 1975, 1976, 1980, and 1981. He was one of only two coaches to both play on and coach national championship teams (the other is Dean Smith). Knight led the Pan American Team to a gold medal in 1979, and has conducted clinics in Spain, China, Japan, East Asia, Europe, South America, Canada, and Finland. In 1984, he became one of only three coaches to win college basketball's "Triple Crown": NCAA and NIT titles and an Olympic gold medal (the other two were Hank Iba and Dean Smith). Sixteen of Knight's former assistant coaches have gone on to become head coaches at the collegiate level.

In March 2000, Knight became head coach at Texas Tech University. In his first season, he led the team to a 23–10 record.

In February 2003, Texas Tech defeated Nebraska 75–49. With that victory, Knight had compiled a personal career record of 800 wins against 303 losses.

He went on to lead Texas Tech to its first NCAA tournament since 1996, and to participation in the Final Four playoffs of the 2003 NIT.

Many people in the sports world believe (although there is no proof) that Bobby Knight must have originated the phrase, "It's my way or the highway." Perhaps he did, but there is another saying: "You can't argue with success." His methods may be questionable, but they are his, and they work. For proof, one need only refer to the astounding record of achievements of this remarkable man.

Knight is still with Texas Tech. So there is as yet no period to his career. Will there be more record-setting achievements? Only time will tell, but if history is any indicator, nobody in his right mind would bet against it.

Every sports fan has an opinion about Coach Knight. Some believe his coaching style is antiquated and out of touch with the changing landscape of modern collegiate basketball, particularly in light of the many freelance players now in the game. Others believe The General is a much-needed beacon of hope whose in-your-face coaching style is a welcome antidote to an increasingly self-involved, self-absorbed culture of young athletes for whom Knight may be the first taste of discipline in their lives.

I have the perhaps dubious distinction of being known in some circles as the guy who couldn't get along with Coach Knight. Even now, there are those who recognize me as the player who transferred from Indiana University. People in hotel elevators have stopped me. "Didn't you and Bob Knight . . ." I usually finish the question for them with, ". . . not see eye-to-eye?" I have spent so much energy explaining and rehashing "the incident" that I keep my responses brief. I think what surprises most people is the respect that I have, and always will have, for Coach Knight in spite of what happened.

It has been more than fifteen years since I first set foot on the Indiana University campus. Yet the memory of the "meltdown" between Coach Knight and me remains fresh. It made regional and national headlines.

For the record, here is my side of the story.

As a little boy, I'd heard of Coach Knight. What little boy hadn't? Back then, cable television was still in its infancy and twenty-four-hour sports channels had yet to arrive, but CBS and NBC aired men's college basketball games every Saturday and highlights almost always featured the Indiana University (IU) team and their mercurial coach. Youngsters, like myself, dreamed of playing in the Big Ten Conference, which was especially popular in the Midwest. Beyond the love of the game, it was fun to watch Coach Knight on the sidelines ranting and raving. Sometimes he was the best part of the show. Of all the things that fueled my desire to play in the Big Ten, the greatest was a chance to play for Coach Knight, a man by whom I was both intrigued and fascinated.

For me the dream met (collided with?) reality when I was at Wherle Memorial High. Several recruiting publications (including *Street* and *Smith* and *The Sporting News*) had placed me among their top five junior and senior year high school prospects. As an All State and All America player averaging 28 points, 14 rebounds, and 6 blocks, I had attracted the attention of almost every college coach in the country, including former OSU player and Indiana coach Bobby "The General" Knight.

> **Be careful what you wish for because you might just get it.**
>
> **—French Proverb**

After several phone conversations, arrangements were made for him to visit the school. Naturally, the whole place was in a buzz. Even my high school coach, Chuck Kemper, himself a tough and imposing figure at nearly six feet and four inches and well over 200 pounds, and a boxer in the armed forces as a young man, was awed by Coach Knight's presence.

I was seated with my back to the door when The General walked in the room. He didn't bother to introduce himself. I guess he knew he didn't need to. Instead, he began circling me like a giant condor zeroing in on an animal carcass. I will never forget his first words to me: "I heard you were a monumental pain in the [rear]."

In the U.S. Defense Department, Defense Readiness Conditions (DEFCONs) describe progressive alert postures for increased combat readiness. Graduated to match situations of varying severity, DEFCONs are numbered 5, 4, 3, 2, and 1 with the following designations:

DEFCON 5: Normal peacetime readiness
DEFCON 4: Normal, increased intelligence and strengthened security measures

DEFCON 3: Increase in force readiness above normal readiness

DEFCON 2: Further increase in force readiness, but less than maximum readiness

DEFCON 1: Maximum force readiness

I have always been a fearless person, but the minute I met Coach Knight, something inside me jumped to DEFCON 3. It was true that I had earned a reputation for marching to the beat of a different drummer, just as he does. Also, and this is not something of which I am proud, I had a bad case of the "entitlement bug" that afflicted (and continues to afflict) most high school athletes. Already lavished with praise, publicity, and media attention, I made the common mistake of believing my own press, a dangerous mode of thinking that has trapped many talented youngsters and prevented them from pursuing an education. Many (thank goodness, I was not among this subset group) see their athletic skills as a "get out of school free" card. If you're going to be a star (and rich) anyway, as the wrong-headed thinking goes, why waste time studying?

Of the many letters I received from Coach Knight during the recruiting process, one in particular stands out. In a letter dated November 9, 1988, he mentioned that he very much looked forward to the possibility of coaching me in an Indiana University uniform. He said that he admired both my intellect and athletic talent, stating that the combination of these two attributes were rarely seen on the high school level. If The General didn't have me hooked already, he reeled me in when he wrote that I had the potential to be successful in pro sports (and once my pro basketball career concluded), and that he would personally help me cultivate my destiny. Keep in mind, I visited Hall of Fame coach Dean Smith and the University of North Carolina prior to this letter being sent to my home. Yes, the one in the housing projects. Coach Knight's candor was definitely an attention grabber.

Coming from one of the best coaches, if not the best, in NCAA history, for me this was like honey to a bee. I admit that it went to my head, not only what he said about me, but also the fact that Bobby Knight, The One and Only Bobby Knight, wanted to coach me, desperately it seemed. Did I use this to my advantage? Of course. Was that right? Of course not. But truth is truth.

Like all of his recruits, I was intrigued by The General's persona. I was also attracted by his ability to maximize a player's skills. I've seen him single-handedly squeeze more talent out of mediocre (and sometimes even star players) than they knew they had. I was mesmerized by the possibility that he could take my skills into basketball superstardom, and by the thought that one day my name might be mentioned in the same breath with:

- Scott May (who was a true mentor to me)
- Mike Woodson

- Quinn Buckner
- Isaiah Thomas (arguably the best IU player ever)
- Randy Wittman (a great shooter, who played with us in open gym)
- Steve Alford (one of the best college players of all time, and whose hair never seemed to move), and
- Keith Smart (whose sixteen-foot baseline jumper with four seconds left in the 1987 Championship game beat Syracuse and gave Bob Knight his third NCAA title).

During the recruiting process, Knight was incredibly persuasive and, ultimately, convincing. Yet, even before I signed the letter of intent for my services, many people were screaming that it wasn't going to work. Many wondered why I had chosen Indiana and Coach Knight when the two of us were so clearly and entirely incompatible. They believed that although Coach Knight and I shared some characteristics, in other more fundamental ways we were complete opposites. The thinking was that a free-spirited player and a stubborn disciplinarian coach were not going to mix and that a confrontation loud enough to be heard from the Atlantic to the Pacific was inevitable. Columnists were even taking bets on how long Coach Knight and I would work together before the blowup came. One of my mentors pleaded with me not to go to Indiana. So did my mother—although she knew nothing about Coach Knight, beyond a few reassuring phone conversations, but she did know me. Too well.

But I was determined to make the relationship with Coach Knight work, and to prove to all the doubters and naysayers how wrong they had been. In retrospect, I believe that desire to prove them wrong was the primary driving factor behind my decision to attend IU.

I was wrong. Had I taken the time, or possessed the maturity, to assess my style of play against Knight's coaching methods, I might have spared myself the repercussions of a poor decision.

The incoming team members consisted of Calbert Cheaney, Greg Graham, Pat Graham, Chris (M.C. Ren) Reynolds, Chris Lawson, Todd Leary, and me—called by some hoop gurus one of the best teams the Big Ten Conference had ever seen, certainly at IU. Other than the Fab Five, led by Chris Webber at the University of Michigan, our group was reported to be one of the most complete assemblages of high school talent to come along in years. We were predicted to win no less than one NCAA Championship and several Big Ten titles. Indiana fans expected nothing less.

In the summer of 1989, we:

- Won the "19 and Under" Invitational Tournament in Jacksonville, Florida
- Came in second place in the "19 and Under" AAU National Championship in San Antonio, Texas, after losing to Shaquille O'Neal's team by a few points, and

- Dominated the Russian Junior National Team at Assembly Hall (former collegiate and NBA stars Billy Knight, George McGinnis, and Scott May coached us).

If expectations had been high before, after that summer they were off the charts. Fans readily embraced us, even though returning players wondered if our hype was warranted. We earned their respect while playing in competitive pickup games. Key returning players, such as Eric Anderson, Lyndon Jones, Jamaal Meeks, and Mark Robinson, tested our resolve and were impressed.

Preseason conditioning was brutal, but we made it through. Grueling Saturday morning runs took their toll on me, and others too. (In the press guide, I was listed as a six-foot-eight, 199-pound freshman. I guess I should have drunk sixteen ounces of water before weighing in.) Being at the track at 6:00 A.M. was increasingly difficult, and I struggled with preseason conditioning, which felt like boot camp.

Thus, it was clear from the beginning that of the seven recruits, I did not fit the profile of a Bobby Knight protégé. Coach Knight had been recruiting the other six for several years. All of them were already familiar with the program. But he didn't begin recruiting me until my senior year in high school, so I came into the picture somewhat late. During a phone call from an assistant coach, I said, "I don't think I can make it here." I was ready to throw in the towel before I ever officially put on the IU uniform I had admired so much as a child.

No doubt the assistant coach with whom I spoke reported our conversation to Coach Knight, who urgently dispatched him to my apartment to coax me into staying, which he did after considerable pleading and even a few tears. Assistant coaches were required to intervene in such situations. Personally, Coach Knight would never shed a tear for a struggling player, nor, quite frankly, would anyone expect him to. As for me, I kept my word and continued in the program, including the weekly Indian Run, which I did carrying a medicine ball. My skinny arms felt like they were going to fall off.

In high school, the coaches let me play my game within their system. But, as I was about to find out, those days were over in October when The General blew the whistle signaling the beginning of the first official practice. One of my teammates, Eric Anderson, tried to warn me (in a way) one afternoon during a pickup game. On offense, your first and only responsibility is to set picks (in other words, the player with the ball uses one of his own players as a shield or screen to allow him to move more freely). So when Eric asked me what I was doing, I was too dumbfounded to answer more coherently than "huh?" I thought what I was doing was obvious, and therefore I didn't know what he was talking about. In high school, the coaches had not addressed the subject of continual picks (in contrast to set picks).

That style of basketball, which is to say, Coach Knight's style, was foreign to me. Of course, his style works. He's got the record to prove it. Even so, I believe our clash was more about ideological differences and playing styles, though I did blend in with his system up until my departure.

In spite of some minor setbacks, I was confident early in my freshman year that coming to Indiana had been the right decision. Coach Knight's keen awareness of each player's every move was nothing short of phenomenal. Scientists have said that the human brain is, in fact, a tremendously sophisticated computer. While I cannot speak for the rest of humanity, Coach Knight's brain is definitely computerized. The way he processes, analyzes, and assesses his vantage point in every game, without forgetting anything, is simply stunning.

Coach Knight was (and probably still is) a perfectionist. So you could rarely atone for a mistake. He was one of the few people I have ever met who could deliver a compliment and an ego-deflating critique at the same time. It is a practice that he has elevated to an art form. During one practice, he said, "Lawrence, you're probably the most talented player that I've ever coached, but you're also the laziest." (Assistant coaches were responsible for rebuilding and repairing bruised egos. "If he gets on you, that means he cares about you," they used to say.)

Perfection is our goal. Excellence will be tolerated.
—J. Yahl

Minor critiques didn't seem to bother me, and I seemed to fly under Coach Knight's radar screen that encompassed players who were perennially in his doghouse. I watched him lay into others, though. His face turned eerily red when he was angry. It wasn't something you wanted to see. I vividly recall a game against Kentucky, which he absolutely abhorred, to put it mildly, and I will never forget how intense he was during a timeout. The color of his face matched his game-day sweater. Everyone on the team was shocked (although returning players were probably immune to it), because Coach's will to win consumed every fiber in his body.

For a while my mistakes were not severely scrutinized, and my teammates resented me for this (a former teammate recently said, "Coach Knight let Lawrence get away with murder"). Some were also resentful of the fact that I didn't have to live in the dorms as a freshman, which I guess they felt put me even further out of the Coach's target range. During recruitment negotiations, I had asked for and been granted my own apartment off-campus. Up to that time, I believe it was standard policy for Coach Knight to forbid freshman players to live off-campus.

One day before practice I was the last player to enter the locker room after a meeting with "Buzz" Kurpius, the academic advisor. "Lawrence, what are you here for, to play basketball or to get an education?" Coach Knight asked. I wondered if it was a trick question, since he knew that education was a top priority of mine, and that I had a passion for basketball as well.

Then, too, his natural stone-faced demeanor made it impossible to tell whether he was serious or joking (which was rare). The room was silent while the coaching staff and my teammates waited for me to answer. "To play basketball," I finally said. My response elicited a burst of laughter, as they had predicted what I would say. I had learned a valuable lesson. If you had an opportunity to humor Coach Knight, take it.

That was one of the few times I ever saw him laugh.

Every IU player knew that Coach Knight's practice sessions were intense and demanding (like the man himself), as well as physically and mentally draining. No amount of preseason conditioning or conversations with assistant coaches could adequately prepare you for the daily practices. Coach Knight is a hard-core believer in preparation and physical conditioning. Because I had worked under Coach Knight, the jump from college to the pros was a lot less demanding for me than the jump from high school to college.

The eruption came in December 1989, when I was kicked out of a practice session for lackluster play. Coming off my best game as a freshman to date (twenty-six points), I was oblivious to what would become the darkest day of my college career. Ironically, Coach Knight had put his arm around me one practice after we had just finished fielding questions from the media, and he said: "Just think about all those $*$#*#*$ who said you wouldn't last this long here." Affection?! From The General?!? Boy, were all those people wrong—the ones who said that this particular coach/player relationship would end in a blowup. I had successfully passed the first litmus test, the initial dog days of preseason practices, and several games. All was well in Hoosierland.

Well, not quite. On that fateful day, the entire team had struggled in practice because we had just completed end-of-semester finals. I caught the brunt of Coach Knight's wrath when I missed a lay-up and committed an offensive foul, barreling into Jamaal Meeks and forcing him to fall backwards. Coach Knight stopped practice and unloaded point-blank in my direction—both barrels. Later, he sent the team to the locker room where we were chastised, primarily by assistant coach Joby Wright. Through Wright, Coach Knight relayed the following message: "I want everyone to return to the floor except Lawrence. I want to enjoy the remainder of practice without him messing it up. As a matter of fact, I don't want him in the building. Tell him to go home."

I never knew the reason for that decision. As I said, it had not been a good practice day for the entire team. Everyone was a little sluggish, which to Knight seemed only marginally less egregious than a capital crime. That I was singled out to get the boot is as baffling to me now as it was at the time. I have considered the possibility that the decision was a ploy to humble me after the recent success of scoring twenty-six points and being named to the All Tournament team. I guess it was my turn to become the proverbial whipping boy, as many IU players have experienced through the years.

In military boot camp (and, strangely enough, in much of the artistic world—for example, ballet), the new student very often must undergo a tearing-down process, including a certain amount of ego destruction. The idea being that only by tearing down the young person can the teachers then build a better, stronger, and more disciplined soldier or artist.

> *I don't have high blood pressure. I give it.*
> —Comment from a Corporate Vice President

I can only speculate, of course, but it is well within the realm of possibility that Bobby Knight bases his coaching style on this principle, with which he may have become familiar during his early years as a coach at West Point. Did he feel that I was, by then, ready to face the full force of his wrath? I don't know. I doubt he ever thought very much about what the other person was feeling once his frustration kicked in.

Whatever the reason for the action, I was devastated. Most of my teammates had been on the wrong end of the Coach's temper more than I, so if I was expecting any comfort from them, none would be coming my way. Leaving Assembly Hall, my mind was made up. I didn't know where I was headed, but I knew that had been my last practice in a Hoosier uniform, even though the team was 6–0 at the time.

I didn't have any luggage, so on my way home I stopped at the grocery store to pick up some bags in which to pack my belongings. I returned from my last trip out to the car to find Assistant Coach Joby Wright waiting for me in the living room. "What are you doing? Why aren't you at practice?" I asked. He said he had called my apartment several times and gotten no answer. "Where are you going?" he asked. I told him I was leaving—for good. He said, "No, you're not." When I tried to walk by, he grabbed me and shoved me. The situation turned ugly real fast. Finally, he said what he had come to say: that he and Coach Knight had taken a chance on me and had bent over backwards for me. Then, in the heat of the moment, I didn't believe it. Now, in retrospect, I believe that they both cared about me. A lot.

When I left, he was sitting in a chair, staring at the floor, with his hands on his cheeks. He was distraught, and the look on his face was one of disbelief. I knew Coach Knight wouldn't be happy either. Joby watched me as I drove away from the parking lot. Coach Knight had told me to go home. I just followed his orders.

Whatever the reasons for the clash, IU fans and the media ridiculed me even though I never publicly demeaned Coach Knight, the program, the university or the fans. I've heard it said that some fans even predicted that my untimely departure would cost the program a National Championship. This was preposterous. The team, which would later include Damon Bailey and Alan Henderson, was more than talented enough to win without me, which they did. In fact, the team went on to become one of the best in the country.

For a time after I left, I didn't read or watch the news, nor did I talk to anyone about the incident. I thought I was waiting for the storm to blow over, though it seemed to linger like a bad cold. I accepted then, and have always accepted, some of the blame for what happened. Still, I felt as if all eyes were on me everywhere I went. If that was my fifteen minutes of fame, I didn't want any part of it.

Public relations proved to be a nightmare. National media outlets, CBS Sports, and *Sports Illustrated* covered the debacle. A CBS Sports analyst reported during halftime of a nationally televised college basketball game that I was AWOL and that my whereabouts were a mystery.

I left Indiana for Madisonville, Kentucky, home of Travis Ford, who was attending the University of Missouri. Travis and I were close friends, and his family embraced me. It was well after midnight when I knocked on their door. "Lawrence, what are you doing here?" Mr. Ford asked, clearly shocked to see me. I told him I'd left IU. I stayed with the Fords for several days and then went to Lexington, where I stayed with another friend for a few days. Then I went home to Columbus, Ohio—to face my mother, who let it be known that she was not pleased with my behavior. "Lawrence, you can't keep running," she said. "Be a man, not a mouse."

That was tougher to swallow than any media blast. Suddenly, it came to me how much I had let a lot of people down and that it was time to get my career back on track.

My scholarship had, of course, been revoked. Coach Knight (of course) refused to grant me a release. I threatened to sue the university, which may not have been a good idea. A sportswriter from *Sports Illustrated* contacted my attorney to set up an interview, and promised that my side of the story would be told. It wasn't, at least not completely.

"But even before the start of the season, there was much speculation on how long Funderburke would last in Bloomington," the article said. "Even Knight's son, Tim, was skeptical. Over the summer Tim . . . helped direct an AAU team featuring Funderburke and the rest of Indiana's incoming freshmen. Funderburke made a questionable impression when he refused to sit with the other players at meals. 'Enjoy Lawrence in November,' Tim told his father on a fishing trip. 'You won't see him after December.'"

I was closer to some players than I was to others (and still am to this day with some of my former IU teammates), but I got along with everyone.

The writer added, "Much of Funderburke's life has been anything but a laughing matter. His father left home before Lawrence got to know him; his mother, Laura, is something of a recluse whom college recruiters never saw. They only talked to her on the phone. Says one college coach, 'None of us ever got a home visit. It was obvious Lawrence was embarrassed with his home life.'"

I failed to see the relevance of these comments to what happened at Indiana between Coach Knight and me. Taking jabs at my home life was unscrupulous and uncalled for.

Nor was it, in my opinion, appropriate for the writer to comment on my character. In the article, he painted a dark picture of my true persona that to this day, is slowly being rectified. Although the other six incoming recruits were well acquainted with one another, other than Chris Reynolds, I had never spoken to or met any of them. Beyond that, I have always been one to keep to myself. This is not the time for a lesson in basic psychology, but everyone knows that relationships take time. Best friends are rarely made overnight—or in the space of one summer or semester. People who know me well see my gregarious side. As for my relationship with teammates, I have always been supportive.

Suffice it to say, the article swayed public opinion—just not in my favor.

To say the least, my freshman term at Indiana had been unsuccessful. Coach Knight had publicly stated that he was finished with me. Even so, I seriously considered rejoining the team as a rejuvenated sophomore. Indeed, the thought of becoming a Knight disciple for a second time was enticing, particularly given the backlash from my decision to leave. It might also have meant an opportunity to silence the critics.

In the summer of 1990, a hush-hush meeting in the room next to the court at Assembly Hall was arranged. Coach Knight, his assistants (Dan Dakich, Ron Felling, and Joby Wright), and I were to attend. To my knowledge, the media were not aware of this meeting.

The meeting went well. More than anything, they wanted to hear me say I was sorry, which I did. I was apologetic and candid, and honest in my portrayal of my freshman year at Indiana. Moreover, I accepted my share of the blame (and always have) for what had taken place.

Mistakes are the usual bridge between inexperience and wisdom.

—Phyllis Therous

Alas, as I noted earlier, with Coach Knight you can rarely atone for a mistake, however small or large. As I walked out at the conclusion of the meeting, Coach Knight let me have it again. "See, you haven't changed a bit. We take the time to meet with you and then you can't even thank us when it's over." Then he left, slamming the door in my face. If I think about it, I can still feel the vibrations—in the air and inside me.

I want to say that I was livid, but that word, "livid," isn't strong enough. There may not be a word that is. One thing was certain, however. I knew that going back to IU had been the champion bad idea of all ideas. I didn't know where I was going, but I knew I wasn't going back there.

I asked the athletic director and Coach Knight on several occasions to grant me an unconditional release. They finally agreed, but only on the condition that I agreed to forfeit two years of NCAA eligibility and to accept Coach Knight's (odd) choice of Missouri as my next school. Losing two years was out of the question.

Taking out loans to pay for the out-of-state tuition expenses, I returned to Indiana long enough to complete the one-year requirement so that I could transfer to another school. It was one of the most difficult periods of my life. It is difficult to say which was worse, being baited into fights or the constant cold shoulder from everyone: coaches, teammates, fans, and students. I was the Benedict Arnold of IU, and for many people I always will be. (I have even been booed during Sacramento Kings/Chicago Bulls versus Indiana Pacers games at Conseco Fieldhouse. Friends and family members have heard derogatory remarks all these years later.)

At the conclusion of the first semester of my sophomore year I called Coach Knight once again. To my surprise, he took my call. Not surprisingly, he took aim and, once again, unloaded the full strength of his wrath. "I knew you were no good the moment I laid my eyes on you. I was certain that you wouldn't stay at Indiana any longer than your junior year before you darted for the pros," he screamed. Before he could finish, I ended the conversation.

That was the last time I talked to one of the most brilliant men in college basketball. Years later I was asked by a local television sports reporter whether OSU should interview Coach Knight for the coaching vacancy. I endorsed the idea, albeit mildly. (This was prior to OSU's decision to hire the outstanding coach Thad Matta, whose candidacy for the position had not then been publicly revealed.)

I think my endorsement surprised many people, including me. But whatever may be said about Coach Knight as a personality, his record as a coach is unassailable. In fact, I said that OSU couldn't have gone wrong with any one of three choices: Jim Cleamons (former Chicago Bulls and L.A. Lakers assistant coach), George Karl (former Seattle Supersonics and Milwaukee Bucks, and current Denver Nuggets head coach), or Coach Knight.

Deciding where to go after I completed my requirements at IU was difficult. This time, I wanted to be sure I made the right choice. Kentucky was out (Athletic Director C.M. Newton nixed that). Louisville was a possibility, since I have always admired Denny Crum. Cincinnati was another possibility. (I recently bumped into Coach Bob Huggins, who joked, "You cost us a National Championship by not coming here.") OSU was a dark horse candidate until All Big Ten and All American performer Jim Jackson persuaded Coach Ayers to consider me. In the end, I selected OSU because it afforded me the luxury of playing in my hometown.

Not everyone agreed with Coach Ayers's decision. One day I turned on a sports radio station only to hear, "Guess who's coming back home? Lawrence Funderburke is returning to Columbus to play for the Buckeyes." The talk show host had gotten wind of my decision, which only about half the callers supported.

As a non-scholarship athlete, I had to take out loans once again to cover my tuition. But it was worth it, even though by attending OSU I would cross paths with Coach Knight again—six times. The General wasn't pleased with my choice and, never one to mince words, said as much when Coach Ayers called (as a courtesy) to say that I would be coming to, and welcomed at, OSU.

Many people have asked me how, and sometimes why, I remember so many details about working with Bobby Knight for one semester. In fact, I remember more about that one semester than I do about my entire three years at OSU. Those years were not uneventful, but I don't have to periodically relive them as I do my semester at IU.

I sometimes wonder whether anyone has ever asked The General (or had the nerve to ask him) how it feels to be a living legend. His career being far from over, he probably wouldn't dignify the question with an answer.

Early in life, I had to choose between honest arrogance and hypocritical humility. I chose honest arrogance and have seen no occasion to change.

—Frank Lloyd Wright

Way back in the day, there was a cartoon character called Popeye, the Sailor Man. Part of his theme song was, "I yam what I yam and that's all that I yam." In a way, that sums up Coach Knight. Perhaps, on some level, you have to envy a person who meets life and lives it on his own terms without apologies or (presumably) regrets. Such personalities are rare, and their impact—for better or worse—on the people they encounter is never forgotten. With time, you can put that impact into its proper perspective, but you will never forget it.

Playing in a Hoosier uniform was an adventure because you never knew what to expect. If players practiced and performed well (without errors), then things ran pretty smoothly. If you messed up, you were done for. Anxiety was a player on the court at Indiana; it was a member of the team.

By contrast, competing for the Buckeyes was euphoric for me, though less so than receiving a degree in finance, which was my proudest moment.

As is the case with all geniuses, there was (is?) an aura surrounding Coach Knight. We both might have been spared a great deal of angst had I seen his dark side prior to enrolling at IU, but I never saw it even though I went to several games. In the absence of any "clues," I could not understand why friends and family counseled so strongly against the decision. (True,

Hook Me Up, Playa!

I had seen him at his worst on television, but that was too far away to be real to me.)

Other than kicking me out of practice that day, however, I have to say that Knight never seemed to be the monster everyone portrayed him to be. He is shrewd, hard as nails, and no one underestimates him. Twice.

A character in a British comedy once screamed, "My bite is definitely worse than my bark, and my bark is atrocious!!"

There has been a certain catharsis for me in telling this story, but that was not entirely the point. I want young athletes to learn from my mistakes.

As a business/finance major, I learned that many companies prepare their operating model using best, realistic, and worst-case scenarios. Had I known and applied this technique in choosing a school, I could have saved myself a lot of headaches and heartache. My decision to go to IU was based on emotion, not reason, and reason is essential in the process of assessing and making decisions.

As to what happened at IU, I don't believe in playing the "what if" game. If I had stayed in the program, would I have been a contributor to their National Championship aspirations? I don't know. In fairness to the coaches, my teammates, and Indiana fans, I should have at least stayed the full year, even though I was not prepared for the type of rebuke I received. For what it is worth, I apologize, again, to those who had high hopes for me in an IU uniform. That is the dark side of transferring while in college. Coaches get attached to you, teammates become comfortable and grow to depend on you, and fans embrace you.

Coach Knight once said, "If you need to talk to me, my door is always open." Some coaches, not necessarily Coach Knight, may wonder about the appropriateness of encouraging friendship (though they may offer it) between themselves and the players. Perhaps they feel such a step would only encourage young athletes to overstep the boundaries. That may be true. But it is also true that many young athletes need a friend as much as, or more than, they need a coach.

I do not regret my decision to transfer from Indiana. I do, however, regret the circumstances that precipitated that decision. Although Coach Ayers emphatically stated that, in his mind, I was coming to OSU with a clean slate, he must have prepared himself for the worst just in case his faith in me turned out to have been unjustified. My new teammates at OSU may also have anticipated a volcanic explosion at some point. That never happened.

Understandably, the NBA teams that were considering drafting me were swayed in some measure by the media coverage by which I was publicly tarred and feathered. Many NBA teams would not welcome a maligned player to their organization, although I had changed for the better since my time as a Hoosier. Coach Ayers told me scouts raised the issue of my character in conversations with him. Thus, the impact of the IU incident on me was emotional, psychological, and financial.

Commenting on quarterback Troy Smith's booster entanglements during the Alamo Bowl game against Oklahoma State University in 2004, OSU football coach Jim Tressel said, "Part of life is taking care of your errors."

I agree wholeheartedly. In the end, it is how one responds to adversity that, more than any other factor, determines the outcome. Recent incidents in which OSU has come under scrutiny have proven this to be true. The public relations journey will be long and arduous, but I believe the new athletic director, Gene Smith, Coach Jim Tressel, and Coach Thad Matta will fight to restore the image of this great university.

Student-athletes and non-athletes alike must play their part as well, and be held accountable for their actions. That said, however, it is also important that universities not be too quick to discard a student who has violated the institution's code of conduct. An opportunity to prove themselves worthy of faith and trust can go as far in the interest of higher education for a young athlete, or any young person, as a diploma.

Finally, and on a personal note, I would like to offer some advice to Maurice Clarett, former Ohio State football standout, or any big-time college athlete who feels that he is being used (or has been used) by the system. Do not underestimate the emotional and financial impact of the controversial trail that will follow you for years to come. A reputation as a controversial figure is, in the end, damaging, even for an athlete (or a non-athlete) who goes on to a stellar career.

Experience is the best teacher.
—Unknown

I have watched Maurice Clarett fall (jump? be pushed?) from his pedestal as a media darling, capturing the hearts of football fans around the country. Barely out of his teenage years, he may not fully comprehend the long-term impact of this situation on his life. But it is safe to say that at some point he will look back and wonder what else he could have done in the way of damage control. It is to be hoped that, in time, he will realize the consequences of the present fallout (though he has since been drafted in the NFL). I wish him well and sincerely pray that he will fulfill his athletic potential. He is an incredible talent.

Hindsight is, indeed, 20–20, and for that reason, it is better to correct entanglements in the moment.

Waiting too long can be costly, and it is very likely to be too late. I should know.

Appendix D

References

www.2facts.com/ICOF. "What Is a Collective Bargaining Agreement?";
  "Revenue—Sharing in Professional Sports"; "Key Events in the
  History of Sports Salary Caps."

Acohido, Byron. "Greenspan Marvels at How Effective Sarbanes–Oxley
  Has Been So Far." *USA Today*, May 16, 2005, B3.

Anonymous. "Failure List of the Famous." www.inspire21.com.

Anonymous Source. Personal Interview. August 2004.

"Avoiding Financial Black Holes." Managing Your Finances. *United Church
  of God* www.ucg.org/booklets/MF/blackholes.htm.

www.baltimoreravens.com.

"Bankruptcy Judge Warns Young People of Debt's Dangers."
www.militarymoney.com/columns/1/175.

Bauder, Don. "God's Scammers." *City Lights Magazine – San Diego*
  www.sandiegoreader.com. March 18, 2004.

The Bible. The New International Version (NIV).

www.bizjournals.com.

www.booknutsreadingclub.com/blackbio.

Blackwell, Jeff. Personal Interview. August 2004.

Brown, Mark. "Squeeze Play." June 2000.
www.lib.niu.edu/ipo/ii000631.html.

Bunn, Curtis. "Team Player." honeymag.com.

Byrd, Petri. Personal Interview. August 2004.

Carson, Dr. Ben, Sr. "History/Growing Up," www.drbencarson.com/
growingup2-body.html.

Carson, Ben, M.D. *Gifted Hands: The Ben Carson Story*, (copyright 1990,
Review and Herald),Grand Rapids, MI, Zondervan Books, Reprinted,
1998, pp. 56–57.

CFP Financial Planners Standards Council. "Ten Questions to Ask a
Financial Advisor." www.cfp.ca.org.

Cohn, Patrick. "Sports Psychology Guidelines for Sports Parents."
ArriveNet Editorials, January 21, 2005. editorials.arrivenet.com/spo/
article.php/3386.html.

www.collegeboard.com.

Conrad, Mark. "Details on Payoffs by 'Tank' Black Revealed." *Mark's
Sportslaw News*. September 22, 1999. www.sportslawnews.com/.

Crayton, Lisa. "Dabbling with Debt: Debt Management for Teens."
YouthWorker Journal. youthspecialties.com/articles/topics/
consumerism/teens.php.

"Double Your Money in 90 Days." home.nycap.rr.com/usless/ponzi.

Doyle, Paul. "Trusted Agents, Advisers Scam Clients." *Nineronline.com
Sports. 21*. October 2004. www.nineronline.com/vnews/display.
v/ART/2004/04/28/408edbb182eac.

Draper, Kris. Personal Interview. October 2004.

Dudley, Rickey. Personal Interview. November 2004.

Dunleavy, M.P. "You're Suddenly Rich? Bummer!" MSN Money.
moneycentral.msn.com.

www.en.wikipedia.org.

Farrey, Tom. "Growing Up Next." ESPN.com.

Financial Planning Association. www.fpanet.org.

"Flim Flam Man," written by Laura Nyro, published by EMI Blackwood Music, Inc, New York, N.Y., performed by Barbara Streisand.

www.fraudaid.com. "How Con Artists Set You Up" and "What a Con Artist Won't Tell You."

Fudzie, Vince, and Andre N. Hayes. "Ten Basic Financial Elements," *Your Brain Is A Muscle, Too: How Student Athletes Succeed In College and In Life*. Amistad/HarperCollins Publishers, 2000.

Funderburke, Monya. Personal Interview. October 2004.

Gardner, Marilyn. "A Generation Weighed Down by Debt." *Christian Science Monitor*. www.csmonitor.com. November 2004.

Gerloff, Pamela. "Playing for Life: Athletes and The Big Money Game—An Online Interview with Brent Williams." www.morethanmoney.org.

Gordon, Ken. "One Toy the Boys Can't Resist: Cars." *Columbus Dispatch*, August 7, 2002.

Graham, Stedman. *Move Without the Ball: Put Your Skills and Your Magic to Work for You*. New York: Fireside Books, 2004.

Grisham, John. *Bleachers*, New York, Random House, 2003.

Hannah, Charley. Personal Interview. October 2004.

Helitzer, Melvin. *The Dream Job: Sports Publicity, Promotion and Marketing*. Athens, OH: University Sports Press, 2000.

Hodge, Scott. "Study Finds Controversial Jock Taxes Spreading." *Budget & Tax News*. The Heartland Institute. September 1, 2004.

Hoffman, David. "Study Finds 'Jock Taxes' Continue Spreading to Non-Jock Professions." *The Tax Foundation*. July 9, 2004.

www.hoophall.com.

Hopson, Dennis. Personal Interview. August 2004.

Hyman, Mark. "Why the 'Jock Tax' Doesn't Play Fair." July 2003. www.businessweek.com/magazine/content/03_27/b3840062.htm.

Iacocca, Lee. *Iacocca: An Autobiography*. Bantam Books, 1984.

"I'd Rather Be Rich" lyrics from the movie *I'd Rather Be Rich*. Universal Studios, 1964.

www.jalenrose.com.

Jenkins, Sally. "Athletes–Fans: A Long-Distance Relationship." *Washington Post*, October 11, 2003.

Johnston, Joey. "Courage of His Convictions." *Tampa Tribune*. January 2005.

Katz, Barry. Personal Interview. September 2004.

Kirkpatrick, Curry. "Funderburke vs. Knight." *Sports Illustrated*, January 22, 1990: 52–54.

Knight, Bob. Letter to the author. November 9, 1988.

Lemieux, Martin. "Planning Ahead of Everyone Else to Win." articles.worldvillage.com_planning_ahead_of_everyone_else_to_win. html. January 2005.

Levitt, Daniel. Personal Interview. October 2004.

Lott, John, Jr. "Athletes and Guns." FOX News. January 28, 2004.

Masser, Mark. Personal Interview. September 2004.

Matta, Thad. Personal Interview. November 2004.

McGraw, Phil, Ph.D. "Pushy Parents?" CBS. June 30, 2005.

National Financial Planning Support Center, www.fpanet.org.

www.nba.com/community/webber.

www.ncaa.org.

Neimark, Jill. "The Culture of Celebrity." *Psychology Today*, 1995. cms. psychologytoday.com/article/pto-19950501.0000331.html

www.newjerseydevils.com.

Nyro, Laura. "Flim Flam Man." 1967.

Oliver, Rick. Personal Interview. October 2004.

Paul, Jephtha. Professional Biography.

PBS American Experience, "The Rockefellers."

Pennington, Bill, and Bruce Weber. "Doctors See a Big Rise in Injuries as Young Athletes Train Nonstop." *New York Times*, February 22, 2005.

Piniella, Lou. www.baseballlibrary.com.

Press Release Newswire. www.PRWeb.com.

Rovell, Darrell. "The other Tiger that lurks in the Woods." *Outside the Lines*. ESPN Sports Business. November 3, 2002. www. espn.go.com/page2/tvlistings/show136transcript.html.

Russell, Bill. *Second Wind: The Memoirs of an Opinionated Man*. Random House, 1979.

SanDiegoReader.com. www.sandiegoreader.com.

Sanford, Rob. "Infinite Financial Freedom: What to Do Before and After You Win the Lottery." *TitleWaves*, 1994.

Sax, Steve. Personal Interview. September 2004.

Seckbach, Elie. Personal Interview. October 2004.

"Smiling Faces Sometimes," written by Norman J. Whitfield and Barret Strong, published by Stone Agate Music, New York, N.Y., performed by Undisputed Truth, Motown Records, 1971.
Smith, Stephen A. Personal Interview. November 2004.

Sullivan, T.J. "The Man Behind the Money Pit." *Ventura County Star*, May 20, 2001.

Tarbell, Ida M. *The History of Standard Oil.* McClure, Phillips and Co., 1904. www.reformation.org/john-d-rockefeller.html.

Telford, Anthony. Personal Interview. October 2004.

Toure. "The Star Maker." *Sports Illustrated.* September 2004.

Trent, Gary. Personal Interview. September 2004.

www.turn2foundation.org.

USAA Educational Foundation, www.usaaedfoundation.org.

Vaughn, Greg. Personal Interview. October 2004.

Versari, Cristina. Professional Biography.

Wallace, Amy. "Father and Son, Soaking Up Affection." *New York Times,* June 15, 2003.

Ward, Aaron. Personal Interview. November 2004.

www.washingtonredskins.com.

Wertheim, Michael. Personal Interview. August 2004.

Young, Colleen. Interview with Samuel L. Jackson. Associated Press, January 14, 2005.

Summary Observations

THE VOICE WAS UNMISTAKABLE. IT was always full of elation, well beyond any sense of the mundane, or any trace of monotonous rhythms that bog down the tone of ordinary life.

"Hey B! Hey Mike! Up here, look up here!"

The year was 1987, and we didn't really have to look up to know who it was. Earvin Johnson was flourishing as the larger-than-life athletic icon known as "Magic." Michael Wilbon (long before his ESPN "Pardon the Interruption" fame) and I were in Los Angeles for Super Bowl XXI, and on this particular evening we were strolling through an outdoor shopping mall in the glitzy neighborhood of Century City. And there was Magic, one level above us, leaning over the railing and flashing his signature mega-watt smile.

"What's up, fellas? What y'all doin' here?"

I'd been a sportswriter for fourteen years by then, and I'd always figured I had a pretty good handle on what it was like to be a professional athlete. I'd covered colleges and the pros in football, basketball, and baseball by then, and figured I had a real sense of it. I was pretty much the same age as these guys, and I'd played in a few summer basketball leagues and serious pick-up games in Washington, D.C., with some major college players. I'd gone one-on-one with my fair share of recently-retired NBA assistants (and gotten crushed). I'd been in the same social circles, hung out in the same clubs and bars, and even dated a few of the same women.

I thought I knew. But I didn't really, truly understand until that evening in that Century City mall.

The three of us ended up talking for nearly a half hour, oblivious to the world swirling around us. We were all good acquaintances, and great sports fans, so we chatted on and on about all sorts of things. Then for no explainable reason, Wilbon and I stopped talking for just a moment.

In that lull, we both sensed something uncommon, almost otherworldly around us.

First we looked up. Then we looked around. On three different levels of the mall, there must have been 500 people swarming around us from all sides. They all stood there without saying a word. It was as though the three of us were inside some glass cage, surrounded by gawking strangers. Wilbon and I, unaccustomed to this attention, were a bit nervous. We'd never experienced anything like this before. We were inside the eye of this perfect storm of celebrity, and it was more than a little unsettling.

Out of nowhere, an Asian tourist ran up to me and started shouting in broken English: "*You keep him here!! You keep him here!!* I go back to my hotel and get my camera! *You keep him here!!*"

Stunned and disconcerted, I looked at Johnson and said, "Erv, maybe we oughta . . ." But he quickly interrupted.

"Just pretend they're not there," he said, smiling. "Happens all the time. Welcome to my world."

I tell this story now because after nearly thirty years on the job, I'm still trying to understand the life of a high-profile athlete—a life that is even more unfathomable today. Understanding it is a nearly impossible assignment, but it's my job to try.

So I draw from my own experiences as a former (undistinguished) Division II track and field athlete. I rely on powers of observation and the ability to ask the right questions. I try to develop good relationships, trust, and respect from the men I cover. Sometimes it works, sometimes it doesn't. But over the years, I think I've been able to serve my readers and satisfy my conscience.

Now I have an invaluable guide to help me—*Hook Me Up, Playa!*, by Lawrence Funderburke. He has provided a masterful, almost clinical, breakdown of what life is like for the high-profile collegiate or professional athlete who must dwell on the other side of the microphone, tape recorder, and notepad.

When most athletes decide to write their life story, it reads like an autobiography. Funderburke's story reads more like a hybrid of the sports autobiography. It is a kind of college thesis as well as a how-to guide for aspiring athletes. It is full of cautionary tales that should help any young athlete navigate the increasingly complicated world of big-time sports.

He asked me to try to lend a little perspective from my side of the "poison pen." But as you know by now having read this book, the relationship between members of the sports media and athletes can, and probably should be, on occasion, turbulent. If we're all doing our jobs properly, some conflict is inevitable.

As sportswriters, we'll cover the athletes' conquests, praise their achievements, and reveal their all-too-human failings. We'll record their victories and analyze their defeats. We'll show their good sides, and if they have a bad side, sometimes we'll have to be critical of an athlete or a coach. Sometimes we'll have no choice but to dwell on their faults. That's usually when the turbulence begins.

What I've learned over the years in this business is that the stuff they teach you in journalism school doesn't prepare you for life as a sportswriter. In journalism school, they talk a lot about being "fair and objective," but that stuff only works so far in the sports world.

I think athletes are more interested in sportswriters being "right" than in their being "fair." As a columnist, I believe being right is far more important than being fair. What's the difference?

Well, being fair would mean that everyone gets a chance to play in a thrilling, down-to-the-wire contest in Game 7 of the NBA Finals. But being right means that only the best, coolest, and most calculating and talented men will be on that floor.

Here's something else I know. Athletes and sportswriters are in many ways just alike. Some are jerks. Some are womanizers. Some are good Christians. Some are liars and cheats. Some of them have vast sports knowledge and care deeply about the games they play and cover. Some have incredible athletic and literary gifts, and others are unprofessional hacks and coach-killers.

But most of them, both athletes and writers, are good people. And now, with the help of Lawrence Funderburke's book, maybe both sides will be able to figure out how the other half lives.

—Bryan Burwell

Bryan Burwell is an award-winning sports journalist who has been covering the sports world for more than thirty years. He is currently a columnist for the *St. Louis Post-Dispatch*, and has written for *USA Today*, *The Sporting News*, and the *New York Daily News*. He has also worked for HBO Sports, TNT, and CNN.

Index